European Union History

Also by Wolfram Kaiser

CHRISTIAN DEMOCRACY AND THE ORIGINS OF EUROPEAN UNION

USING EUROPE, ABUSING THE EUROPEANS: BRITAIN AND EUROPEAN INTEGRATION 1945–63

Edited with B. Leucht and M. Rasmussen; THE HISTORY OF THE EUROPEAN UNION: ORIGINS OF A TRANS- AND SUPRANATIONAL POLITY 1950–72

Edited with P. Starie; TRANSNATIONAL EUROPEAN UNION: TOWARDS A COMMON POLITICAL SPACE

Edited with M. Gehler; CHRISTIAN DEMOCRACY IN EUROPE SINCE 1945

Edited with J. Elvert; EUROPEAN UNION ENLARGEMENT: A COMPARATIVE HISTORY

Edited with H. Wohnout; POLITICAL CATHOLICISM IN EUROPE 1918–1945

Edited with C. Clark; CULTURE WARS: SECULAR-CATHOLIC CONFLICT IN NINETEENTH-CENTURY EUROPE

Edited with G. Staerck; BRITISH FOREIGN POLICY 1955–64: CONTRACTING OPTIONS

Edited with P. Catterall and U. Walton-Jordan; REFORMING THE CONSTITUTION: DEBATES IN TWENTIETH-CENTURY BRITAIN

Also by Antonio Varsori

INSIDE THE EUROPEAN COMMUNITY: ACTORS AND POLICIES IN THE EUROPEAN INTEGRATION 1957–1972

EUROPE 1945–1990S: THE END OF AN ERA?

Edited with E. Calandri; THE FAILURE OF PEACE IN EUROPE 1943–48

Edited with M. Petricioli; THE SEAS AS EUROPE'S EXTERNAL BORDERS AND THEIR ROLE IN SHAPING A EUROPEAN IDENTITY

European Union History

Themes and Debates

Edited by

Wolfram Kaiser
Professor of European Studies,
University of Portsmouth, UK

and

Antonio Varsori
Professor of the History of International Relations,
University of Padova, Italy

First published 2010 by
PALGRAVE MACMILLAN

Palgrave Macmillan in the UK is an imprint of Macmillan Publishers Limited,
registered in England, company number 785998, of Houndmills, Basingstoke,
Hampshire RG21 6XS.

Palgrave Macmillan in the US is a division of St Martin's Press LLC,
175 Fifth Avenue, New York, NY 10010.

Palgrave Macmillan is the global academic imprint of the above companies
and has companies and representatives throughout the world.

Palgrave® and Macmillan® are registered trademarks in the United States,
the United Kingdom, Europe and other countries.

ISBN: 978–0–230–23269–3 hardback
ISBN: 978–0–230–23270–9 paperback

This book is printed on paper suitable for recycling and made from fully
managed and sustained forest sources. Logging, pulping and manufacturing
processes are expected to conform to the environmental regulations of the
country of origin.

A catalogue record for this book is available from the British Library.

A catalog record for this book is available from the Library of Congress.

10 9 8 7 6 5 4 3 2 1
19 18 17 16 15 14 13 12 11 10

Printed and bound in Great Britain by
CPI Antony Rowe, Chippenham and Eastbourne

Contents

Abbreviations

AN	Alleanza Nazionale
CAP	Common Agricultural Policy
CDU	Christian Democratic Union
CEDEFOP	European Centre for the Development of Vocational Training
CEH	*Contemporary European History*
CERE	Centre d'études et de recherches européennes Robert Schuman
CIEC	Conference for International Economic Cooperation
COREPER	Committee of Permanent Representatives
DC	Democrazia Cristiana
DG	Directorate-General
EC	European Community / -ies
ECJ	European Court of Justice
ECSC	European Coal and Steel Community
EDC	European Defence Community
EEC	European Economic Community
EFTA	European Free Trade Association
EMS	European Monetary System
EMU	Economic and Monetary Union
EP	European Parliament
EPC	European Political Community
EPC	European Political Cooperation
ERP	European Recovery Program
ESC	Economic and Social Committee
EU	European Union
EUI	European University Institute
Euratom	European Atomic Energy Community
GATT	General Agreement on Tariffs and Trade
HAEU	Historical Archives of the European Union
HEIRS	History of European Integration Research Society
IBRD	International Bank for Reconstruction and Development
IMF	International Monetary Fund
JCMS	*Journal of Common Market Studies*
JEIH	*Journal of European Integration History*

JEPP	*Journal of European Public Policy*
LDCs	Less Developed Countries
MFE	Movimento Federalista Europeo
NATO	North Atlantic Treaty Organization
NIEO	New International Economic Order
OEEC	Organisation of European Economic Cooperation
PCI	Partito Comunista Italiano
RICHIE	Réseau International de jeunes Chercheurs en Histoire de l'Intégration Européenne
SEA	Single European Act
TEU	Treaty on European Union
UEF	Union of European Federalists
UK	United Kingdom
US	United States (of America)
WEU	Western European Union

Acknowledgements

From its very beginning we have conceived of this book as a European collaborative endeavour to summarize and make more easily accessible state-of-the-art historical research on European integration and the present-day European Union. To be able to do so effectively we decided to organize a workshop halfway through the book project to discuss the draft chapters, exchange information, comment on relevant research and confront our assessment and interpretation of the literature. Although all contributors to this volume are multilingual, research on the history of European integration is so fragmented and dispersed that this intensive exchange has allowed us to write a much better book together, with many cross-references to other chapters, which we hope will prove valuable for the reader. We organized this workshop at the University of Padova. We would like to thank, in the first instance, the Department of International Studies of the University of Padova and the Herbert-Batliner-Europainstitut in Salzburg for their generous financial support for holding this workshop. We are also grateful to Wilfried Loth and Eric Bussière for acting as discussants and for their valuable insights. Finally, we would like to thank Brigitte Leucht for her efficient assistance with the final editing stage of this book.

Portsmouth and Padova, September 2009

Notes on Contributors

Giuliano Garavini is Lecturer of the History of International Relations at the University of Calabria.

Michael Gehler is Professor of Modern History and holds a Jean Monnet chair in the History of European Integration at the University of Hildesheim.

Mark Gilbert is Associate Professor of Contemporary History at the University of Trento and Adjunct Professor of European Studies at the Johns Hopkins School for Advanced International Studies, Bologna.

Wolfram Kaiser is Professor of European Studies at the University of Portsmouth and Visiting Professor at the College of Europe in Bruges.

N. Piers Ludlow is Reader in International History at the London School of Economics.

Lorenzo Mechi is Senior Lecturer of the History of International Relations at the University of Padova.

Daniele Pasquinucci is Associate Professor of Contemporary History at the University of Siena.

Morten Rasmussen is Assistant Professor at the Saxo Institute at the University of Copenhagen.

Katja Seidel is postdoctoral Research Fellow at the German Historical Institute in Paris.

Antonio Varsori is Professor of the History of International Relations and holds a Jean Monnet chair in History of European Integration at the University of Padova.

Introduction

Wolfram Kaiser and Antonio Varsori

We cannot hope to make sense of contemporary Europe without understanding the history of European integration and the present-day
European Union (EU). Its geographical scope and institutional form,
the extent and shape of its policies, and the democratic quality of its
governance have always been highly contested – within and among
governments, political parties, interest groups, new social movements
and European citizens. But without doubt, European integration has
had, and is continuing to have, an enormous impact on the state of
Europe: through transforming the nation-state; creating new supranational institutions and forms of joint policy- and decision-making; integrating markets and liberalizing trade; fiscal and social redistribution;
and through fostering the formation of transnational elite networks and
growing identification with Europe, although not necessarily allegiance
to the EU; but also through accentuating social frictions resulting from
its liberal competition policy, raising concerns about the remoteness of
supranational policy-making and serving as a focal point for anti-elitist
'Eurosceptic' discourses and political mobilization.

European integration has not only transformed the member states of
the EU, however. It has also had a huge impact on third countries: by
drawing peripheral European countries into its orbit resulting in the
various enlargements, supporting the liberalization of global trade in
industrial and service sector products; and propagating new forms of
global governance and rule of law; but also by savagely protecting its
inefficient agriculture and attempting to impose its norms and policy
preferences on others in international relations. In short, the history of
European integration is inextricably intertwined with many of the most
important dynamics in post-World War II Europe and international

1

relations: the transformation of the welfare state, the Cold War, and the North–South conflict and globalization.

Not surprisingly, therefore, research on the history of European integration and the EU has vastly expanded since its origins in the 1970s. This research is not easily accessible, however, as it is highly fragmented. National historiographical traditions have influenced the choice of conceptual approaches and topics as well as historians' normative assessments. Conceptually and methodologically very different approaches like history of ideas, diplomatic history and economic history have existed in parallel and, more often than not, ignored each other, with little cross-fertilization. Moreover, as research on European integration originated in the 'core Europe' of the six founding member states of the present-day EU, most of the research has not been, and continues not to be published in English, but instead in French, German and Italian in particular. Finally, historians of European integration have utilized a vast variety of different sources, from government archives with different formal rules and practical conditions for access, to those of the supranational EU institutions, political parties, interest groups, media reports and oral interviews, but this diversity of sources and historical evidence has also made synthesis more difficult. This in turn is also one important reason among several for why most general histories of Europe in the twentieth century or since 1945 treat European integration in a superficial and cursory form and not as the central feature that it has actually been.

The historiography of European integration and the EU has now entered what Katja Seidel in her chapter in this book calls a third phase of 'refinement'. Historical research has gone decisively beyond the analysis of national policy towards 'Europe', although it continues to discuss the role of the member states as crucial, but not the only relevant actors. Some historians have begun to conceptualize and research the EU's complex political system in historical perspective. Others have broadened the research agenda to include the role of national and transnationally constituted political parties and interest groups and of the media. More and more research also analyses the origins and evolution of single policy areas, widening the perspective from an exclusive focus on policy- and decision-making to explore its connections with socio-economic transformations and Europeanization effects of supranational policies on the member states. Historians are also becoming more interested in the various external dimensions of European integration, not just western Europe's relationship with the United States (US), but also the role of the Community in the Cold War and the impact of its policies on less developed countries. Moreover, an increasing number of historians are also keen to integrate their research more closely with the historiography of modern Europe more generally, going backwards in time before 1945, and with social science research that in turn has become more interested once more in the long-term historical evolution of the present-day EU.

This is the ideal point in time, therefore, at which to take stock and make sure that the rapidly expanding research on the history of European integration and the EU is made more widely and more easily accessible. Thus, this book's objective is not to provide yet another descriptive narrative of the EU's history, as so many textbooks published in the major European languages do more or less reliably. Instead, it aims to provide a sophisticated and comprehensive introduction to research trends and themes and debates in the historiography; or, in other words, to sketch the partly competing answers historians have given to questions of why and how European integration developed, on the basis of a chronology of facts that readers can access elsewhere. With this objective in mind, it is hoped that this book will prove useful for different audiences who need to make sense of the history of European integration and the EU: postgraduate and advanced undergraduate students who are not satisfied with their grasp of the basic facts of the EU's history and institutional structures; researchers in the field of European integration itself, who wish to transgress linguistic and conceptual boundaries to write more sophisticated narratives; political, social, economic and cultural historians of modern and contemporary Europe, who increasingly feel the need to integrate integration history more fully into their work, but do not know where to start, as it becomes increasingly clear to the non-specialist how fundamental the EU's broader impact has been in the longer run; social scientists who utilize conceptual approaches like historical institutionalism, for example, that require a better empirical grounding of their research and improved knowledge of the historiography; and finally, practitioners in EU policy-making in the broadest sense in Brussels and elsewhere, who wish to take a step back from their daily concerns and delve deeper into a history that is also their history, institutionally and sometimes also personally.

To facilitate access to the historiography of European integration and the EU for these and other readers we have divided the book into three sections. The first section comprises three chapters that discuss the context in which historical research has developed over the last decades. In his chapter, Antonio Varsori sketches the origins of European integration research by historians, its institutionalization, formal and informal networks, funding and major collaborative projects, all of which have structured this historical sub-field to a significant extent. Katja Seidel goes on to discuss more recent research trends in integration history through a quantitative and qualitative analysis of major publications including the biannual specialized *Journal of European Integration History* founded in 1995. Subsequently, Wolfram Kaiser explores the integration, or lack thereof, of this historiography within modern and contemporary European history and with the social sciences, exploring the benefits and pitfalls of greater cross-disciplinarity in European Studies research on the present-day EU.

The three chapters in the second section are devoted to particular conceptual approaches to understanding the history of European integration and the EU, or important dimensions of it. Daniele Pasquinucci traces the origins and evolution of the federalist historiography of European integration, which was especially influential in the early stages and in Italy, and its slow reorientation towards an approach that is somewhat less driven by a strong normative commitment to a federal Europe. In his chapter, Michael Gehler studies the extensive and nationally highly fragmented historiography of national European policy-making, combining insights into research on specific country cases with larger conclusions about the role of the nation-state in European integration. N. Piers Ludlow then goes on to show how historians have begun to explore the emerging complex European political system and, especially, the changing role of the various supranational institutions in policy- and decision-making.

The final section consists of four chapters that cover different thematic dimensions of the history of European integration and the EU. Thus, Morten Rasmussen discusses the strengths and weaknesses of different conceptual approaches utilized by economic historians to understand the nature of integration as well as, more specifically, the role of business actors. Closely connected to this economic dimension, Lorenzo Mechi looks at how historians have studied social and cultural aspects of European integration from its contribution to the convergence of national societies to the making of policies with significant social impact, the growth of transnational social networks, the emergence of a European public sphere of sorts and the growth of European identity and allegiance. Whereas these chapters focus predominantly on domestic dimensions of the present-day EU, the remaining two chapters are devoted to analysing how historians have conceptualized its external relations and impact. Thus, Mark Gilbert analyses how historians have studied and interpreted the role of the US in European integration and the changing relationship between the EU and its member states on the one hand, and the US on the other, research that developed out of the sub-field of history of the Cold War and remains closely attached to international history. Finally, Giuliano Garavini explores the various ways in which the Community in conjunction, but also in competition with the member states, increasingly has had an impact on third countries, especially through its trade and development policies, but also in other areas, and how this can help us to understand its currently much more far-reaching competences in external relations and its growing influence on global politics.

Naturally, research on the history of European integration and the EU is developing fast, and is also moving forward in time into the 1980s and later periods. We hope, nevertheless, that with its very systematic approach and comprehensive coverage of trends, themes and debates, this book will serve as an indispensable introduction to the state of the art in historical research in this sub-field for some years to come.

Portsmouth and Padova, September 2009

1
From Normative Impetus to Professionalization: Origins and Operation of Research Networks

Antonio Varsori

At an international history conference an Italian historian and columnist once stated that, in his opinion, the Jean Monnet Professors of History of European Integration, named after the French leading civil servant who is regarded as one of the founding fathers of the European construction, were not too different from the professors of Marxism-Leninism in the former Soviet Union. This was a provocative remark from a mildly Eurosceptic historian. Nevertheless, the co-funding by the European Union (EU) of such university chairs in the history (as well as law, economics and politics) of European integration is a peculiar phenomenon. For example, there are no Dwight D. Eisenhower chairs in the history of the Atlantic Alliance co-financed by the North Atlantic Treaty Organization (NATO) or Ronald Reagan chairs in Cold War history supported by United States (US) administrations. In fact, before any EU funding for university chairs, the French President Charles de Gaulle opposed the creation of a European university in the 1960s for fear that it could become the hotbed of what he called 'apatrides', or European civil servants responsible to no one. Since then, Eurosceptics have been suspicious of any political intentions behind the EU's growing role in education (Palayret 1996, 103–58).

In a recent study on the cultural politics of European integration the British anthropologist Cris Shore has argued that in the field of education, the EU has tried to 'invent Europe as a category of thought'. In this perspective, history and historians have a significant role in such a strategy: 'Typically, EU historiography represents the last three thousand years of European history as a kind of moral success story: a gradual "coming together" in the shape of the European Community and its institutions.' According to Shore, 'French historians seem to have made a particular contribution to the EU's attempt at re-writing history.' In this context, his criticism focuses especially on Jean-Baptiste Duroselle's *Europe: A History of its Peoples* (1990), which appears as a 'story of reason and unity triumphing over disunity and nationalism ... It is invariably a selected, sanityzed and heroic re-reading of the past, one that systematically excludes or ignores the darker side of European modernity such as the legacies of slavery, anti-Semitism, colonialism or imperial conquest' (Shore 2000, 57–60). Of course, such normatively influenced narratives are not limited to French historians. In fact, Mark Mazower (1998), while exposing the 'dark sides' of twentieth-century European history, seems to regard European integration as one of its few success stories. In any case, Shore's observations address an important issue. Is the historiography of European integration a political creation by Eurocrats in Brussels? And if this is so, or at least to some extent, are the historians of the present-day EU some kind of court historians ready to comply with the will of supranational institutions just as many nationalist historians in nineteenth-century Europe contributed to nation-building processes and national integration?

These questions are highly relevant, as the origins and the developments of the historiography of European integration are characterized by the following core features: firstly, the key role played by some large-scale international research projects in initiating greater research on the integration history; secondly, the creation and activities of large European networks with a focus on teaching and research on integration history; and thirdly, the initiatives and the support of European institutions for such projects and networks. Large-scale transnational research projects have also played an important role in establishing other fields of historical research. Thus, in the related field of Cold War history, the Cold War History Project and the Parallel History Project were instrumental for developing and sustaining transnational and collaborative research. However, in contrast to the case of the EU and European integration history, these projects had no direct link with US or other countries' government agencies. Against this background, this chapter will reconstruct the origins of research and research networks in European integration history. It will highlight in particular the transition from its more normative origins with substantial EU funding to the more recent professionalization and conceptual diversification and sophistication and declining interest by EU institutions in this research field.

Origins of the historiography of European integration

In its origins, the history of European integration was only one topic amongst others addressed in other, larger historical fields, especially the history of political thought, the history of international relations, and economic history. Successively, the three main preconditions for the emergence of EU history as a more distinctive research field were the growing availability during the 1970s of archival sources on World War II and the immediate post-war period owing to the change in the US and western Europe to the 30-year rule for access to state archival sources, from various stricter rules that operated before; the development and wide diffusion of Cold War historiography that at least in its early stages, treated Europe's role in the confrontation between the US and the Soviet Union as one of its main topics; and the growing involvement of western European historians in the study of the Cold War.

Until the late 1960s and the early 1970s, European integration, in part because of the lack of access to archival sources, did not attract the attention of historians. There were few exceptions, mainly former European civil servants, journalists and historians of political ideas who were mainly interested in federalism as a political theory (Varsori 2001b, 69–70). In this early period, the ongoing Cold War provoked (especially in the US) several contemporary historical studies that mostly belonged to the so-called 'orthodox' school, which essentially blamed its outbreak on Soviet expansionism, albeit with a growing influence exerted by 'revisionist' historians (Westad 2000). The flourishing of studies of the early Cold War was enhanced by the availability in the US of official records related to World War II and the immediate post-war period. During the 1970s archival records dealing with those years became available in some larger western European states, too. A number of western European historians began to show a growing interest in Cold War history, and focused on its European dimensions. They included especially the US influence in shaping post-war Europe through bilateral relationships, the launching of major multilateral initiatives, such as the Marshall Plan, and the creation of a western defence system (Varsori 2008).

During 1979–80 the French historian René Girault from the historical school of the history of international relations founded by Pierre Renouvin and Duroselle, launched an ambitious international research project on 'the perception of power politics in western Europe'. The project focused on four nations – France, the United Kingdom (UK), Germany and Italy – and dealt with three different periods: 1938–40, 1945–50, and 1950–57. Four major international conferences were held: in Sèvres in 1982, in Augsburg in 1984, in Florence in 1987 and in London in 1992. Historians from different fields were involved, mainly diplomatic history, military history, history of political parties, and economic history; four volumes deriving from the major conferences and some books based on national perspectives were published during the 1980s and the first half of the 1990s (Girault and Frank 1984; Becker and Knipping 1986; Di Nolfo 1992; Dockrill 1995). This research project had two consequences: firstly, the creation of a European network and, secondly, the emergence of a new conceptual and methodological approach to the history of post-war Europe.

The project had four national groups led by senior historians, who coordinated the activities, and research by several younger scholars. At the same time, however, the international conferences offered the opportunity for exchanges of views and opinions among senior and junior scholars. This collective experience lasted for about a decade and facilitated the emergence of an informal transnational network of historians, who shared common interests, learned to work together and became more and more aware that the history of post-war European nations could only meaningfully be analysed and interpreted in a wider international context utilizing a multinational research approach. Girault pushed for such an approach. Other senior historians, who were in charge of the various national groups, included the Italians Ennio Di Nolfo and Brunello Vigezzi, the Germans Josef Becker and Franz Knipping, and the British Donald Watt and Geoffrey Warner. Younger scholars, who played an active role in Girault's project, would be involved later in most initiatives and projects related to the history of European integration. They included inter alia Robert Frank, Gérard Bossuat, Wilfried Loth and Antonio Varsori.

Concerning the project's second consequence, its research results led Girault to develop a revised interpretation of post-war European dynamics. In its early stage the project mainly aimed at understanding how the four major western European states had lost their role as 'great powers' to the US and the Soviet Union from the late 1930s to the 1950s. This approach was tied to questions related to the end of Europe's central role in international affairs, the influence of the Cold War on this process, and the European states' reaction to their decline. In this context Girault emphasized the importance of the 'perception of

power' influenced by psychological and cultural factors as well as material capabilities which could shape the rise and fall of a 'great power'.
The multinational research programme led Girault to partially reassess
its goals. It became clear that understanding the international reality
of post-war western Europe could not be limited to the Cold War and
Europe's descent from power, but needed to include another crucial
phenomenon, namely European integration. This was especially true as
European integration after 1945 had become both a goal and an instrument that some European states, especially France, used with partial
success to recover some of their lost power. Girault's views influenced
several historians from France and other European countries involved in
the project. Reflecting the shift towards greater emphasis on European
integration, the subtitle of the third volume in the series was *The Origins
of the EEC 1952–1957* (Girault 1992, 553–62).

As well as being motivated by historiographical considerations, this
shift may well have been influenced by political developments in
Europe in the first half of the 1980s: the election of François Mitterrand
as President of France (Girault being not a member of, but close to the
French Socialist Party) and the renewed strengthening of the Franco-
German relationship with a 'grand design' for rejuvenating European
integration. Clearly, this cultural and political milieu which evolved
around Mitterrand's 'grand design' favoured the launching in France of
new contemporary historical research initiatives, projects and changing
interpretations.

Enter the European Community

An important change in the European Community's attitude and policies towards higher education and cultural policy proved to be another
catalyst of change. Initially, the European Economic Community (EEC)
had no competences in these fields. In the 1960s, France and Germany
were fiercely opposed to Italy's aspirations for a common European cultural policy, especially the setting up of a European university. In the
view of the Italian governments, its focus would be on the humanities,
and its natural location in Italy and, more specifically, Florence as a
important centre of the Renaissance. The European Commission at first
showed little interest in higher education and culture. It was more concerned with fostering vocational training. However, from the late 1960s
onwards the division into vocational training and education (including
higher education) became increasingly blurred, and the Commission's

commitment to developing the latter stronger (Varsori 2006a; European Commission 2006). In contrast, the European Parliament (EP) had always shown a strong interest in the creation of European cultural and educational policies that would be based on, and strengthen, the ideals of European supranational integration (Paoli 2006). Finally, as a consequence of the summit at The Hague in November 1969, the plan for a European university developed further and in 1976, the European University Institute (EUI) was created in San Domenico di Fiesole, on the outskirts of Florence.

The EUI was not a full university, but a research institute with a post-graduate school for doctoral studies divided into four departments: Politics, Economics, Law as well as History and Civilization. In the beginning the EUI was a small institution with few professors and a small group of research students (Palayret 1996, 182–98). Its first President was the Dutch Max Kohnstamm, a close collaborator of Monnet's. It was clear from the beginning that European integration would be one main research focus at the EUI. Thus, one of the few professional historians interested in the history of European integration at that time, and a committed federalist, the German Walter Lipgens from the University of Saarbrücken, held one of the first chairs in Modern European history (Kaiser 2002a; Loth 2006). A younger British scholar, Peter Ludlow, became associate professor. The EUI had financial and organizational resources that allowed the development of larger international projects. It initiated a project for a large-scale edition of documents on the history of European integration. In a memorandum submitted to Lipgens in 1979, Ludlow retrospectively summarized this project's origins: 'This collection of documents on the European allied governments and the developments of European integration and cooperation will form part of a larger documentary series on the history of European integration and cooperation in general. The origins of the series lie in a request from the European Commission to the newly appointed President of the European University Institute in 1975 to investigate the prospects for an international research project on this theme. ... Consultations took place with international historians all over Europe, and as a result of these consultations ... it was decided to organise a programme of collective research ... aimed at producing a series of documentary volumes covering the period from 1939 onwards.'[1] Ludlow pointed out that the project aimed at creating something similar to the *Foreign Relations of the United States* collection: 'As an experiment in international collaborative research alone, it should prove productive, since historians have not on the whole been as conspicuous as the representatives of certain other disciplines in developing techniques appropriate to a closely coordinated research programme involving scholars in many countries.'

In line with his strong federalist commitment Lipgens stressed the project's more political 'pro-European' features. In a letter of invitation to participate in a conference that took place in Florence in 1977 as a major project milestone he argued that: 'Europe's history is now shaped by two different dynamics: on the one hand the continuing development of nation states' history, on the other the common integration process with common institutions, common archives, etc.... The History Department of the European University Institute believes that it is its duty to favour forms of multinational cooperation that are necessary in order to enhance the study of Europe's common history. For the European Community it is important to develop an autonomous consciousness and a historical consciousness based on sound scholarly foundations.'[2] Among the historians who took part in this conference were Karl-Dietrich Bracher and Hans-Peter Schwarz from Germany, Pierre Gerbet, Pierre Guillen and Raymond Poidevin from France, Warner and Watt from Britain, as well as Andrea Chiti Batelli, Enrico Serra and Sergio Pistone from Italy. The project eventually led to the publication of four volumes, the *Documents on the History of the European Integration* published between 1985 and 1991, with Lipgens as editor and after his death in 1984, Loth (Lipgens 1985–91).

It turned out, however, that this project did not lead to the establishment of the EUI's History Department as the main centre for the study of the history of the European integration. In 1980 Lipgens left the EUI and Ludlow moved to Brussels where he created the Centre for European Policy Studies and became a specialist in current Community affairs. Lipgens' successors, the British economic historians Alan S. Milward and Richard Griffiths were no federalists and also less interested in promoting larger collaborative research projects relying on close links with the Commission. While Griffiths co-edited a few books (Griffiths and Girvin 1995; Griffiths and Ward 1996) and Milward and some of his research students published a collectively authored book on theory and history of European integration (Milward et al. 1993), the study of integration history lost its initially central role in the History Department. Despite of this development, the opening of some western European states' archives based on the new 30-year rule, especially in the UK, led several leading officials in the Commission, notably Emile Noël, Klaus Mayer and Christopher Audland, to push for the creation of archives of the Community institutions. In 1978 it was decided that from 1982 onwards the Community would also adopt the 30-year rule and that its archives would be established both in Brussels and at the EUI in Florence. Finally, in June 1984 the Commission officially opened its archives in Brussels. Later on, the present-day Historical Archives of the EU (HAEU) were inaugurated in Florence (Audland 2007). The opening of the Community archives reflected the growing interest of some within the Commission in propagating and supporting research on the history of European integration which they essentially regarded as the history of the European Communities. Eventually, one result of this growing interest was the publication in 1993 of a history of the High Authority of the European Coal and Steel Community co-authored by French historian Poidevin and Dirk Spierenburg, a former member of the High Authority (Spierenburg and Poidevin 1993). With the support of the Commission, this project had begun in 1987, and the book featured a preface by Commission President Jacques Delors.

The initiative with the greatest long-term impact was the formation of a liaison group of European historians with an interest in the Community, however. In the early 1980s the Commission, especially Jacqueline Lastenouse from the Directorate for Information, developed contacts mainly with French and German historians like Duroselle, Schwarz and Becker. At the time, these historians asked for more support by the Commission, especially by making Community archival sources accessible. As a result, in late January 1982 the Commission and the Luxembourg University Centre organized the 'International Conference of Professors of Contemporary History' in Luxembourg, which was to focus on the 'study of the beginnings of European integration: the value of source material and records'. Some 80 historians attended this conference. Alongside a session on public and private archives and another with a number of eyewitnesses, including Etienne Hirsch and Pierre Uri, former collaborators of Monnet, and the leading Christian democratic politician Paolo Emilio Taviani, for example, a third session focused on 'current perspectives in historical research on the construction of Europe'. Duroselle chaired this session and Schwarz introduced the discussion with a keynote address. At the end of this discussion Girault put forward a resolution that stressed the need for an organization that could coordinate historical research on European integration. Approved unanimously, the resolution called for the creation of a liaison committee of European historians. 'This committee, on which two historians from each member state or applicant country would be represented, would have the following tasks: 1. To publicize information on work done by historians on postwar European history; 2. To advise the Communities on supporting activities in this field; 3. To help researchers in making better use of source material at their disposal; 4. To initiate or encourage meetings between historians in this area.'[3]

In 1983 the Liaison Committee was created. At the beginning it included Schwarz, Klaus Schwabe and Lipgens, immediately substituted by Loth after the former's death, from Germany, Michel Dumoulin from Belgium, Girault and Poidevin from France, Donal McCartney and Dermot Keogh from Ireland, Serra from Italy, Gilbert Trausch from Luxembourg, Adrien Manning from the Netherlands, and Watt and Milward from Britain. It appears that, at this stage, one place was reserved for the EUI, represented by Milward. Some members left after only a few years, and new members were coopted by the group. The first chairman was Girault who was quickly succeeded by Trausch, not least because the Liaison Committee became an official association under Luxembourg law. For some years the Liaison Committee's main goal was to organize major international conferences. The first of these, dealing with the period from the creation of the Brussels Pact in 1948 to the launching of the Schuman Plan in May 1950, was held in Strasbourg in November 1984, and the proceedings were published two years later (Poidevin 1986). The second conference took place in Aachen in 1986 and dealt with the Schuman Plan (Schwabe 1988). The Liaison Committee invested many resources into its third conference organized in Rome in March 1987, which focused on 'the relaunching of Europe and the Treaties of Rome'. This conference was supported financially not only by the Commission, but also by the Italian foreign ministry and other Italian institutions. In Rome, the Liaison Committee brought together, in addition to historians, eyewitnesses with a view to fostering an exchange of views and the utilization of 'oral history' methods for the reconstruction of the history of European integration (Serra 1989). In the beginning these books usually included chapters in English, French and German. Both the Liaison Committee and the conferences were dominated by historians of international relations, with Milward as an economic historian focusing on historical dimensions of international political economy. In the early stages, moreover, most contributions were based on the newly opened archives of national foreign ministries and attention focused very much on the European (integration) policies of member states as part of their foreign policies.

The main logic in the choice of conference themes was initially to foster chronological progress in research in line with the opening up of national sources, especially those from diplomatic archives. Accordingly, the fourth conference in Luxembourg in 1989 (Trausch 1993) aimed at filling the gap of the period from 1950 to 1955 between the themes of the second and third conferences, precisely to complete the chronological order. Although most contributions to this conference and the resulting book still came from political and diplomatic historians, some younger international economic historians were also included, mainly as a consequence of the influence exerted by Milward at the EUI on some younger scholars from different countries.

During the 1980s the Commision supported the Liaison Committee that met about twice a year in Brussels at the Directorate-General for Information, Communication and Culture, with the direct involvement of Lastenouse, who was the main advocate of the Commission's commitment to enhancing historical research on European integration. The Commission Directorate for University Information created a 'historians' corner' in its bulletin and, most importantly, financed the Liaison Committee's meetings, conferences and costs related to the production of the resulting books that were published by the four continental European publishers Bruylant from Belgium, LGDJ from France, Nomos from Germany and Giuffrè from Italy. All of these publishers already had book lists in related fields, especially international and Community law.

The climax in the Commission's commitment and the historians' reaction

The new integration dynamism in the second half of the 1980s and the early 1990s also impacted on the evolving research on the history of European integration. The Single European Act of 1986 and the leadership by Delors, who was very interested in enhancing the Community's role in the field of education (Delors 2004, 77–8) in the late 1980s led to the launching of the first programmes in the field of higher education: in 1987 the Eramus exchange programme was created, and in 1989 the Jean Monnet Action was established (European Commission 2006, 116–21). While the Erasmus programme was designed to facilitate the transnational mobility of both students and academic staff, the Jean Monnet Action aimed at creating and strengthening European and EU Studies through co-funding Jean Monnet chairs, courses and modules in the four main disciplines politics, law, economics and history. Although the Jean Monnet Action emphasized the teaching dimension, it was now clear that the Commission was firmly involved in fostering and funding university activities focused on European integration. At the time, an optimistic mood resulted from the end of the Cold War, the successful management of German unification and the negotiation and eventual ratification of the Treaty on European Union. Europeanist ideals once more revived in some university milieus and combined with the financial incentives of the Erasmus programme and Jean Monnet Action to involve more scholars in the humanities and social scientists in the study of European integration. They also organized the transdisciplinary European Community Studies Association founded in 1987, with its national branches, which gave a further boost to both formal and informal research networks, with close contacts with the European institutions. At the time, most members of the Liaison Committee also became Jean Monnet chairholders, with Lastenouse playing a key role in the new Commission policy (Torquati 2006, 111–44).

Against this background, in 1989 Girault launched a new large research project on 'European identity' that aimed at identifying and defining the characteristics of such an identity in historical perspective. At the time, the European institutions showed a growing interest in definitions of European 'identity' and identity-building initiatives leading to the adoption of the EU flag and anthem (Lager 1995). The research project, supported by the Liaison Committee and co-funded by the Commission in the context of the newly launched Jean Monnet Action, was ambitious. According to Girault, it had to overcome the chronological and methodological limitations of the Liaison Committee's initiatives and not just treat the history of European integration as that of the EU. Instead, it would focus on the entire twentieth century; involve historians with different backgrounds including social, economic, diplomatic historians and others as well as scholars from other disciplines, including, among others, political science, economics, sociology and geography. Last but not least, Girault and his close collaborators at the University of Paris I, Frank and Bossuat, would supervise the activities of the different research units to guarantee an effective transnational approach. Ten research units with different thematic foci were eventually set up: political elites, cultural elites, Europe's borders, European society, the war experience, small countries in Europe, European institutions, the role of religion, and the historiography of the history of modern and contemporary Europe. Of the scholars in charge of the different research units, ten were French, six Italian, two German, one Belgian, one British, one Hungarian, one Spanish, one Swiss and one from Luxembourg. Six of them were already, or were about to become, members of the Liaison Committee. Every research unit organized one or two major conferences involving about 120 scholars altogether. In November 1993 a first general conference was held in Paris, where every research unit presented a final report. This conference led to a publication edited by Girault (1994). Although the individual research units produced research of some relevance, the overall outcome of this project was partially disappointing in that it appeared impossible to identify common characteristics of a common European identity. As a result, Girault developed a follow-up project. The organizational structures did not change much. However, the second project, which lasted from 1995 to 1999, focused on 'European identities' in the plural. The new coordinators were Frank and Bossuat, as Girault was about to retire (Frank 2004, 8). Nevertheless, some of the characteristics of the first project did not change significantly such as the over-representation of historians from the 'core Europe' of the six founding member states, especially France, and a strong role of historians of international relations.

In the meantime, the Jean Monnet Action gave a boost to historical research on European integration. However, history as a discipline had the least number of Jean Monnet chairs. A Commission report on ten years of the Action's activities published in 1999 listed 491 chairs, of which 206 in law, 125 in economics, 116 in political science and only 44 in history, of which eight each were based in Germany and Italy, seven each in France and Spain, five in Britain, and several others in smaller member states, but none in Portugal, Austria and Sweden, for example (Commission Européenne – Direction Générale de l'Education et de la Culture 1999, 10–12). Nevertheless, meetings of Jean Monnet history professors were held in Brussels with the support of the Commission. In 1995 such a group launched an oral history project for a series of interviews with eyewitnesses of European integration, mainly politicians, diplomats and European civil servants. This project was directed by senior scholars who, however, usually relied on younger researchers for conducting the interviews. The project lasted for several years and led to more than 100 interviews being deposited at the HAEU in Florence (www.iue.it). It was influenced by the growing interest among some historians like Maria Grazia Melchionni (2000) in a different methodological approach from the history of European integration based on oral sources, something regarded with at best mixed feelings by most historians of international relations.

More recently, new technologies have favoured the much wider diffusion of factual information and historical sources on the history of European integration including the oral history interviews deposited in the HAEU. Some websites have been developed for this purpose. They include Europa.clio-online in Berlin (www.europa.clio-online.de) and the European Navigator (www.ena.lu) based in Luxembourg, which has been supported by the Commission and the Luxembourg government. Moreover, the Jean Monnet Action also funded many individual research projects and conferences. On the whole, the group of Jean Monnet professors of history proved to be strongly supportive of European integration and the EU. In the early period in particular, academic selection criteria were not strictly applied, and many junior scholars, overt federalists and former EU officials became Jean Monnet professors or were awarded funding for EU-related courses or teaching modules. Naturally, not only in their teaching, but also in much of their scholarly production, strongly pro-EU attitudes prevailed.

While the Girault projects and the Jean Monnet Action evolved, the Liaison Committee began to widen and deepen its activities. In 1993 another major conference on war time plans for post-war Europe took place in Brussels (Dumoulin 1995), an attempt to reassess the origins of European integration. However, the most important goal was the creation of a journal devoted to the history of European integration. A few years earlier, in 1987, Dumoulin had already created a *Historians of Contemporary Europe* Newsletter. In its early issues this publication, which was financially supported by the Commission and published in Louvain-la-Neuve under the label of the Liaison Committee, mainly aimed at spreading information on research on the history of European integration, especially on new publications, relevant PhD theses, new research projects, forthcoming conferences and other initiatives. Dumoulin and the Liaison Committee also aimed at creating a *Who's Who* for the historical sub-field of history of European integration (Conrad and Dumoulin 1992; Duchenne and Dumoulin 1999). Gradually the Newsletter began to publish articles too, mainly by young scholars, but most members of the Liaison Committee aimed at the creation of a fully fledged journal as a reference point for historical research on European integration.

In 1995 the first issue of the *Journal of European Integration History* (*JEIH*) appeared. The journal was, and still is, published by the German publisher Nomos, which had already been involved in publishing the proceedings of the Liaison Group's conferences. The journal could rely on early support by the Commission and the Centre d'études et de recherches européennes Robert Schuman based in Luxembourg, especially for secretarial support and editing. In order to establish the journal, the Liaison Committee layed down a set of editorial rules, with a high rate of manuscripts rejected or authors asked to make major revisions before publication. As Katja Seidel argues in her chapter, moreover, the *JEIH* reflects, although it does not always set, new trends in historical research on European integration. Alongside the new journal and the Liaison Committee's edited volumes, Dumoulin set up a book series in the 1990s entitled *Euroclio*, which is devoted to the theme of European integration broadly speaking. In the first decade of this series, some 50 research monographs and edited books were published. This book series once more developed out of a European network of senior and junior scholars that was partly supported in its early stage by the Jean Monnet Action, with its centre at the University of Louvain-la-Neuve in Belgium. Again, the members of the network mainly came from core Europe, with 17 from Belgium, 12 from France, seven from Luxembourg, five from Italy, three from the Netherlands and two each from Germany, Spain, Poland, and Switzerland. Seven members of this network were also members of the Liaison Committee. More recently, another book series, Studies on the History of the European Integration, with an exclusive focus on EU history, has been set up. This series is published by Franz Steiner Verlag, under the editorship of Jürgen Elvert. Of the 19 members of its international advisory board, seven are members of the Liaison Committee and many are also Jean Monnet chairholders.

Declining Commission interest and professionalization of the research field

In the second half of the 1990s the Liaison Committee continued with its activities. Its conference in Oxford in 1996 covered the period from 1958 through to 1963 (Deighton and Milward 1999). The next conference in 1999 took place in Essen and focused on the subsequent period 1963–69 (Loth 2001). These conferences were largely based on a traditional approach to research following the opening up of state archival sources, mainly foreign ministry archives. In the concluding session of the Essen conference, Wolfram Kaiser and Varsori, in particular, forcefully suggested that the history of European integration could not be limited to a history of the European policies of member states and bilateral relationships like that between France and Germany. Instead, it would be crucial to adopt a new approach that would address the role of various institutional and societal actors and multilevel dynamics of politics and policy-making in the EU in historical perspective.

One impressive early example of such a different approach was the work of a British historian, Keith Middlemas, who had no links with any of the major networks (Middlemas 1995). Similarly, the next Liaison Committee's conference in Florence in 2001 focused on different actors like political parties in integration in the period from 1958 through to 1972 (Varsori 2006b). Some European bodies like the Economic and Social Committee (ESC) and the European agency European Centre for the Development of Vocational Training (CEDEFOP) also began to support research on their own history (Varsori 2000, 2004). Other historians focused on transnational actors and dynamics (Kaiser and Starie 2005; Kaiser 2007). Moreover, in the late 1990s Frank and Bossuat launched a new transnational project, Les temps et les espaces de l'Europe. The very title of the research revealed the ambition of the two French historians to further broaden the approach to the history of European integration, although most of the participants were the same as those who had been involved in the previous projects developed by Girault. Clearly, this long-term continuity in project-related networks favoured the creation of stable forms of cooperation among some historians who shared common interests as, for example, in the case of Loth and Marie-Thérèse Bitsch concerning European institutions (Bitsch, Loth and Poidevin 1998), Dumoulin, Eric Bussière and Sylvain Schirmann regarding European economic milieus (Bussière, Dumoulin and Schirmann 2006a, 2006b, 2007), and Varsori and Josefina Cuesta Bustillo on European social policies (Leonardi and Varsori 2005).

In spite of the formation and broadening of networks and the intensification of research during the second half of the 1990s in particular, the relationship between the Commission and some historians, who had contributed to the creation of the history of European integration as a research field, became uneasy. The Commission aimed at developing close contacts and common initiatives between the wider group of the Jean Monnet professors of history and the Liaison Committee. However, the Liaison Committee was at best lukewarm and regarded the Commission's plans as interfering in its autonomy. In 1997, on the occasion of the 40th anniversary of the signing of the treaties establishing the EEC and the European Atomic Energy Community in Rome, the Jean Monnet Action actually funded and organized a major conference in Rome. This conference mainly focused on contributions by eyewitnesses, without involving the Liaison Committee directly, although some of its members participated in this initiative as Jean Monnet professors (Commission Européenne 1999).

Subsequently, the relationship between the Commission and historians of the present-day EU changed more fundamentally. Despite the transformation and strengthening of the Jean Monnet Action, which became a fully fledged programme more tied to the Erasmus programme located in the Directorate-General Education and Culture, the Commission increasingly lost interest in integration history and focused on other disciplines. The Commission did start and fund another programme in 2000, which eventually led to the publication in 2007 of a history of the European Commission between 1957 and 1972 (Dumoulin 2007). Coordinated by the Belgian historian Dumoulin, this project, and the resulting edited book, was based both on interviews with former Commission officials and sources from the Community archives. It was easily the most ambitious attempt at writing the history of a supranational institution, with much less emphasis on the role played by the member states in the integration process. Once more, it involved historians from core Europe, who were either members of the Liaison Committee or had taken part in Girault's projects. However, history played no role in any major conferences of the Jean Monnet Action in the new century, which were exclusively aimed at current affairs. In the opinion of the Commission such a focus, for example on intercultural dialogue, favouring other academic disciplines potentially had a greater impact on a much wider audience (European Commission 2005). More recently, history as a discipline has had an increasingly smaller share of newly awarded Jean Monnet chairs, courses and modules, only about 10 per cent of the projects approved and co-financed by the Commission during 2004–06. In history, most successful bids continued to be from historians in 'core Europe' countries, with a high representation of Italy. Typically, three of four 'success stories' nominated by the Jean Monnet Programme for history in 2007 were Italian.

Since the late 1990s the Liaison Committee, although formally recognized by the Commission, has acted independently of its institutional support and without privileged access to its funds, the journal being supported by the state of Luxembourg. Moreover, history has also played almost no role in the subsequent EU framework programmes for research in social sciences. The Liaison Committee had its research activities included in EU-CONSENT, a major political science-dominated project funded under the sixth framework programme, but no projects focused more specifically on EU history ever received funding. Last but not least, on the occasion of the 50th anniversary of the Rome Treaties in 2007, the Commission showed no strong commitment to a historical assessment of European integration. The Liaison Committee and the network Les espaces et les temps de l'Europe decided to organize a conference in Rome. It aimed at a multidisciplinary analysis and at promoting a dialogue with European actors, practitioners and representatives of 'civil society'. Despite the obvious fit with the general priorities of the Commission, it only showed minor interest in the initiative and co-funded the conference, which was mainly supported by the French Ministry of Education (Loth 2009). In the meantime, Frank has launched a new transnational research project, partially supported by the French research funding body the Centre Nationale de la Recherche Scientifique, on 'Dimensions and Dynamics of the European integration'.

While the reduced EU-level institutional support for historical research on European integration has only partially hampered the work of established institutionalized and network-type collaborations in this field, younger researchers have set up two new networks: the Réseau International de jeunes Chercheurs en Histoire de l'Intégration Européenne (RICHIE), mainly led by postgraduate research students and young postdoctoral scholars from France, Germany and Italy, and the History of European Integration Research Society (HEIRS) created in the United Kingdom. Both networks utilize the opportunities for communication offered by the web (www.richie-cines.fr) and promote the transnational exchange of information on conferences, calls for papers, research projects and grant options. They have also organized regular conferences to which more senior scholars are usually invited as chairs or commentators, sometimes publishing edited books resulting from these conferences (Rücker and Warlouzet 2006; Affinito, Migani and Wenkel 2009). These networks were created by a generation of younger historians to partake in the scholarly debate dominated for a long time by a generation of more senior scholars from the Liaison Committee or those involved in the initiatives launched by Girault during the 1980s and 1990s. Although it is too early to assess the prospects or the overall long-term impact of these two networks that also collaborate to some extent, they have quickly become the focal point of new conceptual and methodological approaches in historical research on European integration, so that the Liaison Committee has even shown some interest in developing contacts with them.

Conclusion

Looking at the evolution of the historiography of European integration since the late 1970s, it becomes clear that the present-day EU, especially through the Commission, has played a strong role in developing European (Union) Studies at universities and research institutes across Europe and, in this context, has promoted research on the history of European integration as EU history. The early activities at the EUI and the opening up of the Community archives are cases in point.

During the late 1970s and early 1980s a group of mainly diplomatic historians led by the French historian Girault became interested in Europe's changing international role in the post-war period. They launched several international research projects which fed on the growing interest among historians of contemporary Europe in the Cold War and Europe's role in the East–West conflict over time. Their activities at first led to the formation of an informal community of European historians, who shared common assumptions about post-war European history: although the Cold War had played a role in shaping post-war (western) Europe, European integration was an important independent phenomenon and constituted a historical process worth studying in its own right.

Subsequently, the interaction between these historians' research activities and the Commission's aspiration at developing a university and cultural policy led to some larger joint initiatives and to the creation of, and Community support for, formal networks and research projects, especially the Liaison Committee, the research project on European identity, the Jean Monnet chairs for history (as well as three other disciplines) and the oral history projects. In the late 1980s and early 1990s the creation of the Jean Monnet Action favoured support for politically pro-integrationist historians, and the Commission's funding policy became more and more influenced by contingent political considerations. Owing to the commitment of some top EU civil servants, the Commission supported new research projects by transnational European networks.

At the start of the new century the Commission's commitment to support historical research on European integration declined sharply, while it favoured other disciplines and current issues. At the same time, as the chapters in this book demonstrate, the historiography of European integration has become more diverse and conceptually sophisticated, studying a variety of institutional and societal actors and their role in dynamic political processes in different policy fields including the present-day EU's external identity, all of which represents a move away from the former dominance of a diplomatic history of interstate negotiations. New sources have also become available, not least in the Community archives. At the same time, new technologies offer exciting opportunities for networking for an emerging new generation of researchers.

Despite the greater diversity and innovative potential of more recent historical research on European integration, this research field could still become more professional, mature and established both within contemporary history and in multidisciplinary European Studies. For this to happen, it would mainly need to address three key issues. The first concerns its prevailing narrative approach. To some extent this approach is appropriate for historical research. However, as Wolfram Kaiser discusses in his chapter, with some exceptions (Loth 2008) historians of European integration so far arguably have paid too little attention to theoretical, conceptual and methodological issues of European integration and EU politics, which they have largely left to political scientists, with too little cross-disciplinary cooperation.

The second issue is the autonomy of the historiography of European integration. In the more recent past, changing EU research policies and priorities have necessitated greater autonomy from EU institutions in Brussels, especially the Commission. However, most historians of European integration still need to develop greater academic autonomy from EU agendas. They are often perceived as an inward-looking group, and their works are too often ignored by other contemporary historians, even of (western) Europe. This is especially true of some general histories of Europe published in English (Hitchcock 2004; Judt 2005), which usually rely on not very research-based secondary literature on the EU, while the vast majority of publications on the history of the present-day EU was for a long time, and to some extent still is today, published in other languages, especially French, German and Italian.

The third issue concerns the definition of what constitutes the history of European integration. Can this historiography really be limited to the history of the present-day EU, its member states, supranational institutions and policy-making? Should it not also cover the dynamic relationship between European integration and historical developments at the member state and sub-national level? Would it not be necessary, moreover, to extend the temporal framework to the most recent history, to facilitate cross-disciplinary dialogue, and also backwards to the period before 1945–47, to uncover long-term continuities and discontinuities in European history? Is it possible to conceive of the history of European integration without taking into account the East–West conflict during the Cold War, or the wider international context including decolonization and what is now called globalization?

To become more fully integrated into contemporary history and European Studies and to make a larger contribution to academic debates beyond its own specialization, the historiography of European integration clearly has to conceptualize 'integration' in a way that covers these dimensions as part of a more complex European and international history.

Notes

1. Memorandum Peter Ludlow to Walter Lipgens, (?) March 1979, Historical Archives of the European Union (HAEU), Walter Lipgens Papers, b. 179.
2. Letter Walter Lipgens to participants of the project, 10 March 1977, HAEU, Lipgens Papers, b. 179.
3. The author thanks Jacqueline Lastenouse for the permission to quote a document in her possession and for other information she gave him about the origins of the Liaison Committee and the Commission's attitude.

2
From Pioneer Work to Refinement: Publication Trends

Katja Seidel

In the first issue of the *Journal of European Integration History* (*JEIH*), Alan S. Milward declared the coming of age of European integration history as a sub-field. Accordingly, it had developed into a 'separate historiography' (Milward 1995, 7). Milward also made far-reaching claims about the features and aims of such a new sub-field and the *JEIH*, which was to become one of its main outlets. The *JEIH* should mark 'the beginning of a new period of research where history now has its own theories and a research agenda which derives from them' (Milward 1995, 7).

The founding of the *JEIH* in 1995, the first journal dealing exclusively with the history of European integration, indeed helped to establish European integration history as a sub-field of contemporary history. Much time has passed since the creation of the journal and even more so, since the European Union (EU) Liaison Committee of Historians published the first volume of its book series. These two publications are at the centre of this chapter that aims to sketch the quantitative and qualitative development of the historiography of European integration in the more recent past. The chapter will also consider other journals, book series, monographs and edited books, however, since much innovative work has been published outside the mainstream publications. Building on Antonio Varsori's chapter on the background to the foundation of the *JEIH*, the first section will provide a short overview over the journal's main features. The second section will discuss publication trends as reflected in the themes and time-spans covered by the articles published in the journal since 1995. Finally, the third section will analyse thematic trends in the Liaison Committee's book series and other recent publications on European integration history.

Specialized outlet: the *Journal of European Integration History*

The *JEIH*'s administrative home is the Centre d'études et de recherches européennes Robert Schuman (CERE) in Luxembourg. So far the journal is not commercially viable. It is not subsidized, as one might have expected, by the European Commission, however. Instead, it is financed by the Luxembourg Ministries of State and National Education and Professional Training (Rapport d'activité 2007, 53). This link is not least due to the excellent contacts of the former director of the Robert Schuman Centre, Gilbert Trausch, to the political elite in Luxembourg, especially the ruling Christian democrats. It is also not surprising given that Luxembourg, and its Christian democratic prime ministers in the last 20 years, Jacques Santer and Jean-Claude Juncker, have strongly promoted European integration.

The Luxembourg government does not have a say in the management of the journal or its contents, however. Instead, the 14 members of the Liaison Committee form the journal's editorial board and control its content. Moreover, they partly combine the function of editing with that of peer reviewing the submitted manuscripts. Although external review is used occasionally, internal editorial review prevails over other more systematic and transparent systems such as single or double blind peer review, which other journals, especially in the social sciences, utilize. The process of peer reviewing is vital, however, and can contribute significantly to establishing a reliable body of research and knowledge in the field. While the members of the Liaison Committee have the necessary expertise in most research areas covered by the journal, it would probably enhance the diversity of the journal's content and its reputation of independence and academic excellence to systematically involve other academics as referees in the reviewing process.

The *JEIH* is published by the German publisher Nomos, which, together with the Belgian publisher Bruylant, also publishes the Liaison Committee's book series. The journal appears in print twice a year. Usually, one of the two issues is an open and the other a thematic number. Each issue is edited by a member of the Liaison Committee, although the thematic issues can also be proposed and coordinated by other researchers. The thematic issues often feature an introduction, as do some of the open issues. The issues – whether thematic or open – contain between four and eight articles. They are completed by book reviews, abstracts in English, French and German, general information such as calls for papers and books received, and short notes on the contributors. No statistics exist concerning the number of manuscripts submitted to the journal, accepted and rejected or on the topics covered by the rejected manuscripts.

In what way does the *JEIH* differ from other journals that feature the terms 'Europe' and 'history' in their titles? The self-proclaimed purpose of the *JEIH* is 'to encourage the analysis and understanding of different aspects of European integration, especially since 1945, in as wide a perspective as possible.' The emphasis is on 'European integration' and 'since 1945'. It is this particular thematic and chronological focus, which distinguishes the *JEIH* from its competitors. Looking at other academic journals, the *JEIH*'s main competitor has to be *Contemporary European History* (*CEH*). The quarterly founded three years earlier than the *JEIH*, covers the history of eastern and western Europe in the twentieth century and also publishes articles on integration history. *CEH* articles are exclusively published in English but there are abstracts in French and German.

The *CEH* is a fully peer reviewed journal ranked in the highest category A ('very strong reputation among researchers of the field in different countries, regularly cited all over the world') in the European Reference Index for the Humanities developed by the European Science Foundation. In contrast, the *JEIH* is ranked in category B ('good reputation among researchers of the field in different countries'). These rankings have been criticized for their arbitrary character and need to be treated with caution. Moreover, only between 10 and 25 per cent of all journals are ranked in the A category. However, in the long run, and with regard to the trend to systematically assess research, as for example, in the Research Assessment Exercise in the United Kingdom (UK), these rankings may become more important. The fact that the *JEIH* is not in the group of top international journals could make it less attractive for prospective authors and for libraries to subscribe to the journal. For a relatively new journal, it is important to be recognized as an authoritative publication to gain acceptance in the academic world. Still, whereas the *CEH* features in the Arts & Humanities Citation Index, the *JEIH* is not yet included in this search tool that allows access to data of over 1,100 journals in the humanities throughout the world. An alternative way of measuring the *JEIH*'s recognition and influence would be to analyse the numbers of subscriptions or of citations – the so-called Journal Impact Factor. So far, however, no information is available for the *JEIH*.

The second best option to assess the journal's dissemination and reception is a search in the national library catalogues. The results of such a search merely give a general idea of subscriptions as the journal may also be held by other institutional libraries not included in such library catalogues, or individuals. In France, several major libraries have subscribed to the *JEIH*. At least 20 university, national and institutional libraries hold the journal. However, only nine institutions have held it continuously since 1995. In Germany, too, the major university and national libraries hold the *JEIH*, 38 institutions in total. In Italy, 14 libraries subscribe to the *JEIH*, but only five have done so since 1995. At least in the three large EU founding member states, the *JEIH* is quite well established. Even taking into account the size of the country and the number of its universities, the clear focus is on Germany, however. Of course, the publisher's marketing strategy could be centred on Germany. In addition, as the journal is subsidized by the Luxembourg government, the publisher might not feel any urge to increase the number of subscriptions especially outside of Germany.

What about other European countries such as the UK? According to the Copac catalogue, to which most major libraries contribute, only nine university and national libraries have subscribed to the journal and only four have done so continuously since 1995, namely the British Library, and the university libraries of Cambridge, Manchester and the London School of Economics and Political Science. Researchers and students in large research-intensive universities like Edinburgh and Cardiff with significant European Studies programmes and with European Documentation Centres cannot consult it in their own library. Similarly, in the United States (US) only 16 libraries have subscribed to the journal, among them the Library of Congress in Washington and five of eight Ivy League universities. Starting with issue 1 (2001) the *JEIH* has become an open access journal available on the internet free of charge. This may take away the pressure for some libraries to subscribe to it. Due to contractual constraints imposed by the publisher, however, a new issue can only be uploaded on the CERE website six months after its publication at the earliest. In reality, it is often more than a year until a new issue appears on the website. For the latest issue, scholars and students therefore still depend on libraries subscribing to the journal.

While it can be seen as a competitor of the *JEIH* in some respects, the *CEH* is at the same time much broader in focus, and articles related to European integration are the exception rather than the rule. With its exclusive focus on European integration history, the *JEIH* thus clearly fills an important gap. It reflects the increasing relevance of European integration as a subject matter for historians since the 1980s. In this respect history is something of a latecomer. A number of social science journals are dedicated to Europe and European integration. They include the *Journal of Common Market Studies* (*JCMS*), which was founded in 1962, and the *Journal of European Public Policy* (*JEPP*) founded in 1994. While the *JCMS* is aimed at scholars of political science, economics and International Relations, the *JEPP* has a narrower focus on public policy and only features the occasional article with a long-term perspective on developments in the EU.

Unlike in the case of the *JCMS*, for example, cross-disciplinarity is not one of the explicit aims of the *JEIH*. However, the journal invites the analysis of developments since 1945 in 'as wide a perspective as possible'. In principle, this would make it open to contributions from other disciplines. In practice, however, this is the exception. Like other journals such as the *JEPP*, the *JEIH* hardly enters into a dialogue with other disciplines studying the EU. Not least in the light of the rise of European Studies as a teaching subject at universities in continental Europe as well as the UK, where it has been established in this form for much longer, this is a shortcoming that reflects how fragmented and inward-looking the different disciplines and journals still are.

A distinctive feature of the *JEIH* is its language regime. While the leading political science journals on European integration or the *CEH* publish exclusively in English, articles in the *JEIH* appear in English, French and German. In part, this reflects the strength of research on European integration history in France and Germany. As Varsori shows in his chapter, scholars like René Girault, Raymond Poidevin and Walter Lipgens were among the pioneers of this sub-field. Germany and France are also the most important founding member states of the EU, and the language spoken in Luxembourg is a variant of German while French is an official language in this country. Moreover, in continental Europe it is still expected that historians have at least a reading knowledge of these languages.

In practice the three languages are not equally frequently used by the authors, however. English clearly dominates, with 109 articles or 62 per cent of articles published between 1995 and 2008. French holds its ground with 52 articles or 29 per cent. German is in third position with 16 publications or nine per cent of articles. Comparing the usage of the three languages between 1995 and 2000 and between 2001 and 2008, English is clearly the dominating language (57/65 per cent) with the use of French declining (36/25 per cent) and German used occasionally (7/10 per cent). The use of language depends on different variables such as the nationality and mother tongue of the coordinator of a thematic issue, for example. Moreover, the language distribution suggests that some academic networks are still limited to one country or one language area. The rise in the use of English reflects the general trend of more and more scholars seeking to publish in this language with the aim of reaching a wider audience for their work. The continued relative importance of French in part also reflects the French government's policy to protect the use of French as an academic language against the dominance of English.

An analysis of the gender balance within the journal shows that male authors clearly dominate. Two-thirds (119) of authors were men and only one-third (61) were women. Comparing the gender balance between 1995 and 2000 and between 2001 and 2008, the percentage of articles by women has only marginally increased from 32 to 36 per cent. However, the percentages seem to be roughly in line with the representation of women in academic posts in contemporary history across Europe more generally. Of the senior researchers who are members of the Liaison Committee only two are women.

The Liaison Committee's mission statement says that the *JEIH* aims to be 'a permanent forum for the increasing numbers of young historians who dedicate their research to contemporary Europe' (CERE website). While it was not possible to assess the average age of the contributors, several indicators suggest that this is indeed the case. At least two recent thematic issues were compiled due to the initiative of younger academics, Linda Risso (2/2007) and Morten Rasmussen (2/2008), although they were formally edited by members of the Liaison Committee. Both of these scholars are also involved in the work of the History of European Integration Research Society and the Réseau International de jeunes Chercheurs en Histoire de l'Intégration Européenne, the international networks of postgraduate researchers in European integration history, which have begun to impact on the evolution of the sub-field, as Varsori also underlines in his chapter.

Analysing the authors' institutional affiliations can pinpoint geographical centres of research on European integration history. Given the increasing mobility of academics, the institutional affiliation does not always correspond to the authors' nationality. This is especially the case for academics working in the British university system, which attracts a high and rapidly rising number of foreign scholars. Overall, authors with an affiliation in the six EU founding member states are in the majority (101 out of a total of 180). Among them, authors working in Germany (17 per cent/30 articles), Italy (14 per cent/26 articles) and France (13 per cent/24 articles) constitute the largest groups. However, with 31 articles scholars with institutional affiliations in Britain and

Ireland outnumber those with affiliations in Germany. Authors from Scandinavia published 7 per cent of all articles, which is a high per capita figure, and 7 per cent were by authors based in the US and Canada. All in all, authors from western Europe are still strikingly dominant in this research field. Only one author came from Turkey and Cyprus respectively, and five were affiliated at the time of publication with research institutions in central and eastern Europe. Likewise, Spanish and Portuguese authors have only marginally contributed to the *JEIH*.

While the *JEIH* is dominated by historians from the founding member states of the present-day EU, it does not exclude contributions by researchers from other disciplines. The thematic issue on the break-up of Yugoslavia (1/2003), for instance, is dominated by authors with a background in international relations. More likely than not, however, political scientists will submit articles on the invitation of a special issue coordinator. This is hardly surprising given the ever greater emphasis placed by social scientists on publishing in top-ranking journals in their own discipline. On the other hand, a recent *JEIH* volume (1/2008) dedicated to 'theory and history' arguably reflects a growing readiness on the part of mostly younger historians of European integration to engage with theory.

Themes and time-spans in the *Journal of European Integration History*

In his essay published in the first issue of the *JEIH*, Milward (1995, 9) criticized European integration historians for their strong focus on diplomatic and military history; a perspective that according to him, ignored economic, social and intellectual developments. Further, Milward (1995, 12–13) would have liked to see the inclusion of long-term perspectives into the analysis of European integration, which reach from the inter-war period to post-1945 events. In the light of his remarks, which did not necessarily reflect the position of the Liaison Committee as a whole, this section will analyse the themes and time-spans addressed by the articles published in the *JEIH* between 1995 and 2008. This will allow the identification of more recent research and publication trends. It will also highlight themes that are either missing or not sufficiently researched, at least in terms of publications in the *JEIH*.

According to its mission statement the *JEIH* is committed to covering a wide range of themes: 'The Journal publishes the conclusions of research on diplomatic, military, economic, technological, social and cultural aspects of integration.' For a content analysis of the *JEIH*, the published articles can be grouped into categories roughly matching those listed above: diplomatic, defence, cultural, institutional, technological, social, and economic history and articles with a biographical or conceptual focus. It is no doubt problematic to allocate articles to one particular thematic category as they often address several dimensions. For the sake of the analysis, however, a choice had to be made. The theme dominating an article and its source base were decisive for allotting it to one category. For example, in order to be classified as diplomatic history an article would be based mainly on governmental, often foreign ministry sources and deal with national European policies and interstate relations. The different categories were first used to assess the overall distribution of themes in the journal between 1995 and 2008, before a splitting up of this period into three phases (1995–98; 1999–2002; 2003–08) to test whether the thematic focus has shifted.

Articles from a diplomatic history perspective take up by far the largest space in the journal with one-third or 60 articles falling into this category. Diplomatic history themes dominate both open and thematic issues. For example, several thematic issues are concerned with one country or a group of countries and their policies towards European integration and the present-day EU. In 2000, a thematic issue was dedicated to relations between the US and western Europe from the 1950s to the 1970s (2/2000). Other issues dealt with countries on the periphery of Europe (1/2001), small and neutral states and their attitudes towards European integration (2/2001) or Soviet policy towards European integration (1/2002). A variation of the theme was a special issue in 2003, which dealt with one event, the summit at The Hague in 1969 (2/2003) and the policies of different member states and the Commission towards issues discussed and decided at this meeting. Articles written from a diplomatic history perspective are even slightly on the increase. While in the first period (1995–98) 15 articles had themes falling into this category, the last period (2003–08) had 26 articles, which marks a significant increase even after the greater length of the third period (six versus four years) is taken into account.

Although it constitutes a separate category for the purpose of this analysis, defence history conceptually and methodologically is a variation of diplomatic history. With 15 articles it is in third position of all themes addressed in *JEIH* articles, but its popularity is slowly waning in favour of other themes such as institutional history. The latter is on the rise, as is technological history. The number of articles dealing with European institutions has increased from five in 1995–2002 to 13 in 2003–08. Technological aspects of integration were central in

11 articles in total, six of them in a special issue on research and technological cooperation in Europe (2/2006). Up until 2007 the constitutional
and legal history of European integration was much under-represented
with only one article in the first issue on the European Court of Justice
(ECJ, 1/1995). The situation has changed somewhat, however, with a
recent special issue (2/2008) dedicated to the legal aspects of integration
history, particularly the ECJ.

Economic history in contrast had its peak in the early years of the
journal with six articles published until 1999 including a special issue
(2/1997). The importance of economic history in the early years can be
explained with the influence of Milward within the editorial board and
at the European University Institute, and that of his seminal book *The
European Rescue of the Nation-State* (Milward 1992) on the historiography
of European integration more generally. However, this influence did not
have a lasting effect on the choice of themes in the *JEIH*. Not one article
on an economic topic was published in the period between 1999 and
2002. With three articles published in the period 2003–08, economic
history has seen only a slight revival. Its small role in European integration history is however very much in line with its general decline in the
disciplines of history and economics.

In contrast, cultural aspects of integration became fashionable around
the turn of the century when 14 articles were published within the four
years from 1999 to 2002. In 1999, the *JEIH* published a special issue
on the cultural roots of Europe (2/1999). Overall, a total of 18 articles
dealing with cultural aspects of integration history were published in
the period from 1995 to 2008 of which only two appeared in the six-
year period from 2003 to 2008. Thus, the historiography of European
integration in the *JEIH* clearly experienced no 'cultural turn'. On the
other hand, articles dealing with politicians, bureaucrats and other
actors are slowly on the increase reflecting a more general tendency in
current research to assess the background, actions and role of individuals in European integration. The period up to 1998 saw four articles on
individuals like the leading French socialist politician Maurice Faure
(2/1997) and the first post-war Christian Democratic Italian Prime
Minister Alcide De Gasperi (1/1998). More recently, there seems to be
a shift from biographical studies of the so-called 'founding fathers'
to research on less well-known bureaucrats, businessmen and others
like Émile Noël, the long-serving secretary general of the Commission,
Émile Mayrisch, an industrialist and businessman from Luxembourg,
and Karl-Maria Hettlage, a German member of the High Authority of
the European Coal and Steel Community (ECSC) in the 1960s (1/2006).

In total, 14 articles had such a biographical focus of which seven were published in the period 2003–08.

Moreover, few articles published in the *JEIH* deal with current developments or cover large time-spans. Historians hold different views on the extent to which their research should respond to current affairs issues. In the sub-field of EU history, however, which discusses the origins and evolution of a polity in which most Europeans now live, it would seem especially appropriate for historians to contribute to the discussion of current affairs in a suitable form. In fact, one volume of the *JEIH* dealt with the origins and evolution of the wars in the former Yugoslavia (1/2003) from 1990 to 1995. It brought together contributions from International Relations scholars and practitioners with a background in government crisis management. Yet, most of these articles were published elsewhere before and did not shed new light on the wars in the former Yugoslavia. Instead, it would be preferable if a journal like the *JEIH* were to take recent and current developments as the wars in the former Yugoslavia as a starting point, but with a view to investigating the long-term historical background of such events. It might have been expected, for example, that the *JEIH* published a special issue on historical dimensions of the EU's Eastern enlargement in 2004. However, only two articles addressed the cases of Poland and the Czech Republic, two of the new EU member states.

Milward (1995, 7) predicted that integration history would develop its own 'theories' and a research agenda derived from them. This has not happened. The *JEIH* has published very few theoretical and conceptual chapters although their number has increased slightly in recent years to seven in the period 2003–08 from only two in the period 1995–98 and three in the period 1999–2002. However, these articles predominantly utilize for heuristic purposes theories developed in the social sciences and do not develop or promote original 'European integration history theories', as Milward expected. In 2003 one article dealt with the role of neo-functionalism for decision-making in the European Economic Community (EEC) of the 1960s (1/2003). Finally, in 2008 one issue (1/2008) was dedicated to 'theory and history'. The small number of theoretical, theoretically informed or conceptual articles most likely does not reflect a strategic decision on the part of the *JEIH* editors to exclude such articles. Rather, it reflects the reluctance of most historians, especially in the sub-field of integration history, to work with, let alone generate, theories. As Wolfram Kaiser shows in his chapter, this applies especially to theories as highly generalized law-like statements about social processes based on sets of falsifiable hypotheses.

All in all, as this book demonstrates, European integration historiography as a sub-field has seen a trend away from classical diplomatic history themes and approaches towards exploring multilateral, supranational and transnational perspectives (see also Kaiser 2006, 2009b). The *JEIH* as the key journal in the field has not been a trend-setter in this process, however, but has rather followed such new trends. In fact, diplomatic history has remained the most popular approach for European integration scholars publishing in the *JEIH*.

Research trends can also become visible by analysing the chronological focus of research in a sub-field like European integration history. The articles in the *JEIH* cover six periods: up to 1939, 1939–45, 1945–51, 1952–73, the 1970s, and the 1980s until today. For the purpose of this chapter, the latest date or event covered by an article was taken to determine its categorization. The majority of articles (79) deal with the period 1952–73, starting with the establishment of the ECSC and finishing with the first enlargement of the European Communities (EC) by the UK, Denmark and Ireland in 1973. This history mainly concerns the six founding member states France, Italy, Germany and the three Benelux countries. This focus corresponds to the dominant institutional affiliation of *JEIH* authors and the geographical distribution of *JEIH* subscriptions. Moreover, it has remained almost constant between 1995 and 2008.

Given this dominance of the founding years of the ECSC/EEC/EC, it is not surprising that only two articles deal with the period of World War II. At the same time, however, seven articles cover the period before 1939 and 17 articles focus on the immediate post-war period, namely 1945–51. One explanation for this lack of interest in the period from 1939 to 1945 might be that in the 1970s and early 1980s, Lipgens' main focus had been on the history of European integration ideas in the resistance movements. Long before the *JEIH* was founded, however, Milward in particular had declared this research approach obsolete. Similarly, although many dimensions of the origins of European integration after World War II are either insufficiently researched or still very controversial, interest in the immediate post-war period until the formation of the ECSC appears to have declined. Between 1995 and 2000 ten articles dealt with the period 1945–51, eight focused on this period were published during the eight years from 2001 to 2008. The fact that the balance sheet is not worse for the second period is mainly due to a special issue on communist parties and European integration in the post-war period (2/2007). In contrast, starting from a low level of interest, the pre-war years have become marginally more popular. Only two contributions dealt with this period between 1995 and 2000. From 2001 to 2008, however, five articles covered pre-World War II Europe.

This slight shift in the periods covered by the articles published in the *JEIH* points to a broadening of the chronological as well as the thematic scope of the *JEIH* and integration historiography more generally. This trend is confirmed when looking at articles that focus on the period after 1973. From 1995 to 2000 no article dealt with the 1980s or early 1990s and only five took the 1970s into account. From 2001 to 2008 an increasingly large number of contributions reach far into the 1970s (seven) and even the 1980s and 1990s (25). Again, this is mostly due to special issues such as those on the Yugoslav wars, the European public sphere (2/2002) and the relations of the Soviet Union with Europe and the EU (1/2005). On the whole, publications on integration history follow the general 30-year rule for the opening up of state and Community archives, while articles on the 1980s and 1990s are based on sources other than archival material.

Towards refinement: the Liaison Committee series and other publications

In contrast to its editorial oversight of the *JEIH*, the Liaison Committee can freely choose the themes and participants of all of its conferences, which form the basis of its book series. Nevertheless, this book series reflects to some extent the research undertaken both by many of the most recognized scholars in the field and by some younger researchers. As such, the book series mirrors publication trends in European integration history. To date, the book series comprises 12 volumes of which the first 11 were used for this analysis. The first volume, edited by French historian Poidevin, was published in 1986. It was based on a conference in Strasbourg in November 1984 where researchers presented papers dealing with European integration history in the immediate post-war period up to the Schuman Plan declaration of 9 May 1950. In the introduction to this volume, Poidevin discussed the rationale behind this first volume of what was to become the new book series. Accordingly, the aim of the volume was to present original research based on recently opened archives and newly accessible source material. Poidevin qualified the archives of foreign ministries as being particularly important and he argued that 'Europe in its beginnings was born in Paris, London, Bonn, Brussels, The Hague, Luxembourg, Rome and Washington' (Poidevin 1986, 5). The subsequent volumes followed the chronological approach and the aim of publishing research based on recently released archival sources. This approach has certainly led to the publication of original research. At the same time, however, it bears the danger of publishing contributions that lack in originality as they tend to be based on one set of source materials, mostly governmental (foreign ministry) archives, and to favour a narrative of European integration history as the result of multilateral negotiation of 'national interests'.

In terms of dominant research themes, it is possible to differentiate between two phases in the book series. The first pioneer phase was characterized by narrow chronological time-frames determined by the opening or availability of new archival materials and the dominance of diplomatic history themes. The second phase could be called a period of maturation as it was characterized by thematically more coherent volumes with a greater diversity of conceptual and methodological approaches. This second phase was already noticeable in volume eight (Loth 2001). To some extent, this volume did not just compile chapters that were based on new archival research, without being integrated, however, but marked an attempt at achieving greater overall cohesion. In his introduction, Wilfried Loth argued convincingly that the years from 1963 to 1969 covered by the volume constituted a coherent time-span. He aptly pulled together the threads of the different contributions to form a fairly coherent narrative. Volume nine (Varsori 2006b) marks the real beginning of the second phase, however. This book covers a larger time-span than volumes seven (Deighton and Milward 1999) and eight taken together, namely 1957–72. Most likely, the striking absence of institutions and actors from these two previous volumes as well as the profound criticism of the chronological approach at the conference in Essen, which Varsori refers to in his chapter, triggered this break in the tradition. Clearly, the 1960s were a period in which European institutions such as the Commission, the Council of Ministers and the ECJ began to play key roles in supranational politics, something not reflected in the previous volumes. There has been no fundamental break with the chronological approach, however. In fact, volume 11, edited by Jan van der Harst (2007), deals with the period from 1969 to 1975. Nevertheless, this volume, too, integrates a greater variety of themes and research perspectives. The contributions are not exclusively based on governmental sources but take different types of sources into account. Some also have a stronger conceptual focus such as Jan-Henrik Meyer's discussion of the evolution of the European public sphere(s) in historical perspective and Rasmussen's elaboration of state power and the *acquis communautaire* drawing on the case study of Denmark's accession negotiations at the start of the 1970s.

Throughout the history of this book series, there have been four exceptions to the preferred chronological approach. Volume five (Dumoulin 1995) focused on wartime plans for postwar Europe and volume six (Trausch 2005) on small states and 'Europe'. Volume ten (Bitsch and Bossuat 2005) dealt with relations between western Europe and Africa from the inter-war years to the first Lomé Convention in 1975. European actors and policies were at the centre of volume nine (Varsori 2006b). For the purpose of this chapter, the contributions to the book series' volumes have been ranged in the same categories as the articles in the *JEIH*, namely diplomatic, defence, ideas and cultural, institutional, technological, social, economic history, conceptual and biographical chapters. As in the *JEIH*, the main focus of the contributions was for a long time on diplomatic history. In fact, 101 chapters in all 11 volumes fall into this category. This trend is receding somewhat, however. Chapters dealing with defence issues only account for 12 contributions in total, while chapters dealing with history of ideas and cultural history topics are relatively numerous (37). The majority of these chapters were published in the thematic volumes on wartime plans and Europe and Africa (13 and eight). Thus, this focus does not mark a general trend of the book series.

The increased focus on institutional history and on multilateral dimensions of integration politics also visible in the *JEIH* constitutes a more substantial recent trend in European integration history, however. Since volume eight, 19 chapters examined topics from institutional and/ or multilateral perspectives, compared to only five in the first seven volumes. As in the *JEIH*, social dimensions of European integration remain insufficiently explored with only seven chapters in total. Some 21 chapters cover economic aspects and nine the origins and evolution of common European policies such as the Common Agricultural Policy. As in the *JEIH*, however, economic history has remained weak with the bulk of chapters with such a focus (nine) concentrated in only one book, volume two (Schwabe 1988). Only four chapters have a conceptual focus and 13 chapters a biographical focus dealing with European actors. In contrast to the *JEIH*, there has been no significant increase in chapters with a biographical focus more recently.

Moreover, as the volumes still predominantly follow a chronological approach, moving with the opening of governmental and Community archives, the period before World War II is practically not treated at all. In the first two volumes and in volume four (Trausch 1993), all chapters dealt with the period 1945–52. In volume three (Serra 1989) and from volume seven onwards, all chapters dealt with the period 1952–75.

Only five and three chapters respectively in volumes six (Trausch 2005) and ten focused on the period before 1939. The analysis of the book series thus makes it even clearer than that of the *JEIH* that research on European integration history so far has been mainly confined to the post-war era and, more specifically, to the core period of European integration from 1952 to 1973.

The range of authors publishing in the book series is quite broad. Members of the Liaison Committee contribute, but this core group is extended by other researchers. The volumes include contributions by younger scholars often presenting the results of their PhD research. Depending on the theme or chronological framework, other more established scholars in contemporary European and international history, who are not necessarily specialists in the history of European integration, also write chapters. The trend seems to be towards including more scholars from European integration history, however, which may well reflect the coming of age of the sub-field, with many more researchers specialized in the history of European integration. Again, the geographical distribution of institutional affiliations is similar to that of the *JEIH*. Authors linked to institutions in 'core Europe' of the six founding member states are in the majority, followed by authors from the UK, the US and Scandinavia. Very few authors are affiliated with institutions in Spain and Portugal and only one eastern European author participated in a Liaison Committee conference. This is likely to change in the future, however, if the chronological approach is maintained and the books begin to cover the 1980s and beyond.

The language regime of the volumes allows chapters to be published in the four languages English, French, German and Italian. The use of the latter two languages is especially strongly decreasing, however. Again, this development is similar to the *JEIH*. French still holds its ground to some extent, but in volume 11 for the first time all contributions were published in English.

Obviously, a large number of edited books are published outside of the Liaison Committee series, but still involve some of its members. Some of these edited books based on conferences were published in the book series Organisation Internationale et Relations Internationales published by Bruylant. Two of these volumes have a thematic focus and deal with institutions and identities in Europe (Bitsch, Loth and Poidevin 1998) and political cultures and public opinion and European integration (Bitsch, Loth and Barthel 2007). With their rather well-defined thematic focus they are part of the second 'maturation' phase of European integration history. Since the early 1990s, moreover, other book series with a focus on European history have been established, as Varsori also shows in his chapter. The Euroclio series published by Peter Lang is edited by Eric Bussière, Michel Dumoulin and Varsori. It was launched in 1993 and comprises 45 volumes to date. The series includes monographs, often based on PhD research, and some interesting coherently edited volumes, for example on the history of economic thought in twentieth-century Europe and on national administrations and European integration (Badel, Jeannesson and Ludlow 2005; Bussière, Dumoulin and Schirmann 2006a, 2006b, 2007). The series Europe plurielle – Multiple Europes (Peter Lang) was established in 1989 and is edited by the Swedish historian Bo Stråth. The 43 volumes in this series are not focused on the European integration process strictly speaking, but cover the history of Europe since the French Revolution. The aim of the series is to explore the 'multiplicity of Europe' and to look 'at the variety of ways in which social community and images of cohesion have been constructed in Europe'. Two other series, Fonti e studi sul federalismo e l'integrazione europea and Storia del federalismo e dell'integrazione europea, are edited by the Centro di ricerca sull'integrazione europea at the University of Siena. As also discussed by Daniele Pasquinucci in his chapter, these volumes are published by the publisher Il Mulino, which is part of an organization with very close links to the (Italian) federalist movement. In fact, most of the 19 volumes published to date focus on the history of federalism. Finally, a new series on European integration history, edited by Jürgen Elvert, is currently being established by the German publisher Franz Steiner.

Obviously, as the other chapters in this book show, a substantial number of relevant and influential books, especially monographs and coherent edited books, are published outside of such series, not least by British publishers like Palgrave, Routledge and Cambridge University Press, for example. Two recent influential collective publications stand out as examples of books that push a new research agenda in EU history. The first book, *The History of the European Union. Origins of a Trans- and Supranational Polity 1950–72* (Kaiser, Leucht and Rasmussen 2009) demonstrates how historians can benefit from utilizing social science theories and concepts for improving their research and historical narratives of European integration history. The second volume, *Networks in European Multi-Level Governance*, brings together contemporary historians and political scientists for the study of the role of (policy) networks in politics and policy-making in the EU in a long-term perspective up to the present (Gehler, Kaiser and Leucht 2009). This book demonstrates in particular how fruitful cooperation across disciplines can be, especially for assessing temporal change in integration and EU politics and governance. Both volumes understand the present-day EU as an emerging trans- and supranational polity, which has developed its own governing structures, policies and identities over time. Both volumes also practise cross-disciplinary communication and cooperation. The authors discuss and engage with social science theories and concepts such as liberal intergovernmentalism, networks and social and historical institutionalism, with much greater potential to make a significant contribution to social science debates on the EU. Books such as these, thoroughly edited and with a clear research agenda, are leading the way into a third phase of European integration history, or what could be called a phase of refinement.

Conclusion

While the *JEIH* and the Liaison Committee book series are still characterized by the predominant focus on core Europe and diplomatic history perspectives of the early historiography of European integration, they have slowly widened their scope of themes, research perspectives and periods covered. Authors from, and themes dealing with, southern, central and eastern Europe are heavily under-represented in the sub-field. This under-representation is largely due to the fact that the eastern European 'integration' of the post-war period in the Comecon so far is not discussed as part of European integration history. At the same time, EU history is not (yet) a relevant and developed sub-field of contemporary history in these countries. The *JEIH* and other journals encounter great difficulties in trying to encourage authors from these parts of Europe to submit manuscripts. However, it is likely that as archives release documents on the 1970s and 1980s, journals will soon receive more manuscripts for articles dealing in the first instance with countries such as Greece, Spain and Portugal that joined the EU in 1981 and 1986, respectively. Likewise, with its chronological approach, the Liaison Committee book series should see more chapters about these 'latecomers' to European integration, their European policies, accession to the EU and resulting Europeanization effects, for example. With the continuing highly controversial debate on the Turkish application for EU membership, a historical perspective on this topic could come to the fore.

The *JEIH* and other journals cannot prescribe and control the research articles submitted to them. Yet the *JEIH* in particular could use its special issues to encourage research on neglected topics. Special issues dealing with the emergence and development of new Community policies or with political party cooperation and European integration, for example, could address trans- and supranational dimensions to moderate the national paradigm that still dominates research on European integration. The Liaison Committee should probably widen the chronological, geographical and thematic scope of the *JEIH* and the book series or such research will perhaps still be undertaken, but published elsewhere.

So far, the publication trends in EU history have followed a pattern that is common for newly established historical sub-fields. In a first phase, many publications were informed by a diplomatic history perspective. Previously, this perspective had been applied to understanding international relations before democratization and integration in western Europe. Research during the first phase was characterized by a need to accomplish pioneer work, to consult and utilize newly available governmental archives and to explain national policies and reactions towards European integration. This was vital research that needed to be undertaken, and still needs to be undertaken, although our understanding of European politics and policy-making in pluralist democracies has advanced significantly from the earlier understanding of national European policies as cohesive projections of interests and power. The research conducted during this pioneer phase was eventually criticized as inadequate for analysing aspects of European integration history beyond foreign policy-making by member states and intergovernmental bargaining.

As a result, the pioneer phase was followed by a second phase of maturation of the research sub-field, which entailed a broadening of themes, perspectives and time-spans covered. The origins of common policies, the creation of supranational institutions and the formation and greater activities of non-state actors necessitated a diversification of themes covered, methods utilized and sources selected. It could be argued that the sub-field is currently entering a third phase of research, a phase of refinement. This phase is characterized by research and publications with more sophisticated conceptual frameworks to refine research strategies and historical narratives. The greater reflection by contemporary historians on their own sub-field, its goals and shortcomings (Gilbert 2007, 2008; Kaiser 2008) is similarly characteristic of this third refinement phase. So far, studies and research projects typical of this phase adopt multilateral, multi-institutional and multi-level perspectives for understanding European integration history (for example, Ludlow 2006; Kaiser 2007; Trunk 2007; Gehler, Kaiser and Leucht 2009). The increasing popularity of themes such as crises in EU history and the origins and evolution of 'Euroscepticism' also mark the third phase in which historians begin to interpret European integration less as a story of unstoppable progress towards an 'ever closer union' (Treaty on European Union, 1992). Instead, they call into question this dominant teleological historiography of much of the earlier historiography. Arguably, with its aim of taking stock of the historiography of the EU, this volume also contributes to the third refinement phase of the sub-field.

3
From Isolation to Centrality: Contemporary History Meets European Studies

Wolfram Kaiser

Any discussion of the historiography of European integration needs to address its integration within the larger discipline of (Modern) European history since the French Revolution, especially its contemporary history since World War II, its linkages with other disciplines with a focus on the present-day European Union (EU), and the benefits and pitfalls of cross-disciplinarity. This is understood here in a general sense as the attempt to overcome disciplinary boundaries to better understand the complexities of European integration and EU politics. Arguably, this dimension of research on integration history is especially crucial as this historical sub-field on the whole has been quite isolated within Modern European history and European Studies. With the exception of a few monographs like Alan S. Milward's (1992) revisionist account, most works on European integration history including the edited books published by the Liaison Committee and articles in the specialized *Journal of European Integration History* (*JEIH*) are seldom referenced in general histories of twentieth century or post-war Europe or, for that matter, by social scientists working on the EU. As we will see below, this sorry state of affairs to some extent reflects the weaknesses of these genres and research traditions. To an equally large extent, however, it is due to the fact that for a long time, much research on the history of European integration, especially the federalist hurrah historiography and the conventional diplomatic history of interstate negotiations, has been conceptually underdeveloped.

Against this background, this chapter will explore four core dimensions of the connections of European integration historiography with other research and publications on Europe and the EU. The first concerns the limited integration of this historiography within Modern European history more generally – this at a time when the EU's constitution clearly has many features of a federal polity, even if it lacks some crucial attributes of the nineteenth-century nation-state like common defence and internal policing, and when its policy- and law-making has become increasingly intrusive, with many direct effects on European citizens. In other words, one might expect – as historians of European integration have always done (Ludlow 2009, 42) – that the EU's evolution over time would form a core part of any analysis and narrative of European history. The second dimension is the lack of cross-disciplinary integration of this historiography – this at a time when political science research on the present-day EU in particular, which already started in the mid-1950s, has seen exponential growth over the last 30 years, which historians cannot ignore; and when researchers in other disciplines have in fact become more and more interested in understanding European integration in a larger sense than interstate bargaining and supranational policy-making.

The third dimension addressed in this chapter concerns the existing limited (but much greater future potential for) cross-disciplinary cooperation with three broad fields selected for this purpose as especially relevant: political science, sociology and cultural studies. In all cases, a broadening of our understanding of what constitutes European integration or EU history could open up new vistas for research. Linked to this analysis, the conclusion, fourthly, assesses the more general potential benefits of greater cross-disciplinary cooperation as well as its pitfalls. Such pitfalls undoubtedly exist and are probably one reason why so far, most historians of European integration have shied away from reaching out to, and working with, researchers from other disciplines to better understand the origins and current state of integrated Europe.

European integration historiography within Modern European history

Over time the present-day EU has acquired substantial powers shared by the member states and different institutions involved in policy-making, and it has developed legislation and regulation with massive impact on national politics, businesses and citizens. From the creation of the European Coal and Steel Community (ECSC) and the European Economic Community (EEC) in the 1950s, European integration has been one of the most central phenomena in the contemporary history of (western) Europe, from its early significance for the six 'core

Europe' founding member states through its subsequent enlargements and including its growing strong impact on non-member states like Switzerland and Norway, for example. Despite the EU's crucial importance for understanding Europe in contemporary historical perspective, however, EU history is only weakly institutionalized in universities and research institutes across Europe. The Jean Monnet chair programme discussed by Antonio Varsori in his chapter gives some politically motivated visibility to EU history. At the same time, the only chair for European integration history at the European University Institute first held by Walter Lipgens from 1976 to 1979 was actually transformed into a general post for Modern European history in 2006–07, leading to the marginalization of integration history at that institution.

Another possible indicator for the sub-field's integration, or lack thereof, into Modern European history is the treatment of European integration history in general histories of modern and contemporary Europe. For a long time such general histories, written in an accessible style for a larger readership, have been a domain of the Anglo-Saxon scholarly tradition. Such general books published in English easily have the largest circulation and readership and are often influential in shaping the dominant narratives beyond specialized sub-fields. Interestingly, however, as part of the recent wave of such general histories of twentieth-century or post-war Europe most books largely ignore European integration. Thus, despite the crucial importance of the EU for market liberalization and the development of the (western) European economy since World War II, the British (economic) historian Harold James (2003) devotes only 15 out of nearly 500 pages to this topic. Similarly, despite his earlier archive-based work on French foreign and European policy after 1945 (Hitchcock 1998), the American (diplomatic) historian William I. Hitchcock (2003) provides no in-depth discussion of European integration either. Originally an expert on eastern European history, even Mark Mazower (1998), who has professed his belief that the EU is the only suitable framework for overcoming internecine ethnic conflict in (eastern and south-eastern) Europe, makes few references to its post-war history.

Other books implicitly or explicitly advance counter-narratives that are highly critical of European integration and the present-day EU. At one end of the political spectrum is the British intellectual historian Tony Judt (2005). He emphasizes integration as a framework for peaceful conflict regulation and highlights its allegedly distinctive social model as setting Europe apart from the rest of the world. However, Judt's treatment of European integration is still largely informed by perceptions of the EU among the political Left in the Labour Party in the 1970s. Typical images range from the Community as the supranational embodiment of the capitalist system to its political and administrative order as the death-knell of participatory democracy. At the other end of the political spectrum lies the American author John Gillingham's (2003) aggressively neo-liberal 'Republican' attack on the EU informed by the Reaganomics of the 1980s. Despite its more limited title, Gillingham's book is an attempt to write the history of (western) Europe utilizing a comparative approach and putting integration at the core. However, his narrative, which was developed before the world financial crisis originated in the United States (US) in 2007, is informed by a view of the EU as a bureaucratic monster that did not at all foster the extension of capitalism, as it should have done and as authors like Judt in fact believe it has done. Instead, in spite of the overwhelming evidence pointing to the crucial role of the European Commission in market liberalization, Gillingham accuses the EU, and the Commission in particular, of supranational over-regulation that has severely undermined Europe's economic competitiveness. In fact, Gillingham followed up his first general history with an even more blatantly political treatise (2006) on how to reinvent the EU from scratch to turn it into a bulwark of neo-liberalism, with the liberal economist Friedrich August von Hayek as intellectual inspiration and the former Conservative British Prime Minister Margaret Thatcher as 'founding mother'.

In the case of the first set of general histories of twentieth-century or post-war Europe, the authors clearly know little about European integration and even less about its historiography. In the case of the second set of more politicized general histories, they deliberately foster negative counter-narratives as the flipside of the enthusiastic federalist historiography discussed by Daniele Pasquinucci in his chapter. These counter-narratives have a similarly teleological view of the EU except that they see it on an unstoppable path towards disaster and disintegration.

Alongside these and other structural weaknesses of Anglo-Saxon narratives of contemporary European history including the almost exclusive reliance on literature published in English, the normative and teleological nature of much of the early historiography of European integration (Gilbert 2008) probably contributed to its initial lack of integration with Modern European history. In the long run, however, four factors appear to account for this lack of integration. The first of these is the almost exclusive focus of EU historians – with the partial exception of 'latecomer' countries where EU membership was controversial from the start – on politics and decision-making in the supranational centre.

This research has failed to make sufficient connections with either domestic contestation of EU politics or the Europeanization impact of integration on the member states, their politics and societies. However, it is precisely the far-reaching domestic impact of European integration which could help historians of national, regional and local history connect with EU history.

Secondly, the traditional diplomatic history of national European policy-making and interstate bargaining also identified by Katja Seidel in her chapter as still the dominant conceptual and methodological approach to the history of European integration has alienated social and cultural historians in particular. Paradoxically, despite the fact that the present-day EU has always been a polity in the making, the diplomatic historiography of the EU as national policy-making and multilateral negotiations has lagged behind relevant debates and innovations in international history (especially of the nineteenth century) like transnational history and cultural transfer, for example (for example, Loth and Osterhammel 2000). For too long, historians of the EU treated it as an international organization to be explained in a realist interest-based framework. Usually, such interests were implicitly regarded as given, for example resulting from a certain geographical position or economic structure of a country, or as defined by small foreign policy-making elites. Even Milward, who has been just as scathing of this traditional diplomatic history of integration as of Lipgens' history of the European idea and European movements, utilized the idea of 'national interest' in an astonishingly superficial manner until his book on British European policy (2002b), when he replaced it (not very convincingly) with the term 'national strategy'.

Thirdly, the existing textbook-type introductions to the history of European integration and the EU, which could help integrate the sub-field within Modern European history more generally, amount to reasonably reliable, but very descriptive narratives (for example, Dinan 2004; Bitsch 2008). With a few partial exceptions (Gilbert 2003) these books fail to provide sophisticated introductions to debates and controversies, which in turn could put down crucial markers for the wider academic importance of the sub-field. Moreover, without exception the English-language textbooks, which are most widely used, are written by political scientists or historians who have not themselves done any substantial primary research on European integration history. While such views from outside of a research field can be refreshing, they are often not sufficiently informed by recent and ongoing research.

Fourthly, with few exceptions (Benzoni and Vigezzi 2001) historians of European integration have almost completely failed to establish connections across World War II (or across the Cold War divide, but see e.g. Enderle-Burcel et al. 2009; Kirschbaum 2007), further aggravating its isolation within the field of Modern European history. It has only been attempted in conventional histories of European ideas, which have traced such integration ideas back to the resistance movements, as in the case of the German historian Lipgens (1982), or the medieval philosopher Thomas Aquinas in other histories of ideas, but failed to demonstrate their impact on the actual integration process. Neo-Marxist historians like Thomas Sandkühler in his pointed introduction to an edited book (2002) and Patricia Commun (2002) in one of its chapters have raised interesting questions, but provided very ideologically driven answers concerning continuities across World War II. In essence they have claimed (without much supporting evidence) that the ECSC was a German capitalist plot to establish the hegemony of a kind of Fourth Reich over (western) Europe. Although, as Seidel shows in her chapter, some books and articles in the *JEIH* discuss integration plans in inter-war Europe, they usually fail to study continuity and change across World War II – this at a time, however, when national historiographies everywhere have for a long time questioned and revisited the idea of 1945 as a 'zero hour' and as an entirely fresh start.

European integration historiography and European Studies

European integration history is not only marginal within Modern European history, but also in the multi- and interdisciplinary field of European Studies. While European Studies has been well established for a long time as one of the 'area studies' in the British academic system, it is only emerging in Germany, for example. In most countries, however, it is dominated by political science research (and teaching) on the EU's institutions, policy-making and external relations. When scholars like Pierre Gerbet, Raymond Poidevin, Lipgens and Hans-Peter Schwarz initiated research on European integration history between the mid-1970s and the mid-1980s, no sharp disciplinary divide existed as yet between contemporary history and political science. In fact, Schwarz, who induced the early multilateral studies of the formation of the EEC and the European Atomic Energy Community by Hanns Jürgen Küsters (1982a) and Peter R. Weilemann (1983) largely based on the private papers of the German Commissioner Hans von der Groeben, held posts in political science at the universities of Hamburg and Bonn;

this despite the fact that for a long time all of his research and publications such as his biography of the first west German Chancellor Konrad Adenauer (1986–91) qualified as source-based contemporary history. At that time, contemporary history was still considered as a legitimate component of political science alongside International Relations, political theory and ideas and comparative politics.

Since those early days of integration historiography, however, political science as a distinctive social science discipline has become much more professionalized, with its own agendas and methodological standards, increasingly excluding contemporary history from its remit. In some countries like Italy, for example, political science and (international) history are quite hermetically sealed off from one another. In France, political studies has retained a greater interest in history, has a primarily empirical orientation and is closer to politics. At the same time, 'rational choice' political science research, which is largely driven by US institutions and researchers, has made strong demands for the theoretical framing and 'scientific' grounding of the discipline. This tradition, which tends to prioritize quantitative research and is geared towards law-like statements and predicting future developments, has made massive inroads into the more empirical European traditions of the study of politics, especially in Britain, Germany, the Netherlands, and Scandinavia, a trend that increasingly extends to the study of EU politics. Theoretically and methodologically, however, scholars working in this tradition as a general rule tend to be less interested in what they regard as 'case study'-type empirical narratives by historians.

At the same time, the estrangement between contemporary history and political science appears to be even more pronounced in the field of European Studies than elsewhere because the traditional diplomatic history approach has dominated EU history for so long. As a general rule, studies in this tradition are averse to theories and concepts and their narratives tend to be highly descriptive. Crucially, as they focus on national foreign policy-making and multilateral negotiations, they depend on access to new state sources. Thus, scholars, whose work is embedded in this tradition, tend to stick much more closely to the predominant 30-year rule for the opening of government archives than social and cultural historians, for example. This in turn results in a gap of several decades in the coverage of the EU by political scientists and contemporary historians. As Seidel points out in her chapter, most publications on the more recent past in the *JEIH* are by political scientists, not historians. To date, no significant historiography (also) covering the most recent past (Angerer 2001) exists in the sub-field of European integration and EU history.

This growing gap between contemporary history and political science research on European integration at the most basic level results in political scientists not utilizing (and referencing) the empirical results of historical research sufficiently for their understanding of the EU, especially its change over time. At the same time, the exponential growth of political science research and literature on European integration since the late 1970s in particular poses a challenge that historians of European integration should take up. While they legitimately can and should define their own research agendas, they must not develop self-contained discourses largely ignoring the existing body of social science research. Equally importantly, only by daring to generalize more from their empirical findings and linking these to larger theoretical debates in the social sciences can historians hope to instigate, or become more integrated in, cross-disciplinary debates about European integration past and present including tentative guidance on current and future issues based on past experience – thus addressing the question raised by Wilfried Loth and a team of historians (2009, 14), 'How can the present be understood in the light of this past?'

Where contemporary historians have addressed theoretical issues, they have in the first instance discussed the influence of economic and political science theory and theorists on European policy-making. Thus, Ludolf Herbst (1986) first investigated the (limited) influence of neo-functionalism – the dominant integration theory until the early 1970s, most coherently formulated by Ernst B. Haas (2004 [1958]) – on the thinking of policy-makers at the time of the Schuman Plan. More recently, Jonathan P. J. White (2003), Laurent Warlouzet (2008) and Philip Bajon (2009) have discussed to what extent policy-makers, especially in the Commission, were motivated before and during the EEC's 'Empty Chair' crisis of 1965–66 by neo-functionalist assumptions about package deals and 'spillover' – that is, from one sector to another, from economic to political integration, and to new member states. While the direct influence of neo-functionalist authors was probably limited, their ideas might have been mediated by networks and press reporting, for example. In any case, these publications address valid research questions about the rationale and motivations of supranational policy-making. This was illustrated, for example, when in an interview (Peterson 2008) Commission President José Manuel Barroso, who actually holds a political science degree, ventured to nominate five disciplinary political science publications that he found most instructive and influential. Still, such research on the importance, if any, of 'theoretical' assumptions and academic publications for EU policy-making is at best marginal to the relationship between contemporary historical research and theorizing about European integration and EU politics.

Several historians like Varsori (2001b), Loth (2001) and Wolfram Kaiser (2006, 2009b) have contributed chapters on the historiography of European integration to (mostly) political science dominated anthologies on the state of the art of research on the EU and of theoretical debates. For a long time, however, Milward was the only EU historian to engage in a more systematic way with theoretical assumptions, testing them against the evidence from his empirical data, first in his controversial monograph *The European Rescue of the Nation-State* (1992) and subsequently in a collaborative volume on history and theory (Milward et al. 1993). Milward attempted to debunk traditional integration theory. In his contribution to the first issue of the *JEIH* (1995, 7) he even suggested that its publication would mark 'the beginning of a new period of research where history now has its own theories and a research agenda which derives from them'. He boldly predicted a reversal of 'the theoretical flow' from 'historical research to the social sciences'. Milward did not spell out clearly enough what he meant by 'historical theory', however. He probably thought of conceptually sophisticated empirically grounded narratives that would be more analytical than the heavily descriptive earlier historiography, not shying away from generalizations about the driving forces of integration such as global economic competition, strategies for enhancing national power and influence and core integration ideas guiding European policy-makers. Most likely, Milward did not think of a set of falsifiable hypotheses to allow generalizations about social or political phenomena, which social scientists would consider as proper theory, and he certainly never used such an approach himself.

Such epistemological differences need to be spelled out clearly, however, to enable cross-disciplinary cooperation. More seriously from a political science perspective, Milward's criticism of integration theory in his two books, and again in a short contribution to a handbook of EU politics (2007), was informed by an outdated understanding of the neo-functionalism of the 1960s. In fact, he even conflated (Warleigh-Lack 2009) functionalism as an inter-war theory, which was actually opposed to regional integration, and neo-functionalism. As a result, Milward essentially rephrased many criticisms of neo-functionalism advanced by political science scholars such as Stanley Hoffmann (2006 [1966]), Charles Pentland (1973) and Reginald J. Harrison (1974)

20 years earlier. By the early 1990s, however, political scientists like Jeppe Tranholm-Mikkelsen (1991) and others had substantially revised neo-functionalism, discarding in particular all simplistic assumptions about semi-automatic spillover in integration. Moreover, beginning with an article by Simon Bulmer (1983) about the domestic politics of West German European policy, comparative political scientists began to engage in the study of EU politics. This shift generated a whole new set of conceptual approaches and analytical insights increasingly marginalizing all International Relations integration theory, not just neo-functionalism, but also (liberal) intergovernmentalism, something Milward totally ignored. As a result, Milward only debunked what the political scientists themselves had discarded much earlier, so that his intended contribution to 'theory' formation was obsolete and largely ignored.

More recently, some historians of European integration have made renewed attempts at engaging more systematically with political science theory and research. Thus, one group of historians (Kaiser, Leucht and Rasmussen 2009) focused on European integration until the Community's first enlargement in 1973 as the slow emergence of a trans- and supranational polity. Bringing together contemporary historians and political scientists, another group (Gehler, Kaiser and Leucht 2009) utilized the (policy) network concept from comparative politics and public policy research on policy-making with a view to reconstructing the highly informal network-type character of policy- and decision-making in the EU across time. Unlike Milward, the contemporary historians involved in these and similar projects (for example, Kaiser, Leucht and Gehler 2010) do not claim to be able to produce better 'theory' than social scientists, however. Instead, in the first instance they recognize that historians of European integration cannot ignore the work of social scientists on the EU published during periods that they are beginning to investigate. More importantly, they propose to utilize social science theory pragmatically as a heuristic tool for developing new research perspectives on European integration as more than national European policy-making and intergovernmental bargaining; for enhancing their conceptual and terminological precision; for structuring more analytically sophisticated narratives; and for facilitating medium-range generalizations to strengthen the interpretative quality of their work with results that can make a larger contribution to cross-disciplinary dialogue and cooperation.

Towards cross-disciplinary cooperation

European Studies research on European integration and the EU increasingly has a much broader disciplinary remit than in its early days, when it was largely dominated by political scientists, lawyers and, to a much lesser extent, economists; something that is still reflected in the allocation of Jean Monnet funding discussed by Varsori in his chapter. Nonetheless, given that the reconstruction of supranational politics and policy-making will remain a core concern of EU historiography, contemporary historians could relate in the first instance to recent theoretical approaches in political science (Rosamond 2007). When Andrew Moravcsik first discussed historical case studies in the search for evidence to prove his already elaborated theory, he deterred historians from cross-disciplinary learning, let alone cooperation, more than encouraging it. Moravcsik's *Choice for Europe* (1998) as well as his discussion of French President Charles de Gaulle's European policy in the 1960s (2000) appeared to be too theory-driven and badly documented. Moreover, the quality of his interpretation of sources, especially from the 1960s, was seen as deficient not only by historians of European integration, but even by political scientists who examined it (Lieshout, Segers and van der Vleuten 2004). Moravcsik's interpretation seemed to be almost apolitical in its lack of historical contextualization. Thus, de Gaulle's European policy in the 1960s appears as totally unaffected by his background as a French officer and his experiences as leader of the Free French with the US and British governments during World War II, for example. Just as Milward created the misleading impression that historians would in future produce better 'theories' of integration than political scientists, Moravcsik failed at writing a more appropriate empirically based historical narrative and advancing a convincing interpretation of de Gaulle's European policies in particular.

In any case, rational choice liberal intergovernmentalism is not helpful for overcoming the diplomatic history perspective, which is the most crucial conceptual and methodological challenge for historians of European integration and the EU. Integrating liberal International Relations theory with trade theory, liberal intergovernmentalism essentially interprets interests as derived from domestic economic preferences and articulated by member state governments in interstate negotiations as a 'two-level game' (Putnam 1988). Up to a point, this emphasis on economic dimensions of integration is useful. Although, as Morten Rasmussen shows in his chapter, Milward succeeded in nurturing important research on economic policy-making by his 'disciples', the impact of this research on other important parts of the integration historiography has remained limited. However, the exclusive focus in liberal intergovernmentalism on intergovernmental conferences and bargaining in the Council of Ministers is not helpful. It merely treats supranational institutions as designed to 'facilitate' and secure such bargains and completely ignores the role of non-state political actors at supranational and transnational level within the Community. Moravcsik has conceded that his theory fails to account for the independent and crucially influential jurisdiction of the European Court of Justice, which contemporary historians are only beginning to conceptualize and research (Rasmussen 2008). Nor can it explain why Commission policy initiatives in fields like agriculture often passed the Council without much discussion or many amendments, as was the case in the early stages of the evolution of the Common Agricultural Policy (CAP) (Knudsen 2009); why the European Parliament (EP) succeeded in amending legislation although it had no formal powers to do so, as happened in the case of the crucial competition policy Regulation 17/62 (Seidel 2010); and how transnational expert communities and business actors (for example, Bussière, Dumoulin and Schirmann 2007) increasingly organized and attempted to influence agendas and detailed policy-making.

From this perspective, two alternative 'institutionalist' approaches seem much more promising for cross-disciplinary cooperation (Knudsen and Rasmussen 2008): historical institutionalism and sociological institutionalism. Unlike rational choice institutionalism, both actually require history as an independent variable for explaining present-day EU politics. One of the most important arguments of historical institutionalism is that original constitutional and policy decisions create long-term 'path-dependencies' by closing off alternative development options and narrowing down the choices available to policy-makers. From this perspective, it is crucial to examine these original decisions to understand the long-term development of the present-day EU. At this general level, this basic argument would appear natural enough for historians. It is evident, for example, that the formation of a more integrated core Europe without Britain in 1950–52 was a precondition for more supranational forms of constitutionalization. Equally, the basic EEC decision in favour of price subsidies over deficiency payments in the creation of the CAP in the 1960s created important path-dependencies which made CAP reform extremely tedious later. Empirically, moreover, historians find that policy-makers often reconsider past decision-making situations to inform current choices such as when British governments went back to previous decisions against membership in an integrated core Europe during the 1950s and for EEC accession after 1961, using almost identical arguments (Kaiser 1999). This example demonstrates the degree of institutional inertia and the conservative character of policy-making, especially in highly complex settings like the present-day EU.

At the same time, historians could also derive useful generalized insights into policy-making from sociological institutionalist approaches. Opposed to rational choice analytical frameworks, they emphasize the crucial importance of social context for social interaction, supranational institutional cultures and decision-making. Important factors would include collective historical experience and guiding norms and values, for example. Given that historical research, unlike political science, has never been characterized by a similar deep ontological divide between rational choice and what is now usually called 'constructivist' assumptions about what guides human behaviour, most historians – even diplomatic historians – of the EU would probably accept that such factors have influenced policy-making by individuals and in institutions. The challenge remains, however, how to conceptualize and empirically trace in a sophisticated manner their precise role and relative importance – for example in the case of the formation and evolution of an ordo-liberal competition 'culture' in Directorate-General IV of the Commission in the 1960s (Seidel 2010), which has had such crucial long-term effects on economic liberalization in the EU.

Some political scientists have sought to employ constructivist and sociological institutional perspectives for their diachronic analyses of European integration. As they attempt to trace change over time in the politics and governance of European integration, these works are of special interest and value to historians. This is true, for example, of Sieglinde Gstöhl's (2002) comparative study of the European policies of the European Free Trade Association states Norway, Sweden and Switzerland, in which she argues forcefully that rational choice factors alone do not explain accession or abstention from EU membership when states have faced very similar economic and political circumstances, but took diverging decisions. Markus Jachtenfuchs' work (2002) on the evolution of federalist constitutional conceptions since the formation of the ECSC would be of special interest, too. In this study, Jachtenfuchs traces the evolution of constitutional preferences and policies in the Community as informed inter alia by ideological commitments and domestic experiences. Finally, in his book *Building Europe's Parliament*, Berthold Rittberger (2005) has attempted to integrate different institutionalist approaches in his explanation as to why member states progressively delegated more powers to the EP despite the fact that, as Moravcsik would argue, it was not in their interest to share sovereign decision-making powers with a supranational institution.

Some contemporary historians have begun to utilize concepts and insights from the different institutionalisms. These institutionalist approaches have a potentially problematic structuralist bias, however. Looser, more actor-centred concepts like (policy) networks and political entrepreneurship, for example, have recently been employed for a sophisticated reconstruction of the role of individuals and their 'agency' in EU history. One example of this emerging trend is a recent study of transnational Christian Democratic party networks and their role in the formation of core Europe after 1945 (Kaiser 2007). The network approach aims to conceptualize the informal character of policy formation and decision-making, emphasizing the network-type relations between different state and non-state actors within the EU at large and in particular policy domains. The informality of EU policy-making is a phenomenon already highlighted (albeit without utilizing the network concept) by Keith Middlemas in his book *Orchestrating Europe* (1995). Middlemas' work covers the more recent history of the Community, but is largely based on interviews, not institutional or other sources that were not yet accessible at the time. The concept of political entrepreneurship on the other hand attempts to identify conditions for the exercise of political leadership. Such exercise of leadership appears to be increasingly difficult in the highly complex and often enlarged present-day EU of 27 member states. Moreover, typical dimensions of leadership in a national polity like personal charisma or the utilization of media campaigns are not suited to the EU. In fact, leadership is often exercised through networks, which provides an important link between these two political science concepts.

Like sociological institutionalism, the concepts of networks and political entrepreneurship are also partially informed by what could be called with some justification the 'sociological turn' in recent political science research. This has re-emphasized social context and begun to analyse phenomena such as the 'socialization' of actors and institutions (for example, from accession states) into formal and informal behavioural rules and patterns within the EU. As a result, these concepts could (potentially) establish bridges to the study of European integration as something much larger than politics and policy-making in

Brussels, that is, the slow emergence over time of what Loth (2005b) among others has called a 'European society' in the making. For a long time, sociology as a discipline, and especially political sociology, was dominated by a national paradigm. More recently, however, there has been a strong shift (for example, Rumford 2002; Kauppi 2005; Hettlage and Müller 2006; Mau 2007; Favell 2008; Outhwaite 2008) towards focusing much more on cross-border 'transnationalization' processes and emerging multiple identities within Europe and beyond as well as other sociological dimensions of (political) society formation beyond the nation-state.

For a long time, the work of social historians was equally guided by the national paradigm. At best, social historians took a comparative national approach to studying Europe. Characteristically, as Lorenzo Mechi also shows in his chapter, in his early works the influential German social historian Hartmut Kaelble (1988) aimed at demonstrating societal convergence through the statistical analysis of allegedly growing social similarities between national societies in Europe compared to North America and Asia. This early *Gesellschaftsgeschichte*, or history of society of nation-states and of Europe was hardly interested in EU politics and policy-making. Many social historians regarded historians of European integration with disdain. As a result, they failed to make crucial connections between 'Brussels', cross-border societal links in the present-day EU and possible forms of 'Europeanization' as the impact of integration on the member states and their citizens as well as possibly resulting broader convergence processes. More recently, however, social historians of contemporary Europe, like many sociologists, have begun (Kaelble 2007) to integrate transnational linkages more systematically into what is still a predominantly comparative research framework using national units of comparison, and to develop a keener interest in cooperation with historians of European integration (Bauerkämper and Kaelble 2010).

Sociologists have also started to address questions of the social integration of Europe as a culturally heterogeneous space, such as in studies of 'Europe' as a communicative space with mostly ad hoc constituted public spheres (for example, Trenz 2002). The main question here is to what extent a (transnational) public sphere has emerged in Europe which addresses the politics of the EU and holds the European political system accountable (Trenz 2005). Jan-Henrik Meyer (2010) has been the first to examine this question in a contemporary historical study, focusing on ad hoc European public spheres created by the EU summits between 1969 and 1992. Similarly, social historians increasingly address

European dimensions of youth culture and the new social movements in the 1970s, for example. Some contemporary historians with connections with the comparative social history tradition like Kiran Klaus Patel (2008) have argued forcefully for a more fully transnational approach to (contemporary European) history, which would no longer be a subsidiary dimension of comparative history. So far, however, historians of European integration have mainly studied the institutional politics and policy-making of fostering transnational links including, for example, cultural exchange programmes.

For a broader history of European integration, however, the crucial void in these emerging research agendas appears to lie precisely at the intersection between EU politics and policy-making and social developments on the ground, within and across national societies – a history of what could be called individual and collective integration experiences, and the memory of these experiences, not only of political, academic and business elites, but new social movements acting across borders in regional spaces, students exercising new opportunities for study abroad and workers affected by increased competition forcing them to seek new jobs within the internal market. Some younger contemporary historians have recently chosen such a focus on the EU as an institutionalized space of experience in studies of actual cross-border cooperation on the ground. Instead of continuing in the teleological politicized tradition of federalist historiography, for example, François-Xavier Lafféach (2009) has studied the federalist movement as a site for inter-cultural encounters that, at least in the case of some participants, had a strong impact on their identities and preferences for 'Europe'. Similarly, it would be fruitful to focus on the particular effects of EU policies such as the free movement of people and the abolition of border controls in the Schengen Agreement or on the hybridization of cross-national border regions with their own characteristics and identities, not just the institutional dimension of cooperation as in the context of Euro Regions established since the 1970s. Naturally, such research necessitates the use of different methodologies such as oral history techniques, which is not limited to decision-making elites for whom interviews have been more and more utilized (see also Varsori in this book).

Alongside such cross-disciplinary cooperation with sociology and social history in the reconstruction of the EU as a space of experience in historical perspective, historians of European integration could also employ tried social anthropological perspectives on the social construction of Europe and 'Europeans' (for example, Bellier and Wilson 2000). Authors like Thomas Risse (2010) have recently observed a growing importance of a 'supranational' European identity as part of the prevalent multi-layered identities within the EU. He has traced this growth to the experience of tangible benefits of integration like the abolition of border controls and the introduction of a common currency. In a more long-term perspective, however, historians of European integration may find that conscious attempts to 'construct' such a European identity, or what Milward (1995) called 'allegiance', have played a role in this process as well. In any case, European political and academic elites – including many historians (see Durchardt et al. 2006–07 for examples) – have certainly tried to 'imagine Europeans' to adapt the title of Benedict Anderson's (1983) influential study of national identity creation and nation-state formation since the eighteenth century. As at the national level in the nineteenth century this process has involved multiple state and non-state actors and has been partially funded by the emerging 'integrated' political level, in this case the present-day EU, its supranational institutions and member states, whether through its funding for academic research as outlined by Varsori in his chapter or various other initiatives such as the cultural capital of Europe, for example. As historians of countries like Germany and France have emphasized more recently, the national and/or Republican integration agenda was challenged by regionalist identities and demands in the nineteenth century, and it always remained contested and fragile. Similarly, imagining Europeans since World War II has been challenged by national and nationalist programmes from de Gaulle to the more and more Eurosceptic British Conservative Party, for example, while most regionalist movements have actually harnessed the EU agenda of 'unity in diversity' for their own means.

With few exceptions (Delanty 1995; Lager 1995; Shore 2004), social scientists and contemporary historians so far have only devoted shorter articles and book chapters to specific dimensions of such attempts at imagining, constructing and representing Europe and 'Europeans' with the assistance of political symbols like the European flag and anthem, annual prizes like the Aachen Karls Prize, and summit photos of EU leaders, for example. In fact, supranational institutions, member states and regions as well as museums in various member states have even begun to showcase the history of European integration, or links between regional devolution and identity with supranational integration, in exhibitions and museums. Examples of this most recent trend include the temporary exhibition 'C'est notre histoire!' shown in Brussels in 2007–08 and in Wroclaw in 2009 and the House of European History planned by the European Parliament (Kaiser and Krankenhagen 2009). In the processes of national integration, such musealization usually took place once a fairly broad consensus was reached within the integrated national polity. In contrast, putting 'Europe' and the EU into museums is used strategically to foster or strengthen such a consensus.

To date, historians have not really conceptualized and addressed in a long-term diachronic perspective this process of social evolution and cultural construction of Europe and the Europeans. The project on European identity originally initiated by René Girault and discussed by Varsori in his chapter, had a strong French bias and insufficient conceptual and methodological coherence. Without minimizing the structural societal and politico-institutional differences, such a new research agenda would suggest a potentially instructive comparison with nation-state formation in the nineteenth century which has been totally absent so far. Curiously, Milward of all EU historians, raised the issue of European level identity formation in his article on 'allegiance', without following up on his suggestions, however. Yet his was a narrowly rational choice definition of Europeanization resulting from welfare state provision at EU level, which implicitly rejected a more cultural studies type historical approach to understanding the process of imagining the community of Europeans. At the same time, as Mikael af Malmborg and Bo Stråth (2002) and others have shown, cultural barriers to further Europeanization persist and the process of European society formation is both slow and highly contested.

Conclusion

As this survey of options for greater cross-disciplinary learning and cooperation indicates, a better integration of the historiography of European integration within European Studies (as well as Modern European history) promises distinctive benefits (Kaiser 2008; Warleigh-Lack 2009). Some benefits concern conceptual and methodological issues while others affect the substantive empirical focus of European integration history.

Firstly, cross-disciplinary cooperation, especially if it is not limited to political science, could help historians to reconceptualize European integration as a process that extends beyond politics and policy-making in 'Brussels'. EU history needs to be discussed as highly institutionalized 'connected history' (Werner and Zimmermann 2006) in which politics and policy-making by institutions and networks and legal and economic integration and penetration have both facilitated and been influenced by the slow formation of a European society of sorts with dense transnational linkages.

Secondly, cross-disciplinary cooperation can help EU historians to bring out more clearly why the EU matters not just as a supranational history of institutions and politics, but for contemporary Europe and its links with the wider world, something that should facilitate its better integration with contemporary historical and social science research on Europe more generally. It can also encourage EU historians to make bolder judgements about what matters most in and for European integration. While avoiding ontological polarizations prevalent in the social sciences, which often generate reductionist mono-causal explanations, they should go beyond the timid listing of factors that *also* mattered and prioritize those that mattered most. To date, only Milward has advanced such a bold thesis about the nature of integration.

Thirdly, a greater familiarity with social science theories and concepts would be crucially important methodologically for developing more analytically sophisticated historical narratives of European integration (Kaiser, Leucht and Rasmussen 2009, introduction). Too much historical research during the past 30 years has been highly descriptive and narrowly focused on short time-spans.

Substantially, cross-disciplinary cooperation that goes beyond mutual learning from each others' research would allow historians of European integration – fourthly – to address diachronic issues of temporal change in the EU much more systematically than has happened to date. Common projects covering continuity and change in EU history could ask, for example, how institutional cultures develop and change over time. They could also test the widespread assumption among political scientists like Paul Hirst (2000) that policy networks have only played a major role in EU politics and policy-making since the 1980s (Kaiser 2009a). In fact, contemporary historians have already found substantial evidence for the crucial influence of transnational party and expert networks in earlier periods of integration. One particularly useful objective of such collaboration could be to identify critical junctures at which the nature of integration and EU politics might have changed. Through such collaboration, historians of European integration could also demonstrate much more convincingly how historical research can help explain not just the EU's past, but also its nature and future prospects.

Cross-disciplinarity also has potential pitfalls, however. From the perspective of historians of European integration, two stand out. Firstly, cooperation with the social sciences requires the search for somewhat aligned research methodology and academic language. The methodological issue is potentially problematic. Cooperation will mainly have to take the form of qualitative research due to the character of historical sources and the predominantly qualitative orientation of social scientists with an interest in EU history. Cross-disciplinary communication is also facilitated by the utilization of aligned academic language, however. To enhance the cross-disciplinary compatibility of their research, historians may have to utilize some social science terminology. This in turn could thwart another desirable innovation in the history of European integration, that is, the writing and publication of more popular historical narratives – not textbooks for students – in an accessible language to make sense of EU history for a larger non-academic audience with historical interests.

Close collaboration with social scientists – secondly – could also deflect from the need to integrate EU history with a *longue durée* history of modern Europe as in a major research programme on European technology integration since the mid-nineteenth century, for example (for example, Misa and Schot 2005). Exclusive cooperation with the social sciences could lead historians of European integration to adopt the 'presentist' focus of much of their research, where research questions are only considered relevant if their clarification makes a direct contribution to explaining the present-day EU. In fact, various research funding programmes, especially EU framework funding, encourage such a presentist attitude.

For the time being, however, the historiography of European integration has been relatively isolated both within Modern European history and within European Studies. To date, historians of European integration have only related to social science theoretical debates and empirical findings to a very limited extent. More recently, however, some contemporary historians have begun to utilize social science theories and research for heuristic purposes to refine their conceptually more sophisticated historical narratives.

Greater cross-disciplinary collaboration clearly holds great potential for European integration historiography, especially for conceptualizing European integration more precisely in terms of concepts and terminology used; upgrading the analytical dimension of historical narratives compared to earlier more descriptive and predominantly diplomatic historical studies; and addressing much more comprehensively than hitherto questions of continuity and change over time up to the present. Different research perspectives from political science, sociology, social anthropology and cultural studies sketched in this chapter open up new vistas for contemporary historical research on European integration and for cross-disciplinary cooperation. The potential benefits of such cross-disciplinary collaboration outweigh the potential pitfalls that are largely avoidable.

However, such cross-disciplinary cooperation would require that contemporary historians broaden considerably their understanding of what constitutes European 'integration' beyond national European policy, supranational policy-making and intergovernmental bargaining; that they make the transition, as Jost Dülffer (2009, 17) has called it, from integration history to the 'history of the integrated Europe'. Yet such a larger conceptualization of European integration seems inevitable anyhow, if contemporary historians want to be at the centre of the evolution of our understanding of the EU's and the wider Europe's present and future as well as its past.

4
Between Political Commitment and Academic Research: Federalist Perspectives

Daniele Pasquinucci

Federalist-minded historians have undoubtedly made a significant contribution to promoting knowledge of the process of European integration. Therefore, no assessment of the state of the art of the historiography of the present-day European Union (EU) would be complete without considering this research tradition and its publications. While a federalist school of European integration history clearly exists, it is less clear whether it consists of distinct national 'schools' or of individual scholars whose work transcends nationality and specific historiographical traditions. Crucially, federalist historians have adopted similar methodologies, used common interpretative criteria and most importantly, have identified with shared moral and political values, on which they have based their research.

Two closely related characteristics seem to unite individual federalist scholars: their political militancy and their emphasis on historical change coming from the bottom up. According to the latter, pro-European and federalist movements and their leaders have crucially contributed to the construction of a united Europe. These scholars view the unification of Europe as a necessary response to the crisis of the nation-state. In fact, federalist historians have often held influential positions in various pro-integration organizations. This overlapping of academic research and political commitment obviously entails risks. As it is still ongoing, the process of European integration seems to offer even more opportunity than some other contemporary historical research fields for interpretations influenced by strong ideological and political preferences. The Italian federalist school, which has been the most prolific, although it has never exerted a monopoly on Italian EU historiography, is a case in point. As Sergio Pistone (1977, 156), a leading exponent of this school, has argued, historiography has 'an eminently practical role' to play to create 'enlightened' political awareness, which must be based on 'valid knowledge of the course of history'. This course of history can only be interpreted correctly by adopting a 'federalist point of view', as European political integration appears to be the inevitable end-point of the history of the 'old continent' (Varsori 2001a). From this perspective, European integration is not a journey towards an unknown destination. On the contrary, federation is written in the destiny of Europeans, and the role of scholars is to disclose the true path of history.

This strongly teleological approach poses many methodological and interpretative problems, such as the selection and use of sources. In both the history of European movements and that of the larger process of European integration, federalist historians prefer to work with documents of federalist origin. This results, among other consequences, in a lack of attention to other dimensions of integration and of a contextualization of historical events (Graglia 2001, 134). Moreover, their political commitment makes it more difficult for federalist historians to draw and respect the line between direct reporting and a detached historical analysis. For example, the British historian John Pinder, a member and former chairman of the Federal Trust for Education and Research (founded in 1945 in the context of Federal Union), was forced to speak of himself in the third person in an essay aiming to demonstrate how the network of British federalists (of whom he was one of the main leaders) played a determining role in Britain's decision to finally join the European Communities (EC) in 1973 (Pinder 1996, 87 and 89).

These and other significant problems of historical research by federalist scholars are discussed in greater detail below. However, the chapter, firstly, analyses the main characteristics of the research carried out by the German historian Walter Lipgens and his school. The work of federalist historians often remains confined to their milieu, without having any larger influence on academic debates. As one of Lipgens' fiercest critics maintains, he 'is not now much read' (Milward 2002a, 15). Nonetheless, his research has influenced European integration historiography more generally, and made an enormous contribution to raising the academic standard of debate in federalist historiography. Secondly, the Italian federalist historiography is discussed in some detail, as it has made a significant contribution to the historiography of European integration, of pro-European movements and of the political and intellectual leaders who have supported European integration. As we shall see, their research reflects a concept of federalism as an 'independent ideology'.

This notion can be traced back to Mario Albertini, who was a professor at the University of Pavia, leader of the Movimento Federalista Europeo (MFE) and President of the Union of European Federalists (UEF) from 1975 to 1984. Albertini attempted to formulate an academic critique of the idea of the nation-state and elaborated a theory of federalism not 'as a mere constitutional technique...but as an ideology that highlights the new sense of the path of history' (Levi 2002, 140).

Finally, the last part of this chapter is dedicated to British historiography. British federalism has a solid tradition and has influenced the thoughts and actions of many continental federalists. The epic story of the Federal Union, founded in November 1938, is a case in point. British federalist thought was also Altiero Spinelli's main source when he wrote, together with the liberal Ernesto Rossi, his manifesto *Per un'Europa libera e unita*. The document is now better known as the *Manifesto di Ventotene*, named after the island on which both authors were interned for their opposition to fascism, and is considered as the founding text of contemporary federalism.

Walter Lipgens and the origins of federalist historiography

Federalist historiography owes a great deal to the work of Lipgens, whose studies represent an essential reference point for anyone dealing with the history of European integration and, more generally, the history of Europe. Lipgens was born in Düsseldorf in the German Rhineland in 1925 and was called up for military service in the *Wehrmacht* in March 1943. He was discharged in April 1944 due to injuries he suffered in the war. Lipgens was subsequently able to dedicate himself to his studies and in 1960, became lecturer in contemporary history at the University of Heidelberg, where he taught until 1967. He then moved to Saarbrücken, where he worked until his death in April 1984. Between 1976 and 1979 he also taught contemporary history at the European University Institute (EUI) in Florence (Kaiser 2002a, 120). Lipgens' research for his doctoral dissertation and *Habilitationsschrift* was fundamental in determining the interpretation of European history that he would later apply to his research on supranational integration. These two studies were dedicated to two Catholic figures: the humanist Johannes Gropper, who lived at the time of the Reformation, and the Archbishop of Cologne, Ferdinand August Graf Spiegel, who lived during the transformation from the *ancien régime* to the modern nation-state. Both actors tried to identify a suitable form of 'Catholic renewal' in times of change and contributed to redefining the role of

Catholicism in modernity. The link between these early research interests and the ethos that permeated Lipgens' studies on European integration lies in his attribution to European unification of a persuasiveness similar to that of Christian humanism. Christian humanism endured in the ideas of a European federation, and especially in the plans made in the context of European resistance to national socialism (Fehrenbach 1984, 758). In line with this idea, and like many Catholic intellectuals of his generation, Lipgens maintained that the origins of the catastrophe in Europe lay in the decline of the church and religious belief. In this sense, his works belonged to a well-established current of academic tradition, which underlined how the unity of European civilization lay in deep-rooted traditions that needed to be considered in order to discover the fundamental social and spiritual strengths that could contribute to forming Europe (Dawson 1939, 282–3).

As is clear from an exchange of letters with the German Christian democratic parliamentary party leader Heinrich von Brentano, who was a staunch Catholic and leading proponent of the 'core Europe' concept of the six founding member states in his party, Lipgens habitually voted for the Christian Democratic Union (CDU). Lipgens claimed that he had voted for the CDU ever since its formation after World War II above all because its foreign policy was geared towards European integration. He feared that further integration would be jeopardized by the formation of a new coalition between the CDU and the liberal Free Democrats in 1961 and by Konrad Adenauer's subsequent resignation from the post of chancellor in 1963. If the new government were to reverse Germany's pro-European policy, which he strongly supported, he would vote for the social democrats (Kaiser 2002a, 127).

One of Lipgens' other academic interests was German unification in the nineteenth century. Federalist historians have strongly rejected nationalism and have criticized the nation-state tradition. Characteristically, in his studies Lipgens strongly criticized Otto von Bismarck for his *Kulturkampf* against the Catholic Church and for his aggressive policy towards France including the annexation of Alsace-Lorraine. For Lipgens, Bismarck represented a typical exponent of Prussianism based on the idea of a strong state (Loth 2006, 321), which was incompatible with European unity.

Lipgens' first works on European integration history date back to the early 1960s. The European Economic Community (EEC) was in the midst of a crisis at the time, and Lipgens, like other federalist historians (Pinder and Pryce 1969), feared that French President Charles de Gaulle intended to undermine the EEC and replace it with a national

French hegemony over Europe. In this context identifying the historical reasons for the process of European integration appeared to be both
a political task and a moral imperative (Loth 2006, 323).

The most well-known of Lipgens' works, and the ones that have
prompted most debate amongst historians, are his *Documents on the
History of European Integration* (1985–91), which cover the period between
1939 and 1950. The *Documents* comprise four volumes, completed with
the crucial cooperation of Wilfried Loth and the participation of a
large international network of scholars and experts of the history of
European integration. The *Documents* gather the pro-European views
and declarations of politicians, intellectuals, writers, and members of
non-communist resistance movements against national socialism and
fascism from across Europe.

Lipgens did not intend to simply collate in these *Documents* the very
wide range of proposals and projects for European union that were put
forward after World War II in response to the crisis of the nation-state.
Instead, he argued that these individuals and groups were broadly in
agreement on the analysis and interpretation of international politics
at the time. The common condemnation of nationalism and of the
international anarchy generated by individual sovereign nation-states
seemed to make a supranational structure for the continent inevitable
after the war. From this point of view, such a structure seemed to be a
historical necessity rather than one of many options for the reorganization of the post-war international system. Thus, the very concept of
European resistance seemed to acquire real meaning. Moreover, the
choice of period covered by the *Documents* was to underline the existence of continuity between the war years and the launch of the process
of integration (Dell'Acqua 2005, 152–3).

Alongside the *Documents*, a book on the first attempts at European
integration between 1945 and 1947, published in German in 1977 and
translated into English five years later, constitutes a fundamental element of Lipgens' historiography. In the introduction to this book, he
claims that European civilization is founded on four unifying principles: '1) Respect for the human personality, the freedom and dignity
of the individual ...; 2) Respect for small communities and their right
to self-government ...; 3) Respect for objective truth, the belief deeply
rooted in Christian and Greek conviction that truth can be objective ...;
4) The sense of social responsibility for the weak springing from respect
for the individual; the basic principles of help and protection, of justice
and human brotherhood; hence the awareness of Europe's mission, a
universalism that seeks to understand and penetrate the civilizations of

other people and includes as its final goal the unification of mankind' (Lipgens 1982, 22–4).

On this basis, Lipgens' research focused on the importance of the integration projects developed by the resistance movements during World War II for the creation creation of a pro-European ideal – an assertion common to all federalist historiography (Brugmans 1970, 93–101). Such projects seemed to show a common awareness of the allegedly objective necessity to end national sovereignty and establish a supranational system. Why, then, did the crisis of the nation-state not translate into the birth of a European federation during 1945–47? Lipgens believed that the answer lay in the adverse 'diplomatic constellation'. The Soviet Union (SU) and the United States (US) in particular played a decisive role in holding back supranational projects in this period. The Soviet Union categorically opposed European federation because Europe's fragmentation into a jumble of states suited its goal of spreading communism across the European continent (Lipgens 1982, 451–7). At the same time, the US were under the illusion that international order could be achieved based on collaboration with the SU. Only when this became impracticable did the US government become a fervent supporter of European integration. The growing hostility between the two superpowers was accompanied by the re-emergence of nationalism in Britain and France. The British Labour government elected in 1945 attempted to maintain Britain's role as a global power, while in France de Gaulle 'had not only deprived the Resistance organizations of their power, but even in 1945 he was thinking of out-manoeuvring the parties and steering French foreign policy, which he considered his personal prerogative, back to the old Clemenceau line, which could not have been more remote from the spirit of the European federalists' (Lipgens 1982, 130).

One of the most innovative features of Lipgens' research is his reconstruction of the organizational development and political role of movements in favour of a united Europe. Lipgens assumed that this network of organizations played a determining role in integration history. Between 1945 and 1947, while national governments were setting supranational projects aside, the pro-European movements were keeping the public aware of the demand for a united Europe. Moreover, their actions demonstrate that a desire for unification existed prior to the pressure later exerted by the US (Pistone 1977, 162–3). In this context, Lipgens placed particular emphasis on the role played by the UEF, founded in Paris in December 1946 under the guidance of the Dutch federalist and first rector of the College of Europe from 1949 to 1950, Henri Brugmans. A longer-term perspective allowed Lipgens to affirm that in the crucial decade between 1945 and 1955, 'when the policy of European union was taking shape, the political pressure groups advocating union or federation were especially important' (Lipgens 1980, 119).

One of the criticisms of Lipgens' work concerns precisely the excessive emphasis he places on the importance of federalist movements. The idea that they played a determining role in the creation of the European Coal and Steel Community (ECSC) does not seem to be corroborated by convincing evidence, for example. The negotiating strategies of the six national governments and their motivations for the creation of supranational institutions did not seem to derive from a commitment to the federalist project (Dedman 1996, 11–12). In fact, French civil servant Jean Monnet was not influenced by the projects of political groups pushing for European integration between 1945 and 1948. It is therefore no coincidence that Monnet 'is not once directly mentioned' in Lipgens' study (Milward 1992, 335). With somewhat sarcastic overtones, Alan S. Milward (2002a, 15) has especially harshly criticized the very foundations of the interpretative model adopted by federalist historians. In his view, some European nation-states were induced to make partial sacrifices of national sovereignty to strengthen their plans for domestic consolidation. If anything, the nation-states were 'rescued' rather than weakened by integration. In Milward's view, the new Community institutions represented an extraordinary opportunity to safeguard 'national interests' more effectively and resolve domestic problems more easily by dealing with them at European level and in an international context (Dell'Acqua 2006, 53).

Federalism as an 'independent ideology'

Italian historians occupy a prominent position in the field of federalist-oriented studies. The main merit of their contribution, although by no means the only one, is having brought to light the role and upheld the memory of pro-European movements as an important aspect of contemporary political culture and thought. They also contributed to moulding the historiography of European integration in Italy, with first general histories of the unification process, a systematic survey of sources and the first hypotheses concerning questions of periodization (Arfè 1989).

The most important focal points of federalist historiography have been the universities of Pavia, Turin and Genoa. The University of Pavia in particular made a significant contribution to federalist studies thanks to the presence of Albertini. The publishing house Il Mulino in Bologna played – and continues to play – an important role in the dissemination of research conducted by federalist writers including the classics of federalism (for example, Alexander Hamilton, John Jay, James Madison, Kenneth C. Wheare) published in the Biblioteca federalista and the series Fonti e studi sul federalismo e sull'integrazione europea created in 2000 and edited by Giulio Guderzo from Pavia and Ariane Landuyt from Siena. The Bologna-based publisher is part of a cultural association of the same name established in 1965, of which the former member of the Christian Democrat Party (DC) Romano Prodi, who would later become Italy's Prime Minister of the centre–left coalition and President of the European Commission, was chair from 1974 to 1978.

The work by Italian federalist historians can be divided into three main fields. Firstly, they have produced several comprehensive narratives of the history of European integration, almost always characterized by the attribution of a key role in this process to pro-European and federalist movements (Chiti Batelli 1979; Levi and Morelli 1994; Pistone 1999; Olivi and Santaniello 2005). Interestingly, Italian federalist historiography frequently compares the dynamics of European integration to the unification of Italy in the nineteenth century. While the national governments are seen as the equivalent of Count Camillo Benso di Cavour's faction and their moderate gradualist approach to national integration, the federalist movements are regarded as similar to Giuseppe Mazzini and his faction. Italian federalists viewed unification as the result of the will of the people (Albertini 2007b [1964], 483–4). In fact, Italian federalist historians see the European movements as the true interpreters of the 'pro-European' will of the citizens. However, this desire for political unification was, these historians claim, thwarted by the decision of political leaders to maintain the prerogatives of national sovereignty.

The second, more highly developed field of research concerns the history of the movements themselves. Italian historians have produced three important edited books on the history of these movements between 1945 and 1986, in which the strong presence of (not only Italian) federalist historians is conspicuous (Pistone 1992, 1996; Landuyt and Preda 2000). These volumes examine the various organizations and individual leaders of the pro-European movement in depth. The periodization chosen by the editors is indicative of the centrality attributed to the movements in the history of European integration. The first book covers the period between 1945 and 1954. The year 1954 is a crucial one in federalist historiography. In August of that year the project for a European Defence Community (EDC) and European

Political Community (EPC) failed, following the refusal by the French Parliament to ratify the EDC treaty. This apparently marked the end of the most positive period of organized federalism, which had begun with the launch of the Marshall Plan in 1947. The interpretation of this period as a sort of golden age of federalism somewhat uncritically accepts the assessment by the Italian federalist Spinelli in his autobiography. According to Spinelli, the years between 1947 and 1954 were those in which the 'great moderate ministers of Europe' effectively worked towards the birth of a European federation, having been pushed in that direction by a fear of communism and by the 'democratic missionary spirit' of the US at the time (Spinelli 1987, 18). This favourable political situation permitted the federalists to effectively influence the course of history. Their influence is, for example, considered decisive in convincing Italian Prime Minister Alcide De Gasperi to request the inclusion of article 38 in the EDC treaty and thus, launch the process that led to the EPC project.

This focus explains why studies concentrating on the years between 1950 and 1954 are among the best in Italian federalist historiography. In contrast to other strands of federalist historiography, works with a focus on this period actually consider the structural context of European integration (Preda 1990, 1994). The alleged prevalent openness towards supranational projects in this period, according to this historiography, was rational at the time in that the choices made by the ruling politicians generally corresponded to the expectations of those who saw (and continue to see) a European federation as the most historically suitable form of political organization (Pasquinucci 2000, 12). Within this research area, works focusing on the Italian Council of the European Movement and the Italian section of the Council of European Municipalities and Regions also stand out (Zucca 2001; Caraffini 2008).

The third field of research consists of biographical studies. They focus above all on the leading exponents of the European federalist movements, especially Spinelli (Paolini 1988, 1996; Chiti Batelli 1989; Levi 1990; Paolini 1996). However, the books dedicated to Spinelli are characterized by two main limitations: often they simply reproduce Spinelli's own writings; and they have a general propensity to uncritically acclaim his work, turning him into one of the 'European saints' Milward has written about so sarcastically. A meticulous biography of Spinelli without these limitations has only recently been published, by a scholar who has adopted a detached perspective partly because he belongs to a younger generation (Graglia 2008). Many studies have also been dedicated to Albertini (Levi 1992; Padoa Schioppa 2007) and Rossi (Braga 2007).

Two new trends can be discerned in the federalist biographies. On the one hand, as Katja Seidel also notes in her chapter on European integration historiography more generally, an attempt has been made to study less well-known individuals who nonetheless played an important role within federalist organizations, like Luciano Bolis (Rognoni Vercelli 2008). On the other hand, in line with Lipgens' approach, Italian federalist historiography tends to include some of the most important members of the Italian political establishment in the federalist pantheon, helping to legitimize European federalism and freeing it from the accusation of being a utopian idea. This approach also emphasizes the role of the federalist organizations in influencing political decision-makers. The best example of this trend is Daniela Preda's (2004) federalist biography of De Gasperi, who was not only prime minister, but also minister of foreign affairs after World War II. Preda portrays De Gasperi as inspired by a clear federalist vision in the key decisions he made concerning Italy's European policy, with the MFE playing a determining role in influencing his foreign policy.

As mentioned above, Italian scholars have defended federalism as an 'independent ideology'. This ideology is based on three elements: the first is its guaranteeing 'perpetual peace' in line with the teachings of the German philosopher Immanuel Kant; the second concerns structure, with the federal state replacing the nation-state; the third is its contribution to overcoming the division of the humanity into social classes and antagonistic nations (Levi 2002, 142–3).

The close relationship between political commitment and academic research is one of the characteristics of Italian historiography. Italian federalist historians have traditionally held positions in the MFE and other pro-European organizations, and their political engagement has been the source of much criticism regarding both their methodology and their interpretation. A case in point is the way in which federalist historians reconstruct the path that led to the first direct election of the European Parliament (EP) in 1979, a key objective in the federalists' strategy. Article 138 of the EEC treaty ratified in 1957 provided for the direct election of the EP. Nonetheless, the national governments, and the French government in particular, avoided the issue for a long time, concerned that direct election to the EP would result in an increase in its meagre powers. Only at the Community summit in Paris in 1974 did the governments decide to proceed with direct elections. According to Italian federalist historiography, the decisive element in this process was the so-called 'unilateral elections' that the MFE under the leadership of Albertini propagated as a suitable strategy in the late 1960s and early 1970s. This idea was to organize a legislative initiative for the direct national election of delegates to the EP (Majocchi and Rossolillo 1979, 90–3 and 118). The example of the Italian Federalist Movement prompted similar legislative initiatives in other Community states, and the threat of unilateral elections was used to pressurize national governments to finally agree to European elections. While it can be maintained that the unilateral elections contributed to creating a favourable environment for the implementation of article 138, it is less convincing to argue that they were fundamental to making governments change their minds, as the federalists claim (Pasquinucci and Verzichelli 2004, 21–30).

Actually, the Italian federalist historiography has largely ignored Spinelli's opposition to unilateral elections. From a normative perspective, one could argue that Albertini was right to support the unilateral elections and Spinelli wrong to oppose the initiative. What is problematic for professional historians, however, is to even ignore the disagreement between these two federalist leaders, not least as Spinelli's reasons for his opposition were fully coherent with the federalist *Weltanschauung*. In fact, Spinelli opposed unilateral elections because he feared that they would become a by-product of national elections.

According to him, the risk was that the unilateral elections would turn the European Movement towards support of a kind of federalism in one country, nationalizing the federalist strategy and objectives.[1] Paradoxically, Spinelli's words must have sounded familiar to Albertini who, in a significant effort to clarify concepts and terminology, had specified since 1959 that 'above all the term "Europe" designates the "field" in which we have decided to carry out our political activity'. This, he argued, distinguished the federalists from the nationalists and national democrats, who were inclined to carry out 'their political action in the national field' (Albertini 2007a [1959], 354).

This may seem to be a minor episode, if it were not for the fact that the direct elections of the EP are crucial to the federalists' interpretation of European integration in the 1970s and beyond. For a long time this decade was considered a period of 'stagnation' in European integration, although more recently, historians have begun to reconsider this assessment in the light of later developments (Gilbert 2005, 95; Varsori 2006). According to federalist historians, however, the end of the 1970s marked a turning point precisely because the EP elections were finally called. They claim that the direct elections paved the way for the EP to launch a first initiative for a European constitution with the draft treaty establishing the European Union adopted in February 1984. It also created a favourable environment for the establishment of the European Monetary System (EMS) in 1978 and for the crucial *Cassis de Dijon* decision by the European Court of Justice (ECJ) in 1979 (Pistone 2000, 48). The *Cassis de Dijon* decision in turn is generally recognized as having paved the way for the Single Market Programme. In short, from this perspective the federalist initiative for unilateral elections influenced the decision in 1974 to implement article 138 of the EEC treaty. This in turn made it possible to overcome the paralysis of the 1970s by strengthening the EP through direct elections and laying the foundation for all subsequent developments. Consequently, European integration was relaunched above all due to the actions of the federalist movement.

This interpretation is founded entirely on 'interpretation based on reason' (Pistone 2000, 69), which seems to relieve the historian of the obligation of documenting in a convincing manner any causal relations between federalist actions and subsequent events. One example of the federalist 'interpretation based on reason' is the idea that the ECJ issued the *Cassis* decision because it was crucially influenced by the expectations aroused by the first direct EP elections, as well as by the creation of the EMS, and the more favourable climate for integration. This may be a reasonable assumption, but it cannot add to historical knowledge until it has been thoroughly documented. Moreover, existing research calls into question the alleged decisive causal relationship. After all, the ECJ has also contributed to the constitutionalization of the Community through its case law in periods characterized by a political atmosphere hostile to supranationalism (Weiler 1991, 24–31). In other words, it seems clear that the ECJ has followed its own decision-making path, working tenaciously to create 'a constitutional framework for a federal-type structure in Europe' (Stein 1981, 1).

The alleged direct causal link between the expectations created by the election of the EP and the creation of the EMS is also less than clear. Firstly, it is misleading to attribute to Roy Jenkins, the British President of the Commission, who was among the protagonists of the relaunch of Economic and Monetary Union, the belief in a 'definite relationship' between monetary unification and direct EP elections (Pistone 2000, 82). In the Jean Monnet Lecture he gave at the EUI in Florence on 27 October 1977, Jenkins suggested that 'we should use the period immediately prior to the first direct elections of the European Parliament to re-launch a major public debate on what monetary union has to offer' (EC Bulletin 10/1977). This remark hardly proves a causal relationship between the two developments. Secondly, it is also debatable, as Pistone has argued, that the direct election of the EP facilitated the creation of the EMS because the 'most pro-European' governments could not have presented themselves to their electorate with a vision of the Community that 'instead of progressing [took] steps backwards' (Pistone 2000, 49). However, German Chancellor Helmut Schmidt maintained that the launch of the EMS should be subject to the Union of the Left between socialists and communists being defeated in the French national elections of March 1978. Thus, as far as Schmidt was concerned, if the communists had won the elections in France, the EMS as a first step towards monetary union would never have occurred (Gilbert 2005, 119). Moreover, the federalist interpretation hardly explains why the British and Danish governments eventually agreed to the direct elections. Thus, maintaining that 'the dynamism that the direct election of the European Parliament leant to European integration was manifested ... in the creation of the EMS' (Pistone 1999, 48) is a highly simplified version of historical developments.

From Federal Union to neo-federalism: British federalist historiography

Alongside Italy, Britain has also produced significant federalist-inspired studies, with the Federal Union as the main sources of their production and dissemination. This organization was founded in the autumn of 1938 by Charles Kimber, Derek Rawnsley and Patrick Ransome, in response to the weakness of the League of Nations and the profound unease about the Munich Conference in September 1938 where France and Britain agreed to the annexation by national socialist Germany of the Czech so-called Sudetenland inhabited predominately by German speakers. The Federal Union's aim was to promote federalism throughout Great Britain, Europe and the world. In fact, at the time federalist theory and practice were unknown to the majority of British citizens. In Britain, federalist theory was primarily based on nineteenth-century liberal constitutionalism, and the works of John Stuart Mill and Lord Acton (John Emerick Edward Dalberg), who focused on multinational federation, and of James Bryce and A. V. Dicey, who wrote influential texts on the American model of federation. In the inter-war period, non-Marxist socialist reformists like H. N. Brailsford, Kingsley Martin, Bertrand Russell, Leonard Woolf and H. G. Wells played an important role in the formulation of federalist ideas. One of the most important writers was Harold J. Laski. In his *Studies in the Problem of Sovereignty* (1917) he 'expressed his opposition to the monistic view of the State' and his preference for a state organization in which power was distributed over several levels (Pinder 1989, 206). Lionel Curtis and Lord Lothian (Philip Henry Kerr) subsequently played an important role in allowing Federal Union to expand its network of contacts to influential thinkers and politicians (Bosco 1989, 289–308). In 1935, Lord Lothian published *Pacifism is not Enough*, in which he criticized the pacifists' naïve idealism, claiming instead that peace could only be achieved through the creation of a world federation, the first stage of which was to be European federation. The organization's research was done by the Federal Union Research Institute, which was founded in 1940 and chaired by William Beveridge. This Institute promoted the publication of influential works by Beveridge himself, Barbara Wootton, Lionel Robbins, Wheare and Ivor Jennings.

The inclusion of the federalist perspective in British political and academic debate, thanks to Federal Union, was clearly one of the reasons for the favourable reception of Winston Churchill's proposal of June 1940 (albeit intended as a strategic device to keep France in the war) to federate Great Britain and France (Mayne and Pinder 1990, 25–9).

By the end of World War II, however, the federalists' influence on public opinion had diminished significantly, and neither of the two main political parties was ready to support federalism. Moreover, the beginning of the nuclear age, marked by the bombing of Hiroshima in August 1945, brought to light divisions between the supporters of European federation and the advocates of world federation (Mayne and Pinder 1990, 50–79). Nonetheless, members of Federal Union continued to produce valuable work after 1945. Thus, Wheare's *Federal Government* published in 1946 analyses the main forms of federal government (Daddow 2004, 86–90). R. W. G. MacKay, who was a member of the Federal Union Executive Committee between 1939 and 1945, was particularly prolific writing five books between 1948 and 1953 and a sixth that was published posthumously in 1961. MacKay criticized the hostility of the Labour Party (of which he was a member) towards the projects for European unification (MacKay 1961, 30–3).

In the meantime, a new generation of federalists emerged, who advocated combining the objective of a European federal constitution with Monnet's method of the gradual creation of pre-federal institutions (Pinder 2005, 393). Historical analysis was stimulated by the initial successes of the EEC and the British attempt to negotiate membership between 1961 and 1963. Some ten books were published by the federalist essayists, political studies scholars and historians in this phase. All of these called for the establishment of a federal Europe including Great

Britain (Kitzinger 1961; Pinder 1961; Campbell and Thompson 1962; Mayne 1962; Pryce 1962; Shanks and Lambert 1962). Subsequently, in the mid-1960s, the Federal Trust, which replaced the Federal Union Research Institute, became the focal point of British federalist studies (Pinder 2005, 395). Although British federalist historians were convinced that the European nation-state was 'out of date' (Pryce 1962, 13), they also pragmatically underlined why participation in the EEC would be beneficial to Britain. In the battle for Britain's accession to the EEC, the federalists were assisted by the pressure group Britain in Europe, created in 1958. They also worked with strongly pro-integration politicians and diplomats like Anthony Nutting, Edmund Dell, Roy Denman, Edward Heath and Jenkins (Daddow 2004, 95–7). Moreover, the pro-Europeans could count on the press, which with few exceptions favoured British membership of the Community until well into the 1970s (Greenwood 1998).

Federalist scholars are part of the 'orthodox' trend in British historiography. They interpreted the British government's initial decision not to join European integration as a 'missed opportunity'. This implied, above all, sharp criticism of the British political elites, who had been incapable of understanding the country's real interests and instead chose a kind of *Sonderweg*, or special path. Britain's abstention from integration also meant that it lost its political influence in Europe and that the country was forced to adapt 'to European situations created by others' (Camps 1964, 507).

The idea of a missed opportunity seems more valid as a political argument than as a criterion of historical interpretation, however. Arguably, the British government's decision not to join the ECSC/EEC was much more rational than the orthodox school maintained. Extra-European interests, the particular British experience of World War II and an understandable scepticism concerning the post-war democratic stability of France and Germany appeared to justify the initial British indifference towards integration (Kaiser 1996, 205 and 210).

From the 1980s, British scholars' endeavour to define their gradualist strategy for achieving European federation with greater theoretical precision began to take shape (Forsyth 1981; Pryce 1987). This 'neo-federalist' strategy was characterized by a pragmatic approach, reflected in their historical interpretation of European integration. One scholar from the University of Leicester clearly expressed this realism in a book dedicated to experiences of confederation, defining them as the first step towards a federal state (Forsyth 1981). The same theory had been proposed many years earlier by Carl J. Friedrich, who defined federalism as a process and considered confederation as a step in the direction of federalism (Friedrich 1968). This definition is clearly incompatible with the classical federalist interpretation defended, for example, by Italian historians. For the latter group, history demonstrates the shortcomings of the confederal model. The leading exponent of British federalist historiography has attempted to identify a solution to this conflict. In his opinion, this divergence in theories is due to a traditional contrast within the federalist world: between an 'ideological' South and a 'pragmatic' North, with potential for 'creative synergy' (Pinder 1985, 161). It is no coincidence that Pinder proposed this view in the journal of the Italian federalists. One of his main concerns was to find points of agreement with the Italian scholars. His priority was to avoid conflicts that would weaken the political effectiveness of the federalist cause.

Crucially, many neo-federalist historians produced very balanced research, avoiding propaganda and providing empirically based explanations. For these scholars the history of integration demonstrates that European federation 'will not happen overnight or by a single major reform' (Wistrich 1994, 161). In line with this guiding idea, they carried out a series of studies with the aim of illustrating 'how a score of substantial steps have taken the Community from its first manifestation in the ECSC up to the point it has reached today' (Pinder 1991, 199) – an achievement to be proud of. Overall, these authors argue, the results achieved by the Community in political and economic terms are considerable (Pryce 1994, 6–11). From this perspective, the EU has made it possible to solve important common problems and, more generally, to build a structure that could be completed by the creation of a federal constitution (Pinder 2005, 401).

Despite the significant contributions by British federalist writers and historians federalism is often considered as an 'alien' doctrine in Britain (Stirk 1996, 16) because of its various associations with American independence, Catholic social teaching, continental European socialist federalism and domestic demands for Home Rule or independence. Some have even demonized it, which 'has made it difficult for British people to consider the development of the Union and its relationship with the federal idea in an objective way' (Pinder 1998, 1). However, as Michael Burgess (2006) has shown, Anglo-American federalism has very solid historical and philosophical foundations: in the tradition of the covenanters, for example, and in the enduring legacy of *The Federalist Papers*. Furthermore, as Burgess demonstrates, federalism has been a constant feature in British political and institutional reform debates. Above all, it was one of a range of possible models on which to base the unwritten constitution of the United Kingdom in certain phases of its history. Moreover, devolution, Home Rule and federalism were proposed as potential solutions to the Irish question before World War I. Lastly, imperial federation was proposed as a way of governing the colonies within the Commonwealth. The principles of self-government, the limitation of central authority and the participation of citizens in public life were also stimulated by the Protestant Reformation. Federalism, and not just supranational federalism, therefore represents an integral part of the British political tradition, demonstrating 'that there is a different way of looking at the basis of political authority in the United Kingdom' (Burgess 1995, 18).

Not surprisingly, Burgess is the author of one of the most incisive responses to Milward's criticisms of federalist historiography. Although Burgess is a political scientist, his analysis is embedded in an excellent understanding of historical developments. It is useful to discuss his response briefly, not least because federalist historians have not always been capable of answering Milward's criticisms, or even wanted to do so. Indeed, Italian scholars have generally chosen to ignore Milward.

Firstly, in contrast to what Milward insinuates, according to Burgess the federalists have never intended to destroy the nation-state. Naturally, there are some exceptions, such as much of the federalist literature in the immediate post-war period and some 'utopian federalists who seek to uncover a European federal society'. However, the vast majority of federalists 'accepted the national state at face value and predicated their respective political strategies upon its continued existence'. Secondly, the theory that European states were 'rescued' by European integration is certainly 'attractive to realists' as it gives the impression that states remain in full control of their own destinies. Yet, as the chapters by Piers Ludlow and Morten Rasmussen in this book also show, the reality is different: the EU member states are internally fragmented, and by sharing and transferring sovereignty, they have favoured the creation of complex European decision-making mechanisms within a federal context which are not easy to steer, let alone control. Lastly, better understanding is needed of the connection between 'the survival of the national State and the timing of the moves toward European integration' (Burgess 2000, 62–3). Indeed, it can be claimed that the European nation-state 'had already reasserted itself successfully' prior to the launch of the ECSC in 1952. Milward and others, who have criticized the federalists' research, nonetheless made a major contribution to it by inadvertently stimulating a revival of a revised federalist historiography. This revival can be seen above all in the research of the neo-federalists, which is characterised by a greater conceptual sophistication and better empirical analysis than the original federalist historiography (Burgess 2000, 94).

Conclusion

The large body of work produced by federalist historians has certainly provided valuable insights into the dynamics of European integration. The studies of federalist movements have illustrated the history of organizations that have contributed to determining the course of European history in certain moments. In many cases, federalist historians have been pioneers, paving the way for the analysis of a phenomenon that had not been universally recognized as worthy of historical research. European integration was for a long time considered a by-product of the Cold War and the American desire to unite western Europe in order to strengthen the anti-communist front. For this reason it seemed that the history of international relations could also deal with European integration history. One of the merits of federalist historiography is to have reaffirmed the relative autonomy of the process of European integration, which was certainly influenced, but not entirely determined, by the Cold War and US foreign policy. The emphasis placed by Lipgens and many other federalist historians on the importance of European resistance movements in the formation of pro-European and federalist thought reflects the focus on domestic European motivations for integration.

Federalist historiography has clear limitations, however, that mainly result from the overlapping of political commitments and academic research. This feature is especially strong among Italian historians, who have sought to theoretically legitimize their political activism by reference to Max Weber, who maintained that all knowledge of cultural reality is always bound by the author's particular point of view. From this perspective, the federalist historian has the sole duty of declaring his ideological preferences to his readers. In reality, however, Weber argued that the particular 'point of view' only influenced the selection of the topic of research. Then, he added, researchers should make a clear distinction between 'knowledge' and 'evaluation'. In other words, he believed that the academic duty to recognize the reality of facts needed to be separated from the practical duty to uphold one's own ideals (Weber 2001 [1904], 157).

This distinction may be difficult to accept for researchers with a very rigid model of historical interpretation. From the federalists' viewpoint, the most important historical fact that allegedly characterizes the contemporary age is what they see as the crisis of the nation-state, which can only be resolved by ending national sovereignty and creating a European federation. The pro-European and federalist movements – and their historians – believe that they are the only ones capable of interpreting this historical process adequately. This has several consequences. Firstly, they attribute excessive importance to the role of the movements and bottom-up action. Secondly, they have a tendency to assess the process of European integration against a particular political and institutional model as the desirable end-point of the EU's evolution. Lastly, they tend to adopt a teleological view of history.

These merits and shortcomings of federalist historiography raise the question about its future prospects and its ability to overcome the limitations discussed above. Lipgens and his followers did not succeed in demonstrating causal links between the ideas of the federalist movements and the decisions made by governments. Among other historians, a realist diplomatic history approach prevailed, based on government sources and affirming the autonomy of political elites deciding national foreign and European policies and defining and negotiating 'national interests'. As several other chapters in this book demonstrate, however, this approach is not satisfactory either, not least because states are not necessarily very cohesive actors nor the only ones in European integration. In fact, many non-state actors, transnational networks and social groups have played a role in, and are increasingly contributing to, politics in the present-day EU (Kaiser 2007, 7–8). Federalist historiography, with its bottom-up approach, can potentially contribute to such a research perspective on contested European politics in a complex trans- and supranational polity. The analysis of the spread of federalist ideas in networks could also become integrated into a new history of ideas in Europe, and more specifically, of federalism, and how such ideas travel across borders. If the federalist historiography succeeds in interacting with the new trends in the historiography of the EU, it can still make an important contribution to our knowledge of European integration in historical perspective.

Note

1. Florence, Historical Archives of the European Union, Papers of Altiero Spinelli 30, Spinelli to Albertini, 19 December 1972.

5
At the Heart of Integration: Understanding National European Policy

Michael Gehler

After World War II European integration became crucially necessary for the reconstruction of the nation-states of Europe, if not for their outright 'rescue', as Alan S. Milward (1992) argued somewhat provocatively in his book *European Rescue of the Nation-State*. The nation-states founded the present-day European Union (EU), and they are still its main supporters. The economic difficulties of reconstruction and the decolonization shock of the 1950s complicated integration. In the 1970s international economic slumps, turbulence in the currency markets and political crises impeded greater progress in integration. These problems in turn led to repeated attempts to reassert the nation-state and national sovereignty within the present-day EU. Subsequently, rapid industrial and technological development across the world and the emergence of new economic and trading powers onwards required the full implementation of the common market in the form of the single market programme, combined with increased pooling of national sovereignty in the Single European Act (SEA) and the Maastricht Treaty on European Union.

Despite this pooling of sovereignty and the increasing complexity of the EU with greater powers for the European Parliament (EP), for example, the member states were, and still are, the main actors in the EU. To a large degree their role transcended the at various times heated debates in the post-war history of (western) Europe and between different organizations of European cooperation and integration about intergovernmental versus supranational institutional forms or 'negative' market integration versus positive integration with greater political ambitions. National governments and the interests they formulated and projected determined not only the response by third countries like the United States (US) to European integration, but also the policies of the member states and their relationship with each other. Thus, national governmental policy-making within the present-day EU consistently had a strong impact on its changing constitutional design and its domestic and external policies. It comes as no surprise therefore that research on national policy 'towards' and within 'Europe' was at the origins of the historiography of European integration, as Antonio Varsori also shows in his chapter, and remains a crucial research field to the present day.

This chapter discusses different ways in which historiography has conceptualized, researched and narrated national policy towards European integration. Due to the vast volume of research on national European policies across Europe, the chapter has to be selective in its treatment of several country cases illustrating different historical traditions and new research trends: the three largest EU founding member states – Germany, France and Italy – are combined with two 'latecomers' that joined in 1972–73, namely Britain and Denmark. This combination also allows for some observations concerning any marked differences in the historiography on the national policies of larger and smaller states. In general, historical research on the European policies of countries that joined in the second and third enlargements or even more recently, during 2004–07, is less developed. To some extent, however, the chapter draws upon this research, too, in the final section designed to compare the different historiographies and country cases, before the conclusion sets out new research challenges and trends.

Germany: 'Europe' as a magic formula

After World War II, what Martin Geyer (2004, 30) has called an 'adaptation historiography' developed in the Federal Republic of Germany, founded in 1949. Accordingly, historiography moved away from the former paradigm of German national history towards the new paradigm of a partial state integrated with the West. From the start, the sub-discipline of contemporary history in Germany was closely connected with contemporary political issues and debates. In this process of adaptation, protestant historians, who historically had been the strongest supporters of Otto von Bismarck's *kleindeutsch* solution to German unification, moved closer to the Rhenish Catholicism of the first German Chancellor, Konrad Adenauer, and a school of mainly Catholic historians, who left their imprint on the culture and historiography of the new western German state. They included Walter Lipgens and Hans-Peter Schwarz, for example, who played a leading role in the origins of European integration research (Schwarz 1981; Kaiser 2002a). For the political culture of the Federal Republic, 'Europe' was a 'magic word' (Conze 2001).

Many German historians saw themselves as active pedagogues in the consolidation of democracy, drawing upon concepts such as the 'modernization' (Wehler 1987) or 'westernization' of Germany (Doering-Manteuffel 1999), and its long 'road to the West' (Winkler 2000). These concepts were always in danger of turning into teleological narratives, with apparently no alternative development options after 1945. Germany's membership in the North Atlantic Treaty Organization (NATO) from 1955 and the European Economic Community (EEC) from 1957–58 were largely uncontested. The integration into western cooperation and integration structures were both politically desired and academically opportune to support. Not surprisingly, the early works on the origins of the EEC by Hanns Jürgen Küsters (1982a) and of the European Atomic Energy Community (Euratom) by Peter R. Weilemann (1983, 1989), largely based on the private papers of the German Commissioner Hans von der Groeben and inspired by Schwarz, reflected this 'pro-European' consensus in politics and academia. The same observation applies to early political science research on integration by authors close to the federalist movement like Heinrich Schneider and later, Wolfgang Wessels.

In addition to German conceptions of Europe and policy on European integration (Loth 1989) early German historical research focused especially on the central role of Adenauer's European policy (Schwarz 1979). Adenauer prioritized European integration over national unification – a policy that was politically highly controversial in the early 1950s and later critically assessed by some historians (Steininger 1985; Foschepoth 1988). Other historians (Klotzbach 1988; Benz 1990) enquired into the motives for the opposition to the creation of the European Coal and Steel Community (ECSC) by the social democratic leader Kurt Schumacher, who argued that this form of western integration would bar unification. Further research discussed Germany's economic reconstruction from the European Recovery Program (ERP, Marshall Plan) to integration in the ECSC/EEC. As American historian John Gillingham (1988) has shown, sorting out the problem of the limits on the coal and steel production of the Ruhr area became a major short-term objective for the German heavy industry (see also Abelshauser 1995). However, the German Bundesverband der deutschen Industrie (BDI) was unenthusiastic about sector integration and a split of the western European market resulting from the creation of a geographically confined 'core Europe' of six member states. Subsequently, as Werner Bührer (1999) has shown, many German industrialists saw Jean Monnet, the initiator of the 1950 Schuman Plan, at the helm of the ECSC High Authority as too *dirigiste* and bemoaned an insufficient alignment of economic policies in the ECSC/EEC. When Britain launched its free trade area plan in 1956–57, the majority of German industrialists enthusiastically supported the creation of a larger western European market (Schulte 1999). Anticipated economic benefits were one reason why German industry and a clear majority in the German parliament supported EEC enlargement, when Britain, Denmark, Ireland and Norway first applied for membership in 1961–62 (Lee 1999). Nevertheless, some authors like Küsters (1982b) have pointed out that the German industry's influence over governmental policy-making was negligible despite the fact that BDI President Fritz Berg had close relations with Adenauer (Bührer 1995, 106–8). In fact, whereas Adenauer strongly supported core Europe integration with Franco-German leadership, his economics minister Ludwig Erhard advocated global free trade and was more open towards the influence of industry, but ultimately unable to shape the course of German policy on European integration in any decisive way (cf. Brenke 1994; Lappenküper 2001).

In security policy matters Adenauer's objective was to achieve German equality and indicated in return that he would be prepared to agree to a control of the German military potential. During 1952–54, the German government fully supported the French plan for a European Defence Community (EDC). Its rejection by the French parliament in 1954 came as a blow to Germany's European policy (Küsters 1993; Volkmann 1999). However, the western Allies quickly found an intergovernmental substitute in the form of Germany's integration into NATO and the newly created Western European Union (WEU) in 1955 (Wiggershaus 1986; Thoß 1995; Krüger 2003). In the context of core Europe integration in the ECSC/EEC and the NATO/WEU, research has mainly focused on the Franco-German bilateral relationship, not least the close cooperation between French and German political leaders including Robert Schuman and Adenauer, Valéry Giscard d'Estaing and Helmut Schmidt, François Mitterrand and Helmut Kohl, but also Willy Brandt and Georges Pompidou (for example, Loth 2007).

To some extent, Germany's European policy reflected its domestic constitutional character as a federal state and the need to take into account the interests of its *Länder*. On the one hand, Germany's federal structure made it easier to accommodate a further supranational level of governance. On the other hand, European integration and its impact on the constitutional rights of the *Länder* under the Basic Law have also led to legal challenges of the Maastricht Treaty and the Lisbon Treaty in the German constitutional court. As early as 1957 the *Länder* sought to be involved in the ratification of the EEC and Euratom treaties. They only secured far-reaching rights of involvement in the ratification of the SEA in 1987, however. Yet as is more or less the case for all other member states, with very few exceptions (Gruner 2009) historians have hardly looked into the impact of European integration on Germany's socio-economic and political institutions and development.

Instead, research has addressed in greater detail German European policy in various policy fields including the liberalization of European trade and payments (for example, Bührer 1997), the coal and steel sector (Kipping 1996; Bühlbäcker 2007) and industry in general (Rhenisch 1999), proposals for integration in agriculture and the Common Agricultural Policy (CAP) (Thiemeyer 1999; Patel 2009a) as well as monetary policy (Thiemeyer 2009). Much of this research is characterized by a fairly stringent multilateral contextualization of German policy-making as in the case of Hubert Zimmermann's study (2002) of transatlantic balance of payments and monetary policy during the 1960s. Several historians have also utilized oral history methods for gaining background information on informal dimensions of policy-making. Thus, in a pan-core European perspective Katja Seidel (2010) has studied the role of German officials among others in the High Authority and the European Commission during the 'pioneer' phase until 1967. A European orientation also became embedded in the policy-making culture of the national government. In fact, as Küsters (2000) has demonstrated, the German government prioritized coordination within the Community and further integration during the process of German unification in 1989–90.

More recently, a younger generation of historians has developed moderately revisionist interpretations of German European policy. Whereas German post-war governments cultivated their self-image as a crucial engine, if not *the* locomotive of integration, at times they actually opposed European solutions, as in the case of the CAP. For a long time, the origins of the CAP in the 1960s have been interpreted as a compromise solution between France and Germany giving French agricultural exporters access to the western German market in return for German export opportunities in the customs union for industrial goods. However, as Ann-Christina Knudsen (2009) and Kiran Patel (2009b) have shown, the German government adopted an inflexible position in the question of EEC cereal prices, only to see its negotiating position collapse later. Later on, German governments often took cover behind France in international trade negotiations, seeking to protect the national agricultural sector that in southern Germany in particular, was characterized by inefficient small-scale family farming. However, even these new studies remain somewhat state-centric and so far have taken into account the role of political parties, interest groups, new social movements and public opinion only to a limited extent.

France: founding member state facing decolonization

In France, history since 1945 forms part of *histoire contemporaine*, which covers the time period from the French Revolution. It has followed conceptual and thematic trends, from the 'intellectual' history of ideas to the study of the experience of the Resistance and the Vichy government. For a long time, moreover, the Vichy complex of collaboration with Nazi Germany impacted on discourses about national greatness within France and on French historiography, with lasting effects beyond the 1980s. French historiography of post-war Europe became rather introspective and inadvertently Gaullist in its conceptual approach. French historians still tend to focus mainly on French issues and more or less ignore social science research. Yet the end of the Cold War and German unification have transformed Europe and called into question France's original political leadership role within it. In many ways France is no longer the leading member state in the EU, and its global role as a military and nuclear power has become increasingly limited. As a result, the concepts of national power, prestige and influence, which also informed French historiography of French European policy to some extent, have become questionable categories.

In other ways, the historiography of French European policy has developed along similar lines to that of German policy. French historians initially concentrated on the study of French policy initiatives in inter-war Europe, especially those of French Foreign Minister Aristide Briand, and Franco-German relations before the Nazi usurpation of power in 1933 (for example, Poidevin and Bariéty 1977; Badel 1994; Badel, Jeannesson and Ludlow 2005). As more archival sources for the post-war period became available they studied French policy towards the founding of the Council of Europe (Bitsch 1986) and the EEC (Guillen 1989). As René Girault (1989) and others have debated, French integration policy in the 1940s and 1950s was torn between Europe and the French Empire. At the time, the concept of *Eurafrique*, which combined both ambitions, played a prominent role in French discussions and policy-making, as Giuliano Garavini also shows in his chapter.

French and German historians have discussed many different aspects of the evolving Franco-German relationship in the first decade after 1945, especially bilateral economic relations (Wilkens 1997) and French policy on the Saar which remained a source of conflict until the referendum in 1955 rejecting its Europeanization (Hudemann and Poidevin 1992). Several French and German historians have studied the importance of the 'German question' and Franco-German relations for French European policy-making in their biographical approach to understanding the views and policies of influential individual politicians like Schuman (Poidevin 1988), Giscard d'Estaing (Weinachter 2007), and Mitterrand (Berstein, Milza and Bianco 2001; Schabert 2002; Bruck 2003). In the early post-war period France was crucially dependent on American support for its policy initiatives. As Gérard Bossuat (1992) has shown, France needed American ERP funding and US cooperation to guarantee its external security, but this also gave the US some leverage over French European policy. Thus, the French push to create a common market for coal and steel in 1950 derived to some extent from the requirements of the domestic modernization plan developed by Monnet, but it was also a response to US pressure to lift all remaining limits on German production and to take a decisive step towards a more federal form of integration (Lacroix-Riz 1988). Just like the Pleven Plan for a European army later in the same year, the Schuman Plan was born out of an emergency situation to avoid leaving the initiative for the formulation of policy towards Germany entirely to the Americans (Bossuat 1988; Poidevin 1990). Several historians have also looked at the economic interests behind French European policy in these early stages of integration, and the attitudes and role of business actors (for example, Bussière, Dumoulin and Schirmann 2006a; Ramirez 2009).

Historians have emphasized the contribution of French politicians like Schuman, leading officials like Monnet and national elites to European integration (Bossuat 2001a, 2005, 2006). Not surprisingly, French historians are also at the forefront of research on European decolonization and any linkages with European integration (Bitsch and Bossuat 2005). Historians now largely agree that the new centre–left French government from January 1956 became committed to the common market project as well as Euratom for a combination of economic and foreign policy reasons (Bossuat 2009b). While the experience of the Suez War in November 1956 was not decisive, it clearly facilitated the complicated negotiations and smoothed the path towards the signing of the Treaties of Rome establishing the EEC and Euratom in March 1957. However, the Evian Agreement of 1962, which ended the Algerian War, had no such stimulating effect on French European policy at the time of Charles de Gaulle's presidency (Bossuat 2009b).

French historians in particular have also conducted research on de Gaulle and his foreign and European policy from 1958 to 1969. One cornerstone of his policy was to achieve the greatest possible freedom of manoeuvre in relations with the US, culminating in the French withdrawal from the military integration of NATO (for example, Soutou 2001; Bossuat 2001b). De Gaulle's undoubtedly dominant role – his policy initiatives, his aggressive rhetoric about supranationalism and the EEC institutions in Brussels, especially the Commission, and his launching of the 'Empty Chair' crisis in 1965–66 – unfortunately has strengthened the pronounced France-centrism in French historiography, which has neglected multilateral dimensions including the role of other member states and European-level institutions. In contrast to the claims made by the American political scientist Andrew Moravcsik (1998), French historians largely agree that de Gaulle's European policy was mainly motivated by a combination of foreign policy goals, especially keeping Britain out of the EEC, maintaining French hegemony over western Europe and controlling Germany. Using the EEC as a suitable framework for economic modernization and guaranteeing the interests of French farmers were relevant, but subsidiary objectives (Bossuat 1993; Vaïsse 1998).

Despite strong disagreements over the nature of de Gaulle's domestic rule French historians have shown that he cannot be easily classified in terms of his European policy as a 'Eurosceptic', an opponent of integration, or a nationalist. After all, although he had previously opposed them, de Gaulle accepted the Treaties of Rome on his return to power in 1958. His embracing of the common market framework not only disproved initial fears among France's EEC partners, but also triggered a period in which de Gaulle used the EEC treaty to advance the economic modernization and liberalization of France. The French economy profited enormously from the common market and increased its exports rapidly, from a lower starting point than Germany's. However, de Gaulle did aim to strip the EEC of its long-term political objectives and to circumvent its supranational character for any future policy initiatives like the Fouchet Plan for foreign policy cooperation, named after Christian Fouchet, French Ambassador to Denmark and chairman of the intergovernmental committee established to draw up a plan for European political union. The initiative failed in 1962 when Belgium and the

Netherlands withdrew from the talks for fear that de Gaulle would sign the new treaty only to veto British EEC membership, as indeed he duly did in January 1963 and again in November 1967.

As research on French European policy is moving more and more into the 1970s and 1980s, the strong focus in much of the more recent historical research on de Gaulle and Gaullism is waning. But even for analysing the 1960s, younger French historians have avoided a de Gaulle-centric view. They have begun to contextualize French policy-making much more internationally, by taking into account the policies of other member states and sometimes utilizing their sources. They have also begun to reconceptualize the nature of the French Fifth Republic, which does not seem nearly as centralized and geared towards decision-making by one individual, especially over European matters, than de Gaulle made it look at the time. As Laurent Warlouzet (2009, 2010) has shown, the French governments were somewhat fragmented. Different departments had diverging policy priorities. French experts colluded with other member states, Commission officials and business represent-atives to advance their particular concepts for the EEC. Indeed, the EEC was for France an ideal vehicle to carry out a controlled, step-by-step opening of its market and liberalization of its trade and also a means to introduce policies through the European backdoor such as the EEC's essentially ordo-liberal competition policy which would never have found majority support within the French domestic political system.

Italy: the smallest of the larger member states

The Italian *storia contemporanea* has largely been preoccupied with the Risorgimento in the nineteenth century and questions related to fas-cism and World War II, especially anti-semitism, the Italian Resistance, the history of the labour movement and communism and social his-tory themes (Klinkhammer 2004). The focus was on matters of national identity in a fragmented society. Historians and many politicians alike, for a long time cultivated the idea of the resistance and anti-fascism not only as a basis for the post-war Italian Republic, but also for providing political orientation for the future. In the wake of domestic upheaval over corruption scandals, the end of communism in Europe in 1989–90 and the collapse of the Soviet Union in 1991, however, the post-war political (party) system crumbled. With Italy struggling to meet the Maastricht criteria for the adoption of the Euro, domestic politics focussed on constitutional and economic reform after the collapse of the Democrazia Cristiana (DC) as Italy's dominant post-war government party. The former neo-fascists, renamed Alleanza Nazionale (AN), joined the centre–right government of Silvio Berlusconi for the first time in 1994 and again from 2001–06 and after the elections of 2008. They changed their political programme and rhetoric. From the 1990s onwards under the leadership of Gianfranco Fini, the AN progressively rejected any link with fascism, condemned the fascist historical experience, accepted Italy's constitution, its fundamental principles and also the Resistance. In the meantime, Fini was welcomed when he visited Israel and regarded as a moderate politician.

In these changing domestic circumstances, new readings of contemporary Italian history by historians thrived. The inclusion of 'anti-fascism' as a principle in the Italian constitution was called into question, which Renzo De Felice, one of the leading Italian historians of fascism and a Mussolini expert, termed an 'insincere dogma' (Jacobelli 1988). A few historians developed the concept of 'civil war' and some journalists began to point out the role of 'partisan justice'. Further, the 'allegiance to western democratic ideals' of the Partito Comunista Italiano (PCI) during the 1940s and 1950s was debated. At the same time, important contributions on the relationship between the PCI of Palmiro Togliatti and Moscow reflected the predominance of left-wing historians and PCI interpretations in the group of contemporary historians in Italy.

Overshadowed by heated debates over Italy's identity the country actually had a strong pro-European tradition throughout the post-war period as is reflected in the prominent role played by Italian politicians from Alcide De Gasperi, the post-war prime minister to Carlo Sforza, Altiero Spinelli, Emilio Colombo and Romano Prodi. For these and other Italian politicians, European policy was more than lip service paid to the federalist tradition, which actually became a mass movement with a high degree of political mobilization in Italy (Pistone 1985, 1996). In the shadow of historiographical debates about national history, an initially small, but growing, group of historians began exploring the history of European integration and Italy's European policy in particular (Romero and Varsori 2005–06). Most strikingly, in comparison with other national traditions of writing the history of European integration, many Italian authors devoted much time to the history and ideas of European federalism, and especially the role of Italian federalists in the European Movement (for example, Levi and Morelli 1994; Preda and Rognoni 2005). As Daniele Pasquinucci also shows in detail in his chapter, many of these historians actually were, and still are, engaged in the federalist movement.

In parallel with this tradition, but with only few links to it, international historians began to write about Italy's post-war foreign policy and its role in the Cold War and NATO (Pastorelli 1987, 1998, 2009; Di Nolfo, Rainero and Vigezzi 1989; Di Nolfo and Pastorelli 2006; Varsori 1997; Nuti 1999). As Varsori also shows in his chapter, this focus on western European countries in the Cold War provided a starting point for further research into European integration as an important dimension of international politics in historical perspective. As a consequence of the problems related to the lack of archival sources for the latter half of the 1950s, Italian historians were among the few who dealt not only with Italian issues but with other countries' European policies or various Cold War issues (Varsori 1988). A younger generation of historians attempted to integrate the Cold War into European integration issues (Varsori 2007).

As Italy was not as central structurally to European integration and the various interstate negotiations leading to the creation of the ECSC/EEC as France or Germany, research on Italian European policy has concentrated much more on key individuals like De Gasperi. While federalist scholars (Preda 2004) have argued that De Gasperi was a convinced federalist from the beginning, others (Magagnoli 1998; Guiotto 2006) believe that he only converted to a greater Europeanism at the beginning of the 1950s. Research has also focused on the role of De Gasperi (Craveri 2007) and Spinelli (Graglia 2008) in conceiving and introducing Article 38 into the EDC treaty. The article provided for the project of a European Political Community (Pistone 1993) as a roof over the planned European army.

Historians of Italian European policy have also discussed the economic motives for participation in integration and its repercussions on the Italian economy. This research was also fostered by Milward during his time at the European University Institute in Florence, as Morten Rasmussen explains in his chapter. Ruggero Ranieri (1988; Ranieri and Tosi 2004) in particular has explored the role of the Italian involvement in the creation of the ECSC. The Italian government and industry hoped to build on the ECSC to modernize and expand the national steel production in the north and its exports. However, full participation in the ECSC mattered to the Italian government not only for economic motives, but also for the overriding foreign policy objective to attain a position of formal equality, if not necessarily equal influence, in relation to France and Germany in any integration project. From a purely economic point of view, the EEC was much more important for Italian industry (Ranieri 1999) as it offered a framework for economic modernization and for dealing with the chronic domestic problem of unemployment in the Mezzogiorno through the introduction of the principle of free movement of people, which facilitated emigration.

More recently, Varsori has instigated new historical research on European integration and the Italian role in this process. He has attempted to integrate international and diplomatic history with a history of European institutions and broader dimensions of socio-economic and political change and the role of non-state actors in European politics and policy-making (Ciampani 1995). Younger scholars linked to this main school of Italian historiography of European integration have produced biographies of individual leaders like Ugo La Malfa – an early anti-fascist, liberal politician and a minister in different cabinets of Christian Democrat Prime Minister De Gasperi – and studies on the modernization of Italy in the context of European integration, its deepening at the end of the 1960s, security policy in the Mediterranean within the framework of the defence system of the West, and Italy's role in European integration in different time-spans and policy fields (Calandri 1997; Mechi 2003; Guasconi 2004; Gualdesi 2004; Ranieri et al. 2005; Petrini 2005).

Other than in the case of the historiography of France and Germany, historians of Italian involvement in European integration have traditionally also focused on its domestic contestation by political parties and other societal actors like trade unions. This emphasis probably reflects, firstly, the fragmentation of the political system and frequent changes of governments, which made it difficult for Italy to articulate and project interests clearly and cohesively in the present-day EU. Secondly, it is a sign of the great difficulty of accessing Italian state archives, which has often required writing about Italian government policy on the basis of foreign governmental sources. In any case, alongside research on De Gasperi and the DC, the focus has been very much on the Italian Left (Scarano 2009). Italian socialists initially did not support European integration unconditionally and were torn between the two concepts of European union and Atlantic community (Decleva 1986). They wanted a united Europe to overcome the East–West confrontation and mediate between the superpowers. Socialists also criticized the lack of trade union representation in the Community's institutions. It was only towards the end of the 1960s that the socialists under Pietro Nenni's leadership focused much more on influencing European politics and policy-making (Pasquinucci 2006). Further to the Left, the Italian communists, who were initially strongly opposed to western integration, gradually moved in favour of 'Europe' in the 1960s and

1970s. In contrast to the French communists, the Italian communists in this period contributed to strengthening positive images of the present-day EU within Italy's otherwise politically divided public. Thus, the Italian communists helped to deepen Italy's integration in the western European system while retaining a critical distance to the US and calling for a better balance between Europe and the US and NATO (Pons 2006). Recently, Piero Craveri and Varsori (2009) have published a comprehensive volume of Italy's historical role in European integration.

Britain: latecomer to core Europe integration

According to the definition prevalent among British historians, contemporary history now only deals with the period since World War II. British contemporary history has been especially strongly influenced by the attempt to reconstruct and discuss the external and domestic dimensions of Britain's decline as a world power to that of a regional power in Europe with some global interests. Dimensions have included foreign policy issues like decolonization, beginning with the independence of India in 1947, the Suez War, the subsequent withdrawal from east of Suez, relations with the US and nuclear policy, but also Britain's relative economic decline and weakness and elite perceptions of this decline as well as changing elite and national identities. As opposition leader, wartime Prime Minister Winston Churchill promoted European integration as in his speech at the University of Zurich in 1946, but Britain initially insisted on intergovernmental forms of cooperation and did not participate in the core Europe organizations of the ECSC/EEC.

Britain's rapprochement with the EEC started with the first British application for membership of 1961 which de Gaulle vetoed in January 1963. To a large extent this rapprochement was precipitated and accelerated by the decline of the British Empire and new uncertainties about the quality of the 'special relationship' with the US. Because the EEC applications were highly contested domestically, British journalists and political scientists were already highly knowledgeable about the topic in the 1960s. The majority of authors who wrote about Britain's EEC applications and early experience inside the European Communities (EC) strongly supported a more proactive British role in Europe. They did not just cover the policy-making by British governments, but also treated political parties and interest groups as well as shifts in public opinion on integration (Camps 1964; Kitzinger 1969; 1973; Lieber 1970; Moon 1985).

In contrast, historical research on Britain's relationship with 'Europe' has been rather state-centric and tends to focus on explaining government behaviour. This literature has discussed British European policy in great detail for the period until the early 1970s. At first, the focus was on Britain's self-exclusion from the ECSC/EEC (Bullen 1988, 1989). Subsequent research focused on the two EEC applications of 1961 and 1967 and Britain's diplomacy in the face of de Gaulle's opposition to its membership (Kaiser 1996; Tratt 1996; Ellison 2000; Young 2000). This research has been highly critical of British government policy. The former Labour Party politician Edmund Dell (1995) in particular strongly criticized the decision against joining the ECSC in 1950. Informed by the assumption that core Europe integration and Britain's membership in it was always inevitable, and that Britain would have done better had it joined much earlier, this set of literature accused Britain of having 'missed the bus' on various occasions. Other authors like Richard Lamb (1995) were mainly critical of British diplomacy and its refusal in 1961, for example, to contemplate substantial concessions to de Gaulle in return for British EEC accession, especially over nuclear cooperation. By the early 1960s, Britain's Commonwealth ties had declined, and the Conservative government led by Prime Minister Harold Macmillan was concerned about the future of the transatlantic relationship and Britain's less than dynamic economic development (Robertson and Singleton 1999). In light of the negative rationale behind the applications, which were informed by the medium-term dangers of continuing to stay outside of core Europe, some authors like Wolfram Kaiser (1996, 2004) have argued that the British applications never amounted to a break in European policy. Instead, British foreign policy objectives remained largely unchanged, but EEC membership was now regarded as a more suitable means of securing them.

Several authors have argued that the first British EEC application was not necessarily doomed from the beginning, despite de Gaulle's scepticism. Instead, a substantial British offer on nuclear cooperation with France could possibly have changed de Gaulle's attitude, but with the exception of a few pro-European politicians like the conservative Peter Thorneycroft, who served as President of the Board of Trade and Chancellor of the Exchequer, the British government never seriously considered making such an offer (Kaiser 1996). On the other hand, N. Piers Ludlow (1997) has argued that the British government could and should have made more concessions in the negotiations faster to exploit de Gaulle's relative domestic weakness before the parliamentary elections in late 1962. Research has now moved on to study the European policies of the Harold Wilson (1964–70) and Edward Heath (1970–74) governments (for example, Daddow 2003; Pine 2007). Milward (2002b) has also published an 'official' history of Britain's European policy. In line with his previous conceptual approach to understanding European integration history, Milward has interpreted British policy from an (economic) rational choice perspective as a largely consensual 'national strategy' and an attempt to manage the transition from the status of an imperial power to medium-sized European power.

As Rasmussen also argues in his chapter, however, this approach neglects cultural and identity dimensions of policy-making. In fact, Kaiser (1996, 2009c) has argued forcefully that the domestic political conflict over 'Europe' within and between the Conservatives and the Labour Party had a major impact on Britain's European policy-making, not least by preventing the emergence of a minimal cross-party consensus on British policy, or even membership in the present-day EU. Similarly, political scientists have made the point that such domestic political, institutional and cultural factors also account for what Stephen George (1992) has called Britain's 'semi-detachment' from integration even after it joined the EC in 1973. Thus, Jim Buller (2000) has shown how much government policy-making during the negotiations about the Maastricht Treaty was determined by the attempt to keep a deeply divided Conservative Party together.

British governments often combined excessive expectations about a British leadership role after EC accession with a refusal to contemplate that membership could also have a fundamental impact on Britain. This half-hearted view indicated the extent to which Britain's EEC application and its subsequent membership never reflected a radical break with past policy preferences and collective attitudes. Several authors have discussed the exaggerated British leadership claims, which were not in line with the realities of EC politics, especially the close Franco-German collaboration. Thus, as Anne Deighton (2001) has emphasized, the Wilson government and especially Foreign Minister George Brown expected to play *the* leading role in the Community after accession. Melissa Pine (2007) has used Kaiser's (1996) argument about the first application to account for the second application by claiming that Wilson, Brown and the Foreign Office hoped that EC accession would actually sustain and broaden the existing relationship with the US. As Kaiser (2002b) has argued, exaggerated claims to leadership and Britain's continuing ambivalence about European integration were culturally embedded, and Britain eventually joined the Community under very unfavourable circumstances in terms of its domestic economic situation and the structures of EC policies, especially the CAP and the budget.

After Heath lost two elections in 1974, British governments only developed a positive agenda for integration once more when Prime Minister Margaret Thatcher strongly advocated economic liberalization in the 1980s by supporting the single market programme. In essence, Labour Prime Minister Tony Blair continued this policy from 1997 to 2007, although his government opted into the Social Chapter. Ever since Britain's EC accession, however, British leaders have been torn between their presumed need to play to strongly Eurosceptic sentiment at home and their general understanding that it would be desirable for Britain to play a more proactive role within the present-day EU. Euroscepticism is part and parcel of a long tradition of relative cultural isolation and of 'othering' the EU partners and treating 'Brussels' as a scapegoat for domestic political failure. Whereas two-thirds of British voters approved of continued EC membership in the referendum of 1975, today only a minority of the population arguably feels at home in 'Europe' (Kaiser 2009c).

Denmark: 'reluctant European' and small latecomer

As in the case of Britain, Denmark's European policy was shaped for a long time by the early decision not to participate in core Europe integration (Laursen 2004). In the early 1950s, Foreign Minister Hans Christian Hansen characterized Denmark's attitude as seeking 'pragmatic solutions to practical problems on an intergovernmental basis' (Laursen 2009b, 221). In fact, his view strongly influenced the early historiography of Denmark's policy towards the creation of the ECSC and the EEC, and even within the present-day EU after its accession in 1973. However, the decision about Denmark's policy towards the ECSC was not a foregone conclusion. Recent research has stressed that opposition to supranationalism, which was played up in the British debate, played no significant role in the discussions in the Danish government during 1952–53 (Branner 1993; Sørensen 1998). In the early 1950s, Danish decision-makers actually shared many of the concerns of the core Europe founding member states. In particular, they were keen to foster Danish industrialization and to secure access to international markets, especially for their agricultural produce, through closer European cooperation. Decision-makers needed to avoid being cut off from the German export market for agricultural produce, which was once more growing in importance, without losing market share in Britain. As a result, Danish governments were keen to prevent a split in the western European market. The early debate about European integration in Denmark was limited to small elites from government, political parties and trade unions and business organizations. Led by the social democrats, the Danish government decided to participate in the European Free Trade Association (EFTA) in 1958–59, but encouraged the British government to apply for EEC membership only two years later in 1961 as a means to overcome the division of western Europe into two economic blocs.

Danish social scientists first became interested in Denmark's European policy in the 1960s, after the country's first EEC application. While Gunnar Nielson (1966) focused on how Denmark was torn between its links with Britain, Nordic cooperation, and core Europe integration, Peter Hansen (1969) mapped the domestic coalitions within and between political parties and interest organizations on 'Europe'. Both authors drew attention to the fact that the social democratic labour movement played a major role in the definition of Denmark's European policy. They showed that reservations about supranational core Europe integration and the preference for Nordic cooperation only really grew stronger in the second half of the 1960s, becoming a barrier to Denmark playing a more proactive role in the EC after accession. In his comparative study of the Nordic states, Toivo Miljan (1977) set in stone the view of Denmark as just another Scandinavian 'reluctant European' alongside Norway, which decided not to join in a referendum in 1972, and Sweden.

When Danish historians first began to study the country's European policy, they focused on the years from 1947 to 1957. In line with Milward's approach to understanding the origins of European integration Vibeke Sørensen (2001) explained Danish European policy as a reflection of a particular domestic political strategy for building a national welfare state. At the same time, Hans Branner (1993) emphasized how much more flexible the Danish government was initially in its attitude to the precise institutional forms of cooperation or integration, as long as Denmark could secure these domestic objectives. Anders Thornvig Sørensen (1998) has discussed this question in greater detail in the context of Denmark's policy towards the abortive Green Pool negotiations over agricultural integration in the first half of the 1950s. In the meantime, these and other dimensions of Danish European policy are also discussed in the larger context of Denmark's foreign policy after 1945 in the fifth volume of the history of Danish foreign policy (Olesen and Villaume 2005).

In his biography of the social democratic politician and Danish Prime Minister Jens Otto Krag, Bo Lidegaard (2001–02) has provided valuable insights into Danish European policy-making. Krag constantly had to fight Euroscepticsm in his own party. To placate such Euroscepticsm he propagated EC accession, which was approved by a large majority in a referendum in 1972, as an economic decision without long-term political implications. However, this in turn had long-term implications for the way in which many Danes regarded core Europe integration and viewed attempts at deepening it, as became clear in the negative referendums on the Maastricht Treaty in 1992 and joining the Euro in 2000. Authors like Johnny Laursen (1996, 2000, 2001) have also shown that the prevailing scepticism in the labour movement reflected real concerns about the future of Norden, economic modernization and domestic political competition with the more 'pro-European' conservative and liberal parties.

Several studies have also treated the second Danish application which eventually led to the accession negotiations and the referendum on EC membership (Due-Nielsen and Petersen 1995; Bo Lidegaard 2001–02). Rasmussen (2003, 2005) has analysed the Danish accession negotiations. He has argued that the Danish government succeeded in developing a clear negotiation strategy and building domestic support for it, eventually succeeding in securing highly favourable conditions for its agriculture, and making Britain pay the bill for EC enlargement. From the 1970s onwards, political scientists were already studying the domestic debate and the referendum about membership, analysing the motivations of the Eurosceptics also in comparison with the Norwegian debate. According to Hans Marten (1979), lavish financial resources, strong organization and unity of action won the vote for the Yes side in Denmark. In contrast, the No camp was ideologically highly fragmented. It was dominated by intellectuals and political groups to the Left of the Labour Party. As a result, the sceptics among the social democrats were cautious about strongly supporting the No camp (Hansen, Small and Siune 1973; Rasmussen 1997).

Until recently, Danish historians of European integration worked almost exclusively on Danish national policy. As the examples of Knudsen and Rasmussen show, however, several of the younger historians now make important contributions to the study of EU multi-level politics, legal politics and the evolution of policy fields from a multilateral perspective. But even the narrower focus on Danish policy has produced revisionist insights that have called into question prevailing self-perceptions among Danish elites and citizens about their relationship with 'Europe' and made a useful contribution to the historiography of European integration. As Laursen (2009b, 223) has provocatively asked: 'If the rationale and continuity of intergovernmental preferences has been exaggerated in Danish historiography, might not also the rationale of supranational integration similarly have been exaggerated in the historiography of say Dutch, French, or German integration history?'

Towards comparing national European policy

Most historical research on national European policies, with the partial exception of Britain and France, has perhaps unfortunately been conducted by nationals of these states. As a result, this literature is particularly strongly informed by national historiographical traditions and experience of contemporary socio-economic and political change in the national context. Accordingly, Germany's European policy has been closely connected with the country's division and the Cold War. The German question returned with a vengeance when the Berlin Wall came down in November 1989. Subsequently, German unification led to a new focus in German historiography on eastern German history and a new emphasis on national history in what could almost be called a process of historiographical 'nationalization', marginalizing German research on the history of European integration generally and German European policy more specifically.

Research on national European policy is highly developed and diverse, which results firstly from better and longer preservation and easier access to sources in state archives. Secondly, this trend reflects the continuing crucial role of the member state governments in EU politics and policy-making. Crucially, with the partial exception of France, the question of participation in core Europe integration was not heavily disputed, and a broad domestic consensus developed soon on the desirability of membership in the founding member states of the EEC. Thus, historiography focused less on why these countries set up the ECSC/EEC in the first place, but on how national positions on institutional and policy issues influenced interstate negotiations. In contrast, with the exception of Spain and Portugal, national policy towards integration in 'latecomer' countries remained highly controversial domestically for a long time, even after accession, as in the cases of Britain and Denmark. As a result, the historiography in these countries concentrated much more on reconstructing the domestic debates for and against membership, the decisions leading up to membership applications and the accession negotiations.

By definition, the historiography of national European policies has shown how member state governments formulated and projected particular interests in interstate negotiations. The first set of interests was of an economic nature. Thus, the hope that integration would be a suitable framework for the stabilization and modernization of France's state industries formed a main argument for French participation in core Europe. The common market also promised new prospects for economies of scale and increased exports. Equally, the wish to avoid exclusion from this larger market motivated Britain's initiative to create a larger free trade area in 1956–57, and was one reason for the EEC application in 1961. The attraction of the common market and later, the single market programme, were strong incentives for other latecomers for reconsidering their attitude to EC membership as in the case of Austria, when it applied for membership in July 1989 (Gehler 2002, 2006, 2009).

On the whole, however, research on national European policy has put greater emphasis on domestic political and especially, foreign and security policy reasons to account for why states joined core Europe or refrained from doing so. For smaller states in continental western Europe, the supranational integration of core Europe served as a guarantee for their territorial integrity. The Benelux countries that had had painful experiences with violations of their neutrality by Germany in both world wars, had a strong interest in protection against any external aggression through membership in NATO and the EEC. At the same time, independent supranational institutions combined with weighted voting in the Council of Ministers, which gave the Benelux countries together one vote more than each of the three large countries and which seemed the best guarantee for their influence over European integration. In contrast, their long-standing traditions of neutrality were powerful barriers to membership in the EEC with its common trade policy and long-term political objectives for countries like Switzerland (for example, Gees 2006) and Sweden (af Malmborg 1994).

Foreign policy concerns were especially important for Britain as a declining global power. What makes Britain a special case is its 'special relationship' with the US. This relationship was crucial for Britain in retaining a national nuclear deterrent that in turn was seen as indispensable for supporting its claim to continued great power status of some sort (for example, Clark 1994). In fact, the new John F. Kennedy administration exerted substantial pressure in early 1961 for Britain to enter the EEC (Kaiser 1995). This motivated the Conservative government to see EEC membership as a new strategy for safeguarding Britain's role at the centre of the 'three circles': the Commonwealth and its relations with the US and western Europe. The importance of the US as a 'third factor' in Britain's European policy, which has played a role to the present day, is exceptional.

Comparing different national European policies further highlights that external developments and challenges strengthened either a strategy for integration with supranational dimensions, or a policy of national sovereignty with intergovernmental economic cooperation. Among the exogenous factors which have impacted on national European policies have been, first of all, the policies of the two superpowers. Clearly, those countries that profited significantly from the Marshall Plan and the ERP funds were bound to trade liberalization in western Europe. On the insistence of Britain and other countries, however, the Organization for European Economic Cooperation had a strictly intergovernmental institutional framework. Subsequently, strong American support for the supranational principle and core Europe formation in the ECSC/EEC posed hard questions for those countries that decided to stay outside. At the same time, the Soviet Union made the argument that neutrality was incompatible with EEC membership and thus minimized the options of several outsiders, especially Austria.

Clearly, historians of national European policy have to write about their topic in a strictly multilateral and comparative context. In fact, Schwarz demanded a consistent multilateral contextualization as early as 1983 (Schwarz 1983). At the same time, the comparative perspective (Kaiser and Elvert 2004) also helps historians to identify the specific reasons for exclusion and self-exclusion from core Europe integration (Angerer 1998). Further, it also becomes clear that the strategies behind membership in core Europe and in intergovernmental cooperation forms like EFTA were not always as different as contemporary actors and observers at times made them look (Laursen 2009b). Thus, both France during the presidency of de Gaulle and Britain, especially in the later stages of Thatcher's premiership, were strongly opposed to supranationalism and further integration. Lastly, several outsiders and latecomers had fairly close relationships with core Europe: Denmark enjoyed observer status with the ECSC; Austria 'quietly' participated in the European Monetary System through its close alignment with Germany's interest rate policy; and most recently, Switzerland decided to join the Schengen Agreement, which was originally signed in 1985 by five of the then ten EC member states to provide for the abolition of border controls, from 2009 onwards.

Conclusion

Despite the decline of the welfare state and the greater fragmentation of national polities, nation-states remain at the heart of the EU, which justifies continued research on national policy towards European integration and, for the member states, within the complex dynamic multi-level governance structures (Gehler 2001). In what Seidel, in her chapter, calls the third period of 'refinement' of the historiography on European integration, however, the weaknesses of the initially dominant focus on explaining one national policy have become clearer. The first of these is the excessive state-centrism which has been too exclusively focused on explaining government policy relying solely on more easily accessible state archives. In contrast, for many countries like Britain and Denmark, for example, earlier social science research actually considered the role of party politics, interests groups and public opinion to a greater extent. More recently, however, historians have begun to go beyond considering only how government decisions are influenced by domestic politics; they are now also researching the importance of transnational links and networks of domestic actors for national governmental policy-making as well as for decision-making in Brussels. This approach appears most advanced in research on political parties and their transnational networks (for example, Gehler and Kaiser 2004; Mittag 2006; Kaiser 2007; Gehler and Schönner 2009).

Linked to the more sophisticated conceptualization of governmental policy-making as embedded in domestic politics and transnational networks and contestation, historians have also begun to reintegrate the role of ideas and ideology for national European policy-making. Diplomatic historians have often assumed that governmental decision-making on Europe has been determined by interests that are given or defined by small foreign policy-making circles. Similarly, Milward and his disciples, as Rasmussen also shows in his chapter, believed that such interests were rationally derived from domestic politics. However, policy-making was influenced by guiding integration ideas at the national level and increasingly, within the supranational institutions. Up to a point, national politicians and officials as well as the members of the EP and officials in the Commission became socialized into new ways of 'doing things' together, including cooperation in the Consultative Assembly of the Council of Europe, the ECSC Common

Assembly and High Authority, the EP (Rittberger 2005; Müller-Härlin 2008) and the Commission (Dumoulin 2007; Seidel 2010). Working together created social ties and loyalties and formed the basis for the emergence of an esprit de corps and Community feeling. Although perhaps still largely limited to elites, over time a form of Community identity took shape (Rochard 2003; Frank and Greenstein 2005). The repercussions of this Community identity for national European policy-making remain insufficiently explored in historical research. Whereas social scientists trace such a Community identity in large-scale data, especially opinion polls, historians could continue to utilize biography as a suitable approach for studying Europeanization effects in the case of individuals involved in EU politics and policy-making.

At the same time, research on national European policy should explore the under-researched linkages between integration issues and the Cold War and its escalation and de-escalation as during the *détente* of the 1970s. The continued geographical broadening of research on European integration in historical perspective beyond core Europe will highlight how important this dimension was especially for countries like Austria and Finland. In this context, research on the relevance of bilateral relationships for national European policy holds significant potential, particularly for the co-called 'unequal partners' such as Ireland and Britain, Austria and Germany (Gehler et al.1996; Gehler and Böhler 2007) or Finland and the Soviet Union.

Apart from such forms of reconceptualizing domestic European policy-making and its international political framework, historians of national European policy also need to go beyond archive-based in-depth studies of short periods of time. With very few exceptions (for example, Gehler 2002, 2009) comprehensive long-term accounts of national European policy on a documentary basis are still missing, even for some larger core Europe member states. Such books could be very useful, however, for making the detailed research on specific time periods more accessible, putting the results into context and studying change in national European policy over time. Similarly, as argued above, comparative studies could contribute to a better understanding of national European policy. Without comparative studies (for example, Wurm 1995; Gehler 1998; Gillingham 1998; Gruner 1999; Kaiser and Elvert 2004) national historiographies tend to develop 'special path' narratives that highlight the alleged uniqueness of particular country cases and neglect the significant similarities. Finally, as in other fields of historical research on European integration, future research will have to expand geographically, in particular to include east-central and south-eastern Europe.

Future research could not only develop these and other dimensions of national European policy, however. While the member states have shaped the EU, the EU has also impacted on the member states. So far, historians have largely neglected the effects of European integration on the member states and third countries, however, a point also made by Lorenzo Mechi and Garavini in their chapters. These Europeanization effects were manifold and included constitutional issues and national law, socio-economic structures and the alignment of political forces. In the social sciences, literature on Europeanization has evolved only in the context of the EU's Eastern enlargement, but the historical roots of these processes clearly go back in time. Here, research on national European policy can connect with the work of Hartmut Kaelble and others. As the outlines of an emerging European society are becoming clearer (Kaelble 2005a, 2007; Kaiser 2006), the past and future role of the nation-state within this changing context continues to be of crucial relevance for understanding the nature of European integration.

6
Governing Europe: Charting the Development of a Supranational Political System

N. Piers Ludlow

From its very outset, the process of European integration has been about the transformation of the economy and politics of Europe through the building of supranational institutions. Early historians of the process recognized as much, faithfully relaying multiple comments by Jean Monnet, the initiator of the 1950 Schuman Plan, about the importance and enduring nature of institutions. And yet oddly, despite this early insight, historians were very slow actually to study those institutions which were established. As Michael Gehler discusses in his chapter, the initial focus of serious historical writing about European integration was overwhelmingly on the different national motivations which underlay the start of European integration and on the various national actors – individuals, governments, and political parties – who committed themselves to the establishment of a supranational Europe. There were admittedly a few notable exceptions. Peter Ludlow's innovative investigation into the birth of the European Monetary System appeared as early as 1982 and contained a great deal of information about both the interaction of the member states within the recently created European Council framework and the role of the European Commission (Ludlow 1982). Hanns Jürgen Küsters' (1982a) study of the negotiations leading to the treaties establishing the European Economic Community (EEC) and the European Atomic Energy Community (Euratom) published the same year revealed much about the bargains which had brought the Community's institutional system into being. But the main thrust of the first decade or so of serious writing on European integration history was not directed at the institutions of the European Coal and Steel Community (ECSC) and the EEC themselves. Scholarly literature about these last hence remained the almost exclusive preserve of lawyers and political scientists, plus the occasional memoir left by some of those involved in the initial stages of the Community's evolution.

There were two key reasons for this initial tendency of historians to ignore the institutions of the emerging European political system. The first was a chronological one, in that the main controversies of early historical writing about the integration process involved the pre-history of integration and the basic motivations which had led France and the other five founding member states to establish the ECSC, the EEC and Euratom in the course of the 1950s. As a result, discussion centred on a period prior to the birth of what would become the key European institutions and dealt with a series of debates that did seem, to a very large extent, to have been conducted either within and between national governments or amongst political and economic groupings, which were still organized on a primarily national basis. More admittedly might have been said about the way in which some of the early institutional experiments like the Organisation for European Economic Cooperation or the Council of Europe contributed to the Europeanization of attitudes amongst some national statesmen and civil servants, as well as encouraging the formation of informal transnational networks of like-minded experts, bureaucrats and politicians. But not only did the methodology of these first studies centred on national government archives tend to screen out such pan-European factors; it may also be the case that some historians were too ready to take the 'founding fathers' at their word and regard those institutions which had preceded the ECSC/EEC as 'failures'. These institutions mattered only insofar as they demonstrated how Europe should *not* be built. In a period which preceded the birth of the better known and most successful European institutions, however, the primary focus on national actors had some degree of justification.

The second factor contributing to the early neglect of institutional history was archival. Efforts to organize the papers and records of the Community institutions began in the late 1970s and were to culminate with the establishment of publicly accessible European Community (EC) archives in 1983 (Audland 2007). It took significantly longer, however, for the system to begin to operate efficiently. Many of the teething difficulties were connected with the somewhat bizarre division of labour between the archival services of the Commission and the other Community institutions which were primarily located in Brussels, and the actual archives which were intended to be housed in Florence. The flow of paper from Belgium to Italy was highly unreliable at first and characterized not merely by delays, but also by substantial gaps in the collections that were transferred. Until the mid-1990s at least this resulted in the somewhat paradoxical situation that whereas the best facilities were undoubtedly located in Florence, the collection of available material was significantly better in Brussels. Any researcher planning to engage in the detailed study of how the Community institutions had originally functioned, thus had to choose between a trip to the well-equipped and well-staffed archives in Florence where working conditions were excellent but the range of papers which could be consulted was highly limited, or a visit to Brussels, where many more documents were accessible but where there was no guarantee of a proper reading room, where much of the archive staff seemed primarily interested in responding to the demands of Commission officials rather than researchers, and where the rules about what could be copied, and even what could be read, seemed largely to be subject to individual negotiation. A further source of frustration was the mismatch between the records of the ECSC High Authority which had been properly catalogued in parallel to the writing of the official history by French historian Raymond Poidevin and Dirk Spierenburg, a former member of the High Authority (1993), and those of the European Commission which were much less well ordered and all but devoid of finding aids. This meant that any enquiry made to an archivist about the Commission would tend, perversely, to elicit an initial response based upon the records of the ECSC High Authority rather than on Commission files, since the former were much more easily searchable than the latter. Still more fundamentally, the fact that both the Community institutions themselves and the majority of EC member states had decided to institute a 30-year rule for the opening of official papers, releasing formerly secret internal documents only after three full decades had elapsed, ensured that detailed archival work on the operation of the EEC or Euratom, as opposed to the ECSC, only really became possible in the first half of the 1990s. It was hence not until the middle of the final decade of the twentieth century that a steady flow of historical literature about the institutional dimension of European integration began to appear.

This chapter begins by describing the main phases in the evolution of a detailed scholarly literature on the Community's institutional system and the start of a historical debate about multilevel politics within Europe. It then highlights a few of the key issues upon which experts disagree, before turning to some of the deficiencies of, and gaps in, the current literature. This last naturally helps identify those questions upon which further research is necessary. And finally, the chapter discusses the need for greater links between the study of Community's development and the wider history of Europe since World War II.

The vanguard

The first salvo of note was the appearance of the detailed official history of the ECSC High Authority, a volume the French edition of which bore the revealing sub-title of 'une expérience supranationationale' – a supranational experiment (Spierenburg and Poidevin 1993). Unsurprisingly, perhaps, this suffered from some of the customary difficulties of an official history. Poidevin was thus distinctly less constrained in his criticism of some of the High Authority's actions when writing subsequent papers than he had been within the co-authored official history itself. But the lengthy volume did demonstrate how much could potentially be unearthed from the previously unused records of the European institutions and how much an account written from the perspective of a supranational actor could add to the existing national narratives. As mentioned above, it also stimulated a systematic effort by the Commission archival service to organize, catalogue and make searchable on the computer the files of the High Authority, thereby significantly facilitating the work of any subsequent historian intent upon working on this pioneering institution. Less high profile, but also very useful, was the multilingual edited volume *Die Anfänge der Verwaltung der Europäischen Gemeinschaft* (Heyen 1992) which brought together a number of historians and political scientists interested in the early workings of the EEC bureaucracy. The appearance of two very detailed and accomplished biographies of Monnet in the course of the 1990s also added an extra level of detail to historical knowledge about the man most frequently credited with being the 'father' of the Community's institutional system (Duchêne 1994; Roussel 1996).

The latter half of the 1990s saw the publication of a further edited volume exploring the institutional landscape of early European integration, edited by Poidevin, Marie-Thérèse Bitsch and Wilfried Loth (1998), and a sprinkling of other contributions to historical conferences that investigated the role of Commission in particular (for example, Griffiths and Ward 1996). Antonio Varsori (2000) led a research team, which examined the early operation of the Economic and Social Committee – a body to which attention had seldom been devoted before. And there was even a first attempt to assess the life and career of the first President of the European Commission, Walter Hallstein (Loth, Wallace and Wessels 1995). None of these yet captured the full complexity of the

EEC institutional system, still less of Europe as a multilevel political system. But they did begin to show, firstly that the major landmarks in the Community's evolution could no longer be studied without greater attention being paid to the role of the Community institutions in general and the Commission in particular, and secondly that the archives in Brussels and Florence did contain enough of significance to be used as a valuable complement to the much better known national archival collections. Neither the materials held by the Commission nor those of the Council of Ministers constituted an effective substitute to papers collected in the various member state capitals – too many of the key decisions were still taken in the national capitals and discussed bilaterally away from Brussels – but the EC archives could shed light on aspects of the Community's operation that were all but impossible to analyse effectively from the national archives alone. This message was further reinforced by Anne Boerger-De Smedt's (1996; see also 2007) substantial, if still alas unpublished, doctorate on origins of the ECSC, EEC and Euratom institutional system and by Piers Ludlow's (1997) monograph on the Community's collective response to the first British membership application of 1961–63 which used documents from the British, French, German and Community archives to piece together as comprehensive an analysis as possible of the EEC's first encounter with the challenge of enlargement. *Dealing with Britain* also posed a challenge to those inclined to interpret the Community's development with exclusive reference to the larger member states, especially France and Germany, since the Council files on the failed British application brought out vividly the highly distinctive and important roles played by the Dutch, Belgian and Italian delegations in particular.

The American challenge

The debate amongst historians about how the early Community functioned was given a further stimulus by the work of Andrew Moravcsik (1998). *The Choice for Europe* was the first major work by a political scientist to discuss the formative years of the Community since the writings of the neo-functionalists over three decades earlier (Lindberg 1963). And like the neo-functionalists it offered a provocative and comprehensive theory about how the European system worked and about the key motivations of those involved. For Moravcsik, decision-making within the EEC, in the 1960s as much as in the 1980s, was dominated by the member states – and the large member states in particular – with minimal contribution from the supranational institutions. His book sought to chart the development of the Community from 1955 right through until the early 1990s almost exclusively in terms of bargaining between the three largest member states, Britain, France and Germany. Member state motivations meanwhile were primarily explicable in economic terms, with particular emphasis being placed on the way in which organized interest groups within the key member states were able to exercise a decisive influence over the way in which their governments negotiated in Brussels. According to Moravcsik, Charles de Gaulle's European policy was thus not the result of the French President's geo-political world view, as most traditional analysts had claimed, but was instead driven by de Gaulle's single-minded attempt to obtain an advantageous European agricultural policy so as to be able to quell the unrest and discontent of French farmers and their collective interest groups (Moravcsik 2000). Most historians were unconvinced by this highly revisionist interpretation. But the eruption onto the scene of a heavyweight political scientist who was prepared to some extent to engage with the historical literature and to challenge a number of scarcely contested assumptions about how the early Community had developed was something which demanded some degree of response.

No historian was prepared to descend straight into the arena and challenge Moravcsik directly. Apart from anything else, the sweeping chronological span of the American political scientist's work was very different from the majority of historical works, which instead tended to zoom in on a rather shorter and less ambitious period of time. The desire to find a single explanatory key for the whole process of European integration was also something which many historians regarded with a degree of perplexity. What a political scientist might refer to as an effort to achieve theoretical parsimony, could instead be seen by a historian as the stripping away of essential historical context and the pursuit of unnecessarily simplistic mono-causality. Gradually, over the next six or seven years, a succession of historical studies would build up a rather more nuanced view of how the early Community operated, would suggest that the member states acted in pursuit of rather more than simply economic aims, and would begin to challenge Moravcsik's tendency to dismiss as largely unimportant the role of the Commission.

One important set of contributions was made by the wave of doctorates which began to emerge in the early years of the twenty-first century, many of which looked in detail at the Community's early policies. The first of these was Ann-Christina Knudsen's detailed study of the origins of the Common Agricultural Policy (CAP) – now revised and published as *Farmers on Welfare* (Knudsen 2009). This was followed by Lucia

Coppolaro's (2006a, 2006b, 2006c) investigation of the Community's behaviour in the Kennedy Round of the General Agreement on Tariffs and Trade negotiations, Laurent Warlouzet's (2010) detailed investigation of French European policy-making in the late 1950s and 1960s which included a sizeable sub-section on the emergence of the EEC competition policy, Simone Paoli's (2007) study of the Community's halting attempts to devise a harmonized approach to education, and Lorenzo Mechi's investigation of the origins of Community social policy (Mechi 2006; Varsori and Mechi 2008). Each of these varied slightly in their emphases and in their interpretation of exactly who proved the decisive actors in the formulation of these early common policies. But all were fairly clear in their rejection of any explanation which concentrated exclusively on the larger member states or which marginalized Community institutions.

A similar emphasis on multi-actor and multilevel interpretations emerged from the range of edited volumes which, in attempting to explore the Community's development during the period from 1958 to 1973, had to weigh in to the debate about the institutional system. Wilfried Loth's volume *Crises and Compromises* (2001) was the first example of this, containing a range of chapters exploring that most notorious of institutional tussles in the Community's early development, the 'Empty Chair' crisis of 1965–66. This was then followed by Antonio Varsori's more thematic volume, *Inside the European Community* (2006), which devoted considerable space to both the early common policies of the Community, and to some of the key political actors and personalities involved in the nascent institutional system. The dynamics of the key Franco-German relationship and the extent to which the Community's development could, and could not, be explained through this prism was the theme of Marie-Thérèse Bitsch's volume, *Le couple France-Allemagne et les institutions européennes* (2001) and this idea was again one of several investigated in a further Loth volume, *La gouvernance supranationale dans la construction européenne* (2005a). The latter also contained further biographical sketches and a number of chapters which sought to home in on key moments in the Community's institutional development and the definition of the Community's policy range. Another volume, meanwhile, brought together a wide range of differing perspectives and interpretations of both the Empty Chair crisis and the famous Luxembourg Compromise, which had brought the dispute between France and its fellow member states about the working of the Community system to a close (Palayret, Wallace and Winand 2006). No single dominant interpretation emerged from *Visions, Votes and Vetoes,* but the sheer range of contributions involved and the diversity of their sources, did highlight how rich and diverse is the archival base on most major episodes in Community history. And the most recent edited collection of note is *The History of the European Union: Origins of a Trans- and Supranational Polity, 1950–72* (Kaiser, Leucht and Rasmussen 2009). This volume is also worthy of attention in its consistent attempt to draw upon some of the theories and ideas developed by political scientists working on the present-day European Union (EU). Studies looking at the first years of institutional evolution in Luxembourg and Brussels thus make use of ideas such as path dependency, principal agent theory, or policy networks more often deployed in the analysis of much more recent European developments. The chapters by two of the three editors, Wolfram Kaiser and Morten Rasmussen, also explicitly discuss the extent to which this dialogue between history and political science can enrich our understanding of how the Community system came into being and functioned during its early years. Many of the same issues are also explored in a special issue of the *Journal of European Integration History* (*JEIH* 1/2008) devoted to the dialogue between integration history and the social sciences.

The *JEIH* has been an important forum for the debate about the Community's institutional system more generally. Here, too, discussion of institutional matters was relatively slow to begin – as Katja Seidel points out in her chapter. The *JEIH* began to appear in 1995, but after a first issue, which included articles on both the High Authority and the European Court of Justice (ECJ), the institutional theme all but disappeared until 1999. It was thus not until the early years of this century that articles about the development of the Community system began to appear with any regularity. Once it had got going, though, many of the relevant articles turned the historical spotlight on areas of Community activity, which had previously been largely ignored. A special issue in 1999 thus looked at cultural cooperation at a European level. Another special issue in 2006 investigated the Community's role in the promotion of scientific research and cooperation. Four articles in a 2008 issue analysed the emergence and early reception of an activist ECJ with an expansive interpretation of the role of EC law. The 2003 volume dedicated to the summit at The Hague in 1969 also constituted the first detailed historical investigation into a gathering, which had often been seen as a major landmark in the EC's advance. Typically, though, the extra information gained about what had happened in the Community's first major summit meeting, while certainly valuable, did not provide an easy answer to the question posed in the journal's introduction, namely whether the summit should be regarded as a success. A more detailed understanding of both the varied expectations with which the different governments had approached the summit and of their divergent assessments after the event led instead to a view of the outcome which was much too nuanced to be classed as either total failure or complete success. A series of other journals have also published important pieces on the Community's institutional development. Véronique Dimier's research into the emergence of Directorate-General IX and the gradual establishment of a Community policy towards its African and Caribbean associates were published, for instance, in *Sciences de la Société* and *Etudes internationales* (Dimier 2001; 2003). *Contemporary European History* and *Relations internationales* have also featured an intermittent strand of pieces devoted to the Community's institutional and policy development.

One of the first historical monographs to grapple with the complexities of the Community system was Ludlow's *European Community and the Crises of the 1960s* (2006). This drew upon sources in a wide range of national and Community archives in an attempt to reconstruct the way in which the Community coped with the Gaullist challenge of the mid- to late 1960s. Naturally this included several chapters devoted to the Empty Chair crisis and its aftermath, but it also encompassed the crisis that beset the Community in the aftermath of de Gaulle's 1963 veto of British membership and the further round of turmoil triggered by the French President's second veto in 1967. Throughout it sought to emphasize the importance of interplay not simply between the member states and the Community institutions – this was very definitely not a reading of Community history reduced to a struggle between France and Germany alone – but also between different policy areas. The Empty Chair crisis was thus not presented merely as a clash of institutional visions, but instead as something which was as much a product of the unequal distribution between member states of gains and costs in the emerging CAP as it was about attitudes towards the powers of the Commission or the European Parliament (EP). Similarly, the laying to rest of the Gaullist challenge, accomplished at the summit at The Hague in 1969, entailed a deal which covered what the Community did and who should be in the Community, as well as an agreement to leave largely unaltered the institutional operation of the EEC. Eleonora Guasconi's (2004) study of the Community in the early 1970s is another example of a book which attempts to analyse the EC's operation from a thoroughly multinational and multi-archival viewpoint. This, too, brought out some of the complexity of the institutional system, the variety of actors involved and the interconnections between policy areas.

A somewhat different approach to institutional history was adopted by the official history of the Commission written by a team of historians led by Michel Dumoulin (2007). *The European Commission, 1958–72: History and Memories* mixed portraits of some of the more prominent figures of the early Commission such as Hallstein, Sicco Mansholt, or Emile Noël, with chapters, which sought to trace the Commission's activities in various policy areas. It also drew upon a wide range of recollections of this era, gathered in interviews with surviving Commission officials – although sadly this emphasis on oral history, which was largely of the Commission's own choosing rather than that of the historians involved, did mean the volume was not accompanied by the same type of effort to organize and catalogue the archival base that had been carried out to facilitate the Poidevin and Spierenburg project on the High Authority. The outcome is rich in detail but somewhat lacking in overall analytical thrust. Future historians will therefore be able to raid its pages profitably in search of ammunition for their own research projects – and may well be able to derive even more benefit from the full texts of the eyewitness interviews which have been made available online. But they will look in vain for any strong assessment either about the Commission's own evolution, or about its place in the wider Community political system. An official history of an institution which, unlike the High Authority, was still very active and very sensitive to its public image, was perhaps not the ideal forum for a genuinely open debate about the efficacy and success of the Commission during its early years.

A further category of recent writing about the Community's institutional system which ought to be mentioned is that produced by a younger generation of scholars emerging through the History of European Integration Research Society and the Réseau International de jeunes Chercheurs en Histoire de l'Intégration Européenne, the twin associations created to promote interchange and discussion amongst the newest specialists in integration history. So numerous indeed are the next cohort of researchers to work on projects with a strong institutional dimension that it seems almost invidious to single out any for a special mention. A few of these projects though do deserve to be highlighted, if only because they have either been recently completed or have reached a sufficiently advanced stage for their findings to have been widely disseminated. Into this category fall Seidel's (2010) work on the officials who composed the early Commission, their backgrounds, and their experiences of working within the nascent European administration; Arthe van Laer's (2006) groundbreaking study of the Community's efforts to promote technological cooperation at a European level during the 1970s and early 1980s; Brigitte Leucht's (2008, 2009b) findings about the role of transatlantic networks in the Schuman Plan negotiations; Philip Bajon's (2009) in-depth study of the Empty Chair crisis and in particular of the divisions within the Commission that were produced by the confrontation with France; and Laura Schichilone's (2008) exploration of the origins of the Community's involvement in environmental policy-making. These, and many others, underline both the vitality of the debate about the Community's early operation and the imagination and creativity being shown in the search for new topics and for unused or underused sources.

Finally, it also important to acknowledge the contribution made to our understanding of the Community system of the numerous studies of key bilateral relationships within western Europe. Studies of the Franco-German relationship such as those by Georges-Henri Soutou (1996) or Ulrich Lappenküper (2001), of that between Germany and Italy investigated by Carlo Masala (1997), or of the bonds and the tension between Germany and Britain analysed by Martin Schaad (2000) amongst others have the great merit of exposing the amount of business within an integrating Europe which took place (and still takes place) at a bilateral level rather than in a multilateral context. Many Community deals – and non-deals – are hence impossible fully to interpret without knowledge of what has been said and agreed away from Brussels in face-to-face meetings between the representatives of just two countries. Indeed, the series of bilateral meetings prior to every key summit or Council meeting has become an EU ritual for the leaders of the country holding the Union's rotating presidency. Other countries too seek to coordinate their positions bilaterally before going into the fully fledged Community negotiations. Bilateral studies can provide extra understanding of this dynamic, helping to contextualize agreements or disagreements about Community matters within the wider frame of relations between France and Germany, France and Italy or Germany and Britain. And they also can be more effective than purely EC-centred work at picking up the extent to which non-Community related tension or disagreements adversely affected negotiations in Brussels. Having said this, it remains the case, however, that purely bilateral studies can at times play into the hands of those who wish to explain all that goes on at a Community level as a simple function of one or two key relationships between national leaders or some of the bigger member states. Such studies do need to be read in conjunction with those which adopt a more multinational approach, not to mention those works that factor in the role of the Community institutions themselves.

Where does power lie?

Perhaps unsurprisingly, this proliferation of work on the institutions of the first Community structures and upon their interaction with one another and with the more traditional bureaucratic and political structures of the member states has not led to a single dominant view of how the early EEC operated. Consensus may exist that too simple a model for explaining decision-making in Brussels is to be rejected. Few of the historians referred to above would hence be happy with an attempt to interpret the development of the Community between 1958 and the early 1970s which relied either on nothing more than the preferences and ambitions of a small number of the larger member states, or on the actions and aspirations of the Commission alone. But within the field there are differing emphases on the precise balance of power between the Community institutions and member states, and upon the lines of causality connecting disputes about how the Community should operate with discussions of what it should do – that is, which policy areas should be prioritized.

A clear example of this occurs in the recent literature about the autonomy and degree of initiative held by the Commission. In Knudsen's account of the CAP's birth, the Commission held the initiative throughout the gradual and highly contested emergence of the agricultural policy. Mansholt and his officials thus fully merit their reputation as the true 'fathers' of the CAP. This contrasts not merely with Moravcsik, who is largely dismissive of Commission influence and who identifies France as the driving force behind all of the key CAP decisions, but also with Ludlow's account which, while recognizing the importance of the Commission contribution, nevertheless places equal if not greater emphasis on the role of those states, France and the Netherlands particularly, who pushed for the policy's completion within the Council of Ministers (see also Patel 2009c). Similarly, Lise Rye's (2009) reading of how the Commission managed to escape from attempted member state control in the realm of information policy, differs significantly from my emphasis on the rise of Committee of Permanent Representatives (COREPER) as a mechanism used by the member states to control the activities of the Commission, including within the field of information policy (Ludlow 2005a). And within the literature on the causes of the Empty Chair crisis, there is again a divergence between my talk of 'decommissioning the empty chair crisis' and interpretations like that of Matthias Schönwald (2001) or Philip Bajon (2009) that strongly emphasize the role of the Commission in general and its president in particular in triggering the French boycott.

Such differences of opinion are of course, to some extent, just that, namely differences of opinion arising from divergent readings of the same body of evidence. To some degree such differences of judgement may reflect differing overall opinions over how the Community system functioned – which may in turn sometimes be linked to more normative judgements about how it *ought* to function. In some cases, the influence of particular political science theories about how the EU works and has developed may also play a role – although as noted above, few historians are comfortable with the inevitable generalizations that such theories involve. But equally important is the sheer complexity of the system and the huge profusion of possible archival sources on the basis of which its history can be written. Both of these mean that several of the divergent views outlined above – as well as many others like them elsewhere in the literature – owe as much to the different source bases used and the different overall foci of the studies in question as they do to simple differences of view. Thus Knudsen's highly detailed study of how the ideas that underpinned the CAP emerged naturally highlights the role of the Commission where many of these ideas were transformed into precise policy recommendations and then assiduously defended throughout the tense Council negotiations. My somewhat broader-brush interest in the wider politics of the Community during the same period de-emphasizes the Commission role by contrast, and picks up instead much of the political give and take between member states as well as the trade-offs made between agricultural policy and other aspects of the Community's development. Neither account is necessarily wrong or incorrect. They are simply both trying to describe somewhat different aspects of an enormously complex whole, and doing so moreover, on archival foundations which overlap but are nevertheless significantly different from one another.

Mind the gaps

While this plurality of views is something to be welcomed and the proliferation of studies outlined above is also encouraging, the study of how the Community developed as a political system has not been a field entirely without problems. The first of these is the imbalance of research devoted to the various European institutions. Thus while there has been considerable attention paid to the Commission, much less has been directed towards the Council Ministers, and hardly any at all towards the ECJ and the EP. The European Council has also been barely studied by historians, the sole exception being Peter Ludlow's (for example, 2004) series of largely interview-based analyses of a succession of recent summits. An uneven distribution of research like this is perhaps not entirely surprising. There has always been a tendency to view the Commission as both the most original and the most dynamic of the Community institutions – and therefore that most worthy of scholarly attention. Its role as initiator of all legislative proposals also makes it an obvious first stop for anyone seeking to study the birth of a particular EC policy. And access to its papers, while far from perfect, has also tended to be more straightforward than it is for some of the other Community institutions and especially the ECJ. But for all this it remains essential that sufficient research is directed towards the other components of the Community system.

The importance of the Council of Ministers should be in little need of emphasis, given that no major Community decision could (and can) be taken without there having been agreement amongst national ministers. Explaining such decisions, moreover, can seldom be done purely from the papers of single member states, vital though national records remain for any interpretation of what happened when national ministers gathered in Brussels. So some attempt to reconstruct Council discussions either by using the Council's own archives or by building up a more complete picture of Council debates through the collation of multiple member state accounts remains an essential step for any serious attempt to explain Community decision-making. Similarly, the value of studying the ECJ ought to be self-evident. Most accounts of the Community's development feel obliged to pay brief reference to the Court's succession of landmark rulings. With the exception of the contributors to the *JEIH* (2/2008), few historians have gone beyond such token references, however, and there is a great need for new and detailed research into how the Court took the decisions that it did, how it interacted with the other Community institutions, and how it managed its relations with the member states. Furthermore, the story of how European law developed, which has been written about at some length by lawyers but seldom by historians, needs to be integrated properly into the wider history of European integration. Joseph Weiler's provocative ideas about the legal revolution carried out by the Court driving institutional change within the Community were first published nearly two decades ago, but so far at least historians have been strangely reluctant to respond to his challenge (Weiler 1991).

Even the comparatively powerless EP is worthy of greater study. For a start, the records of EP debates and of EP committee meetings, constitute probably the fullest record of European debate and discussion preserved anywhere. They thus offer both a valuable window into the thinking of the multiple Commissioners and Council representatives who explained and justified themselves before the Strasbourg assembly and a means of gauging the mood of 'Europeans' more generally. What was expressed openly in Strasbourg may well provide a fairly accurate insight into what was also felt around Community Brussels but was rarely written down in such detail. Furthermore, there is sporadic but intriguing evidence that the EP may have had rather more political impact than might have been expected from an institution with so little formal power until the Maastricht Treaty on European Union. There are at least two reasons for thinking this. Firstly, there appear to have been occasions when the Commission was so anxious to hasten the development of a genuinely democratic Community, complete with proper parliamentary oversight, that it acted *as if* the EP had much greater power then it really did. Hallstein's deference towards the assembly's views in the run-up to the Empty Chair crisis in 1965 would be a case in point. Secondly, there are also a number of incidents which suggest that even a comparatively powerless assembly may have been an important forum for the development of certain ideas which affected multiple European political parties. One example of this was the EP's role in helping to foster strong left-wing opposition to accession of Francoist Spain to the Community in the course of the 1960s. The formal power to decide on this issue did not rest with the EP. But the fact that Spain's case was extensively debated amongst members of the EP contributed to the building up of a strong head of steam behind the anti-Franco cause and led to political parties across Europe voicing similar misgivings about potential Spanish accession (Ortuño Anaya 2001). Within each national context, such vociferous opposition was much harder for member state governments to ignore.

There is also a danger that the multiplication of single institutional studies, focusing, say, just on the Commission, or just on the ECJ, will replicate at the level of the European institutions, the limitations inherent in single national studies so apparent at an earlier stage of integration historiography. Further detailed investigations into the actions, character, and ideological make up of the Commission, the Court or the Parliament would, of course, be genuinely useful. In-depth research into patterns of behaviour in the Council of Ministers, including perhaps lower level but still crucial bodies like COREPER, and within the European Council would also add significantly to our understanding of how the EC/EU system worked. But just as it was vital for the historiography of European integration to break free from the exclusive reliance on studies of Italian European policy, French European policy, Dutch European policy and so on, it is equally important that single institution studies at a Community level are complemented by investigations which seek to look at the way in which the various Community institutions interacted with each other and with the member state governments. For it is only by analysing the workings of the whole system that the emergence (or indeed non-emergence) of particular decisions can be properly understood, or that trends in the development of the Community system can be grasped in their entirety.

In similar fashion, there is also a need for studies which capture the interplay between different policy areas. A large number of the recent books and doctorates that have contributed so much to our understanding of the EC/EU system have been organized around the detailed study of a single Community policy. This approach has much to commend it. Focusing on an individual policy area allows the researcher to acquire both a degree of expertise on the policy in question and a real feel for the individual policy-makers involved, which is likely to be hard to match for someone attempting to review a much wider array of Community policies. Single issue studies are likely, moreover, to have a degree of thematic coherence which is much harder to achieve when dealing with multiple policy areas. And they can also facilitate the drawing of useful comparisons with decision-making in the same policy area at the level of individual member states or even in other political systems. There is, however, a real danger that they overlook the degree of cross-policy linkage which occurred in Council discussions and in bilateral relations between member states. In 1960s Brussels discussions of the CAP, for instance, were seldom free from cross-currents caused by the parallel debates, often involving the same ministers and the same senior officials, about other Community policies and about the wider development of the EEC. Bargains involving one policy area could thus frequently involve 'side-payments' made in another; tension and mutual resentment provoked in the negotiations about agriculture, could easily infect debates about the Kennedy Round also; and tactics used successfully in one field, were likely to be imitated elsewhere. Single issue studies are ill-equipped to capture these patterns entirely, and ought ideally to be flanked by investigations that look at a number of policy areas.

Also slightly worrying is the difficulty which many researchers have had in 'getting inside' the Commission. The Brussels institution is not an easy body to study. Its structure, its purpose and its mode of operation can all appear rather impenetrable to historians more accustomed to working on national governments. Many of its main personalities remain somewhat obscure, with neither the published memoirs nor the biographical studies that might be expected of comparable national politicians readily available for the historians. And above all its record-keeping culture is very patchy, with many decisions either not recorded at all or noted down in the most cursory of terms. The failure of certain parts of the institution to hand over their records to the archive service only makes the problem worse, as does the tradition of each Commissioner viewing the files of his or her personal *cabinet* as a private possession to be disposed of as they see fit. All of this means that it becomes extremely hard for any analyst to go beyond the Commission's public position on any given issue, or the stance adopted by Commission representatives in Council debate, and discover not only why the Commission took the line that it did, but also whether or not this position had been contested internally. And such a lack of transparency leads in turn to an understandable tendency for historians to spend less time analysing and assessing the Commission's viewpoint on any given issue than is devoted to the debate within some of the more open member states.

There are admittedly a few examples of research that prove that an assiduous and imaginative historian can build up a detailed view of debate within the Commission. Laurent Warlouzet's (2010) analysis of the struggle between two highly different visions of competition policy is one such; Philip Bajon's (2009) work on the outbreak of the Empty Chair crisis another. But in both cases the methods used to discern internal discussion within the Commission are as eloquent about the inadequacy of most Commission records as they are about the ability of either historian. Warlouzet was thus compelled to use reports sent to London by the British head of mission in Brussels and preserved in the British archives in order to identify the main parties jousting over competition policy, while Bajon owed much of his insight to the handwritten notes of Noël, the minute taker at the weekly meeting of the Commission. How far either technique will take future researchers with slightly different topics must be open to doubt. The patchy nature of Commission papers does therefore remain a serious cause for concern, and one that makes it all the more regrettable that no overhaul of the archival catalogue accompanied the preparation of the official history of the Commission.

Finally, there is also some danger that as writing about Community history and about the development of the EC/EU system grows ever more sophisticated and ever more specialized, it will also become progressively more detached from the wider history of post-war Europe. The gap between the 'integration story' and the more general debate about how the whole continent has fared since 1945 is already a regrettably wide one. It could potentially develop into an unbridgeable chasm, however, as historians of European integration become steadily more fixated on a set of institutions and personalities within those institutions that mean little to those without an advanced understanding of how the EC/EU system worked and works. The key figures in the launch of the Schuman Plan after all, Monnet and French Foreign Minister Robert Schuman himself, were both personalities with whom any expert on post-war France, or even post-war Europe, was almost bound to be familiar. The protagonists of inter-institutional tussles involving Hallstein's Commission and COREPER, by contrast, are much less likely to trigger any name recognition, nor are the issues about which they did battle likely to mean much to those who are not specialists of European integration. The impenetrability of the specialist debate could, moreover, become even greater were the current fashion for importing political science and International Relations jargon to continue. The presumed merits of easing dialogue with specialists on the contemporary EU might well be outweighed by the dangers of confining integration history to an isolated ghetto within its own discipline.

Conclusion

There is hence a real need for some at least of those working on the historical development of the EC/EU political system to address questions and issues which will underline the relevance of the integration process for the wider history of Europe rather than aggravate the existing divide. This might well include a much more systematic effort to measure the impact of European choices and European policy upon national politics within each of the member states. How much have national decision-makers been constrained by their country's participation in European integration? Or has European involvement instead opened up policy options and possibilities that might not have been available to countries detached from far-reaching multilateral cooperation? How conscious of these constraints and openings have national decision-makers been? And how far have they been open about them to their electorates? Another potential area of study might be to investigate whether there is any sign that national politicians and officials have been 'Europeanized' by their involvement in Brussels-level governance. The amount of time which national ministers and senior civil servants have spent interacting with their counterparts across Europe has, after all, grown steadily throughout the six decades of the integration process, and it would be fascinating to assess whether this has had an effect. It would also be interesting to look much more systematically at the interplay between political and economic change at the national level and change at the European level. How far does the political complexion of European governance alter as governments come and go at a national level? How are the dynamics at European level affected by varying economic fortunes? Is there mileage in the old cliché that integration only advances in the boom times? Or is it in fact times of crisis that are more liable to make European politicians (if not their publics) turn to Europe in search of solutions? And there is need for much more work on attitudes towards European integration at both elite and public levels, as well as on the degree to which policy-making at a European level is responsive to public concerns and sensitivities. What use do politicians make of public opinion constraints and sensitivities at a European level? And how much have governments been able to exploit any leverage they might enjoy at a European level in order to win popularity and party political advantage at home?

Beginning to address these and multiple other potential questions about the interface between European and national level politics might start to lessen the isolation of European integration history. It would also help to assess whether the increasingly sophisticated, methodologically diverse, and plentiful literature on the gradual growth and development of the EC/EU political system is an arcane form of scholasticism, devoted to an issue almost entirely peripheral to the wider development of the post-war world, or instead the study of an important and influential phenomenon that has shaped both the development of individual European nations and the economic and political trajectories of the whole continent.

7
European Rescue of the Nation-State? Tracing the Role of Economics and Business

Morten Rasmussen

The history of European integration has been so deeply influenced by the economic history of Europe after 1945 as to make the two inseparable. There is little doubt that the successful reconstruction of the western European economy and the economic boom that lasted until 1973 facilitated the various integration initiatives of the 1950s and 1960s. At the same time, these initiatives were crucial to the very economic success of western Europe. Thus, it is not surprising that the majority of successful integration initiatives were of an economic nature, whether it was the establishment of the European Coal and Steel Community (ECSC), the creation of a common market for agricultural and industrial goods in the European Economic Community (EEC) or the more recent formation of Economic and Monetary Union (EMU). The historiography of European integration reflects this central importance of the economic dimension of European integration. A significant number of important publications deal with this subject, most notably those by the British economic historian Alan S. Milward (1984, 1992). However, as this chapter demonstrates, there has been little connection between much of this economic historiography of integration and international and diplomatic historiography, the latter having largely dominated the general historiography of the integration process.

While economic history, by definition, draws upon economic theory and methodology in order to analyse past economic phenomena, the literature on the economic history of European integration has made relatively limited use of such theory. Instead, in their qualitative studies historians have focused on the empirical exploration of the interaction between politics and economic developments, or the political economy of integration. One result of this approach has been a great number of studies on the commercial and economic diplomacy of the western European nation-states and the linked European public policies of an economic nature. In contrast, no attempts have been made to systematically employ macroeconomic theory and quantitative tools to explore, for example, the effects of the EEC customs union on the economic development of western Europe after 1945. Thus, considering the current importance of macroeconomic mathematical models and econometrics in the discipline of economics, the economic history of European integration is only marginally related to more mainstream economics. Rather, it shares common ground with the new institutional economics developed by Douglas North (1990). North assumes that political institutions are central in that they define the market of economic transactions. In order to understand economic developments these institutions therefore have to be analysed. Thus, qualitative and narrative economic studies of Europe's post-war development in this tradition such as the recent economic history of post-war Europe by Barry Eichengreen (2007) have drawn extensively on the results of the economic history of European integration. Even if economic historians of European integration should in the future embark on macroeconomic studies of the long-term economic effects of European integration, it is highly likely that most interdisciplinary dialogue will continue to take place with more qualitative and narrative types of economic studies as in Eichengreen's book.

Discussing the political economy historiography, this chapter will evaluate the two leading schools of economic history of European integration. Arguably, Milward's socio-economic and state-centric approach that explains European integration as the European 'rescue of the nation-state' is the more important historiographical tradition. As a consequence, the first two sections are devoted to discussing first, his approach and then the research and publications by economic historians who over the last two decades have employed this approach in their empirical studies of integration in the 1950s and 1960s. The second major school of economic history, which is examined in the third section, has resulted from a large research project on the transnational networks of economic elites and the development of European identities led by Eric Bussière and Michel Dumoulin. Finally, the fourth section explores new directions of research in the economic history of European integration, focusing on recent studies of European-level public policies and the role of business and firms in integration. The conclusion discusses the state of the art in relation to future challenges for historians of economic integration and potential links with research on contemporary European integration and European Union (EU) politics.

The life and teachings of Alan S. Milward

One of the important driving forces in the minds of the first generation of historians embarking on writing an economic history of European integration in the early 1980s was what they perceived as the dominance in the historiography of European integration of diplomatic history and federalist research. To the economic historians led by Milward both the analysis of foreign policy-making by diplomatic and political elites and the focus on the role of European ideas produced an unrealistic understanding of the driving forces behind European integration. These historians doubted that politicians and decision-makers operated in isolation from societal constraints resulting either from parliamentary politics or socio-economic pressures. Instead, the new generation of economic historians wanted to place the various initiatives of European integration in their historical context, namely that of emerging democratic welfare states experiencing a remarkably long period of sustained economic growth in the three decades following World War II. Ironically, one of the leading international historians criticized, René Girault (1982, 1381), had already led the way by arguing as early as 1982 that the economic nature of the treaties establishing the EEC and the European Atomic Energy Community had been overlooked.

Girault's sharp observation was not among the motives behind the first major contribution by Milward, his book on the economic reconstruction of western Europe from 1945 to 1951, however (Milward 1984). Originally, Milward had wished to explore the economic reconstruction of the western European nation-state but, as he discovered during the project, the initiatives for integration were deeply connected to economic (and political) reconstruction. His book caused considerable debate because he argued, inter alia, that the economic importance of the Marshall Plan for economic reconstruction had been grossly exaggerated. However, his analysis of the formation of the Organisation of European Economic Cooperation (OEEC) and the ECSC had a more significant long-term impact on historiography. Milward analysed and outlined the economic foundations of European cooperation of the 1950s. In relation to the ECSC he demonstrated, in particular, the economic nature of what he called a peace treaty between France and Germany.

In 1992, Milward published *The European Rescue of the Nation-State*, his first book dedicated solely to the history of European integration. The underlying concept of the book and his subsequent work was 'that changes in the economy, society and political organizations, which are closely interlinked in the post-war state have been the motivation for the choice of integration, and that it should be possible therefore to design a theoretical approach to identifying those very changes in society which do lead to integration' (Milward et al. 1993, xi). His methodology was much the same as for *The Reconstruction of Western Europe*: primarily based on state archives of multiple countries. As he readily admitted in his first book, he wrote the history of western Europe from the top down, leaving it to others to explain particular national policies (Milward 1984, 464–5). In *The European Rescue of the Nation-State* he included in his overall narrative on the formation of the EEC detailed national histories, for example, the experience of the Belgian coal and steel industry within the ECSC and Britain's responses to European integration. The only archival sources he used were state archives, such as those of political parties or interest organizations, however. This pattern was later repeated in the first volume of his official history of Britain's policy towards European integration from 1945 to 1963 (Milward 2002b).

In accordance with his conceptual perspective, Milward placed the decision to create the EEC, and indeed, all major integrationist decisions, in the context of the history of the European nation-state during the twentieth century. He argued that, after 1945, western European nation-states agreed on supranational cooperation in order to change the international state system in such ways as to guarantee their domestic socio-economic policies. Moreover, he posited that such domestic policies, which aimed at economic modernization, were vital for the stability and rescue of the western European nation-state. By supporting such domestic socio-economic policies, the creation of supranational European organizations in the 1950s contributed decisively to this rescue. Milward argued that European ideology was certainly important to key decision-makers like the German Federal Chancellor Konrad Adenauer, French Foreign Minister Robert Schuman, the Belgian Paul-Henri Spaak, who served as foreign minister and prime minister, and French civil servant Jean Monnet, for example, as he conceded in a provocative, but less than solidly documented essay entitled 'The Lives and Teachings of the European Saints' (Milward 1992, ch. 6). According to Milward, however, their European ideology differed sharply from those of utopian federalists, who had no political influence. These political actors did not denounce the nation-state as the foundation of the post-war European order. Rather, they considered European integration, and the limited surrender of sovereignty to European institutions, as a fundamental means to 'rescue' their own nation-states.

In 1993, Milward developed his thesis further in cooperation with Danish historian Vibeke Sørensen (Milward and Sørensen 1993). They argued along classical intergovernmentalist lines that national governments would surrender sovereignty and choose integration only if it was vital for important national policy objectives. In contrast to inter-governmental cooperation or an interdependence framework, as they called it, supranational cooperation had certain advantages. It instituted a system of law that bound participants more firmly to their commitments, was less easily reversed, and finally, excluded a number of economic competitors. Milward never claimed that political motives were unimportant, for example, for the creation of the EEC. He found, however, that at the end of the day, security concerns or federalist objectives depended on socio-economic objectives. In this sense the more political and more economic dimensions of the EEC were intertwined and the latter of more fundamental importance (Milward 1992, 208). Milward wanted to go beyond the empirical analysis of small decision-making circles and write a broader social history of European integration, as he called it. His conclusion in *The Frontier of National Sovereignty* was that the role of the various interest organizations was actually relatively limited before 1958. Instead, the electoral logic, which at the time was essentially decided by whichever party could best deliver economic growth, full employment and welfare for all citizens, determined policy outcomes (Milward 1993, 186–201).

Dissatisfied with the conceptual weaknesses of this understanding of domestic politics, which made it difficult to connect broader socio-economic developments with empirical explorations of decision-making processes, Milward (1995) proposed to study what he termed the 'allegiance' of national citizens to the nation-state and the present-day EU. According to Milward, allegiance encompassed all elements that induced citizens to give their loyalty to institutions of governance, ultimately securing political stability. Taking as his starting points opinion polls and historical research on nation-state strategies for creating allegiance in the nineteenth century, he argued that people in (western) Europe after 1945 developed increasingly complex demands for 'security' to be provided by the nation-state. Milward argued that historians should study income, and the perspective of future income through the life cycle, which were perhaps the most important determining factors at general elections. Secondly, Milward proposed that historians should explore the rapid transformation of public finances after 1945 and the impact of rising taxes and welfare benefits on people's incomes. Why did national citizens accept rapid increases in taxes in the 1950s and 1960s, and what impact did the welfare state have on allegiance? Finally, Milward suggested analysing what constituted European allegiance in the sense of the symbolic role of 'Europe' in political rhetoric (Milward 1995, 15–18).

The allegiance research programme never got off the ground, however. The type of research required for tracing the first two dimensions was not only extremely demanding, but also required an innovative use of the often scarce source material available. This was especially true of the second dimension. In this respect, Milward ran into the same troubles as those experienced by welfare historians, namely how to understand the extremely complex sets of diverging welfare systems as they evolved in the different European nation-states, and how to compare them when statistical resources were defined and collected nationally. Perhaps for these and other reasons the proposed research programme did not catch the imagination of other historians to the same extent as Milward's state-centric 'rescue' thesis. In the end, Milward abandoned the project when he accepted to write the official history of Britain's European policy.

While Milward's approach had a significant impact outside the field of European integration history and was adopted by a new generation of economic historians, as we shall see in the next section, his work was largely ignored in the broader field of integration history. The main reason for this was probably that his revisionist account went against the mainstream of international and diplomatic history practised by French, German and Italian historians, who dominated the field academically and institutionally in the 1980s, as also becomes clear from Antonio Varsori's discussion of research networks in his chapter. More of an *agent provocateur* than a diplomat, Milward's style of writing and debating did not help to bridge the gap between what became a new school of economic history and the existing, albeit internally diverse school of international and diplomatic history.

In fact, with respect to the analysis of politics at the European level, Milward's work has largely had a negative impact. It strongly reinforced the existing state-centric approach of diplomatic historians. Moreover, by arguing that supranational institutions, transnational networks and European ideas and ideology did not matter much, he probably delayed by a decade or more the emergence of a sophisticated historical analysis of European-level decision-making. Milward's failure to contribute to the understanding of the role of the supranational institutions can perhaps be explained by the fact that his empirical studies concentrated on the period before 1963. Yet why he excluded transnational networks completely from his interpretation is hard to understand. He has recently tried to nuance his approach. To escape the realist implications of the concept of national interest, he has proposed the need to place the latter in the context of a broader, global national 'strategy' (Milward 2002b, 1–9). Likewise, he has become increasingly open to subscribing independent influence to the European Court of Justice (ECJ) and the European Commission. His late pragmatism does not amount to a wholesale revision of his state-centric understanding of how politics has evolved at the European level, however (Milward 2005, 36–7).

Ultimately, Milward's most important and lasting contribution is connected to his analysis of the domestic politics of the nation-state. His efforts to contextualize the domestic decision-making processes underlying the formation of European policies have been important because they have permanently placed the need to write a social and economic history of European integration on the research agenda. Critics have pointed out that Milward does not convincingly link his socio-economic analysis to governmental decision-making on 'Europe', which is at least in part due to his exclusive reliance on government sources in state archives, and that he has neglected the contested nature of decision-making in most European nation-states, ignoring the role of identities and values (Kaiser, Leucht and Rasmussen 2009, 3). While both are valid points, one could ask to what extent historians working on identities and values have actually managed to link developments in public opinion, for example, with decision-making on European issues. The difficulties with linking broader socio-economic or societal developments to elite decision-making constitute a more general problem in the writing of the history of European societies in the twentieth century. Milward's attempt to address this issue probably still stands as the best available starting point for future research.

... and the disciples: state-centric economic histories of integration

The European Rescue of the Nation-State has been the first convincing attempt by any historian to explain the nature of the process of European integration and the only one that received significant attention outside the sub-field of integration history. With this achievement

Milward spearheaded a new generation of historians who did not necessarily share his theoretical ambition, but accepted its implications
for empirical research. The majority of them were educated at the
European University Institute (EUI) in Florence, where Milward held
professorships from 1984 to 1988 and again from 1996 to 2003, and
where his own former doctoral student, Richard Griffiths, held the same
chair from 1988 to 1996. Writing state-centric histories, these historians emphasized the domestic and socio-economic roots of European
integration. The result was a significant number of new studies of the
European policies of single states, national interest organizations, as
well as the different initiatives of European cooperation and integration in the 1940s, 1950s and early 1960s.

The first group of younger historians mainly came from the 'core
Europe' of the six founding member states and explored the immediate post-war years. Several studies focused on the economic reconstruction of western Europe and the Marshall Plan and analysed how it was
received by western European countries (for example, Sørensen 2001).
While Italy's state archives were closed, and largely remain inaccessi-
ble to this day, the exploration of Italian industry (Ranieri 1988; Fauri
2004) and agriculture (Laschi 1999) offered alternative ways to gauge
Italy's role in integration. Likewise, Federico Romero (1991) conducted
an important study of the role of emigration in Italy's European policies
under Milward's supervision at the London School of Economics and
Political Science.

A second group came to the fore from the early 1990s onwards and was
dominated by researchers from outside core Europe. Indeed, Griffiths
made a virtue of this trend in shifting research interests by launching a project that dealt with European cooperation in the larger OEEC
and the European Free Trade Association (EFTA) formed in 1959–60
(for example, Griffiths 1997). The dominant approach among younger
researchers from this group was to study the European policies of single
states, usually their own. In many respects Milward's approach proved
useful for explaining the gradual rapprochement with, and ultimately,
in most cases, accession of the outsiders to the ECSC/EEC, including
Ireland (Fitzgerald 2000), Denmark (Laursen 2004; Rasmussen 2005),
Norway (Frøland 2001), Spain (Guirao 1998), Portugal (Andresen-Leitao
2001), Finland (Paavonen 2001) and Sweden (Malmborg 1994). In these
countries, pro-European feelings had never been strong among the
political elite or the general public (Kaiser and Elvert 2004). Instead,
European integration was first and foremost a question of trade in the
first two decades after World War II. This fact did not diminish the

political importance of European integration to these states, however. In a post-war world where political success, for authoritarian regimes in Spain and Portugal and social democratic-dominated Scandinavia, increasingly rested on the attainment of welfare, the increase of exports to the dynamic EEC market was a key to economic modernization and growth. According to Milward (1992, 119–223), similar commercial dynamics had instigated early European integration. As Frances Lynch (1997) has demonstrated in her study of the socio-economic foundations of French European policy in the 1950s, the common market perspective was also an important factor behind the decision by the governments of the Fourth Republic in favour of setting up the EEC.

While most of the studies discussed here approached their particular topic armed to the teeth with the Milwardian approach, many of them also demonstrated the complexities and ambiguities of each national case. Maurice Fitzgerald, for example, showed how the need for economic modernization, which drove Ireland's first application for EEC membership in 1961, was closely connected with the wish to escape from the commercial and political dependence on Britain (Fitzgerald 2000). Johnny Laursen (2004) and Morten Rasmussen (2005) have shown that to understand Danish doubts about membership and later scepticism after accession can be explained only by referring to the role of national identity – this despite the important economic gains that Denmark expected to derive, and actually did derive from membership, especially participation in the Common Agricultural Policy (CAP). Notwithstanding the qualities of this literature, it is striking how the focus on the economic and commercial diplomacy of the western European states corresponds with the perceptions and attitudes of the political and administrative elites of outsiders before 1973. In some countries like Britain and Denmark the economic approach was characterized as 'pragmatic' in contrast to what was perceived as unrealistic and ideological federalism, as if British and Danish attitudes to European cooperation were less dogmatic. Thus, to some extent the focus on state archives and the economic and commercial diplomacy of states predetermined the outcome of many of these studies and blinded them somewhat to the importance of other historical factors such as the important role played by identity and worldviews (Kaiser 2001).

Another trend among the second group of researchers was to study European cooperation and integration from the 1940s to the 1960s as interstate diplomacy. Analysing the OEEC (for example, Brusse 1997), the ECSC (for example, Witschke 2009), the Green Pool plans for agricultural cooperation (Griffiths and Girvin 1995), the CAP (for example, Knudsen 2009), commercial policy (for example, Coppolaro 2006c), monetary policy (for example, Zimmermann 2002) and the common market (for example, Perron 2004), these studies contributed crucial insights into the economic and commercial diplomacy that characterized many of the negotiations on European integration of the period. Several features unite these studies: they share a socio-economic approach and are almost all based on multilateral and multi-archival documentation. With few exceptions, moreover, most notably Ann-Christina Knudsen's (2009) study of the formation of the CAP, they share an assumption about the pre-eminence of the nation-state in integration. At the most general level this literature demonstrated how the different governments and national administrations did their utmost to ensure that any step towards European integration would strengthen domestic socio-economic objectives, while simultaneously tempering more ideologically motivated attempts to integrate Europe. The greatest strength of this literature was to demonstrate and document how the search for a viable regional commercial solution to underpin continued economic growth, the prerequisite for industrial modernization and the financing of welfare states, became a driving force that contributed to the foundation of the EEC, secured its success and made it increasingly attractive for outsiders to join later.

At the same time, this literature suffered from a number of conceptual and empirical limitations. The primary use of state archives, the assumption of the pre-eminence of states and governments and the socio-economic approach might have linked up nicely to provide a forceful explanation of European integration. However, they also created a circular argument where one link in the chain reinforced the next, leading to these authors largely ignoring evidence of the influence of transnational networks, European ideas and ideology and the institutionalization of the European political space on the course of European integration. The result was a tendency to emphasize the role played by socio-economic dynamics to the extent where other important factors were ignored. Recent research has demonstrated the extent to which this represents a flawed representation of European integration (Kaiser, Leucht and Rasmussen 2009). As Wolfram Kaiser (2007) has shown, for example, Christian democratic transnational networks, their common ideas on Europe and the mutual trust they developed in the late 1940s were crucial for securing the success of negotiations on the treaty establishing the ECSC. Likewise, the revolutionary development of European law in the early 1960s, which transformed the EEC treaty into a federal legal order, not only depended on a transnational network of lawyers that supported the jurisdiction of the ECJ and facilitated its acceptance by national judiciaries, but it was also deeply influenced by the federalist preferences of the key protagonists (Rasmussen 2008). Supranational institutions such as the High Authority of the ECSC and the European Commission were dynamic in the early phases of European integration. The Commission, for example, exerted a significant influence on the establishment of the CAP (Knudsen 2009). Thus, while socio-economic analysis must still be considered of fundamental importance for any account of the history of European integration, it is also clear that it needs to be combined with a history of ideas, institutions and politics.

European business and industrial elites and European identity

In parallel with the launching of Milward's path-breaking ideas on the process of European integration, another group of researchers began to mobilize around a very different research agenda of economic history. At the politically most opportune moment in 1989, Girault launched a large European research project involving researchers from across most of Europe to explore the formation of European identities in the *longue durée* (Frank 2004, 7–12). As set out by Varsori in his chapter, this project represented an attempt to widen the agenda and enrich the school of international history to which Girault belonged. Brought up in the tradition of Jean-Baptiste Duroselle and Pierre Renouvin, who were inspired by the French Annales school's conceptualization of *forces profondes*, Girault had a background as an economic historian (for example, Girault 1982). It was therefore no coincidence that the project included a strong economic dimension. As part of the broader network, a group was set up under the leadership of Bussière and Dumoulin to study the formation of European identities among economic elites, in particular among business and industrial leaders, both at the national and transnational level. Among the participants in the group were Laurence Badel, Ruggero Ranieri, Sylvain Schirmann, Werner Bührer and Robert Boyce. Many of the researchers involved in this group had a background as experts in the economic history of France, Italy, Germany and Belgium in the inter-war years (for example, Bussière 1992). This enabled the group to create a research agenda that connected the inter-war years with the post-war period, even if the main geographical focus remained quite narrowly centred on France, Belgium and Germany and, to a lesser extent, Italy and the Netherlands. Alongside a number of path-breaking empirical studies of economic elites (for example, Bussière, Dumoulin and Schirmann 2007), the group developed a synthesis addressing the question to what extent economic elites contributed to the formation of a European identity (for example, Badel et al. 2004). More recently, this has been turned into a synthesis of the economic dimension of European integration as a whole (Bussière, Dumoulin and Schirmann 2009).

This group's general approach went beyond the institutional history that dominated both the diplomatic and the economic history of European integration. Instead, the focus was on the formation of European identities among economic elites and an exploration of what kind of European organization or integration they envisaged. The ambition was to analyse economic elites in their particular historical context, which included exploring the transnational dimension of their activities. By focusing on their culture, worldviews and the constraints under which they operated within different sectors and firms, it was possible to discern a European identity among multiple identities and to evaluate its properties. However, the researchers made no attempt to link economic elites with a strong European identity to concrete European integration initiatives empirically (Bussière 1997, 5).

The overall conclusion of the research project was that the majority of the economic elites in core Europe did acquire a European identity during the twentieth century. It never became as strong and vocal as the federalist sentiments of the European movement of the 1950s, nor did it develop into an exclusive identity as a result of the establishment of European institutions in the economic sphere, as was originally predicted by neo-functionalist theory. Instead, the European identity they developed remained relatively weak and coexisted with an allegiance towards the nation-state, national political objectives and the daily requirements of doing business. The historical roots of a European perspective among the economic elites seem to be linked to long-term economic interests, and less to short-term political considerations or events. Finally, the establishment of European institutions and their attempt to activate and involve business interests at the European level apparently did not reshape European identities, which had already formed before 1952 (Badel et al. 2004, 21).

The formation of a European identity was shaped by both external and internal challenges to the European economic elites. Externally, the economic challenge of the United States (US) loomed large during the twentieth century. The relative economic decline of Europe compared with the US dominated contemporary discussions. European apprehension was nourished by Europe's financial dependence on

American lenders, the American protectionist tradition and the increasing investments of American firms in Europe. At the same time, new American methods of production and marketing inspired European industries and businesses. The large US market was considered a key to the production of scale and high productivity that characterized the US economy from the 1920s into the 1960s. The ambition to create a similarly large European market became a fundamental element in the emerging European identity of economic elites already in the inter-war years. Within Europe, the experiences of the inter-war period, with plans for economic reconstruction built on political confrontation, were negative. It became increasingly obvious to the economic elites how interdependent the economies of France and Germany, for example, were both technologically and economically. While the American contribution after World War II was important in different ways, it was this shift in European consciousness that was decisive for the integration initiatives after 1945 (Badel et al. 2004, 14–29).

The shape of the particular European identity and the related preference for the shape of European cooperation or integration differed according to what business or industrial sector is examined. The particular culture of the economic elites mattered greatly, as did the concrete interests of the business or industry in question (for example, Badel 1998). Researchers have distinguished two approaches in particular, namely a 'contractual' and a 'liberal' approach. The former describes a tendency among sections of the economic elites to favour a controlled form of capitalism, combined with a European vision that saw a regional organization as an end in itself. Bussière, for example, argues that this tendency found different expressions across time either in the shape of the industrial cartels of the inter-war period or elements of economic planning and European industrial policy that are traceable in the ECSC or EEC, and that this approach remains strong to this day at the national level. The liberal approach is less precisely conceptualized and described in this literature, but is ascribed to certain economic circles in the inter-war years who saw a European market as merely a first step towards global liberalization. Both the ECSC and the EEC had strong liberal traits, in particular in their competition policies. In this view, the ECSC and the EEC represented compromises between the two approaches, the historical roots of which lay in the inter-war period (Bussière 2006).

More recently, Bussière, Dumoulin and Schirmann have argued that the economics of European integration can be analysed as a continuous battle between these two approaches. The authors interpret the various episodes of economic integration in this light. For example, the attempts by French civil servant and Vice President of the Commission Robert Marjolin to introduce macroeconomic planning into the EEC during the 1960s are seen to represent the continued influence of the contractual approach. Likewise, these authors consider EEC competition policy launched in 1962 and the Single European Act of the 1980s as examples of the continued and perhaps increasing influence of the liberal approach. Bussière has also argued that the two approaches relate loosely geographically to a core Europe constituted by France and Germany and a wider Atlantic area including Britain and, after World War II, also the US and Canada. From this perspective, the core Europe contractual approach from the inter-war period became gradually weakened by the geopolitical evolution after 1945. In this view, opting for the core Europe EEC or the broader OEEC framework in the late 1950s also reflected the same basic conflict (Bussière 2006; Bussière, Dumoulin and Schirmann 2009).

In many respects, this research project has been path-breaking although it has not influenced the research agenda in the same way as Milward's work. It has spawned a wealth of new empirical studies of different economic elites and has crucially broken with the state-centric approach that has characterized the historiography by focusing on culture, identity and also exploring the transnational dimension. Likewise, the analysis of European identity formation among continental economic elites is based on a conceptually nuanced understanding of identity. Thus, the project's conclusions should be of interest to historians and social scientists alike.

At the same time, this project also has important limitations. It is arguably a crucial omission that it did not in any systematic way conceptualize and explore empirically how the economic elites, nationally or transnationally, influenced actual policy-making and integration initiatives. As a result, the conclusions about the extent to which competing contractual or liberal visions of the economic elites influenced integration initiatives at the very least seems premature. The lack of solid empirical grounding in this regard is combined with a less than clear definition of the two economic visions of Europe that allegedly constitute two alternative economic models. Subsuming different historical phenomena such as inter-war cartels, sector integration in the 1950s, macroeconomic planning in the EEC in the 1960s and recent national protectionism within one model assumes a degree of continuity that should not be taken for granted and needs to be empirically substantiated. Similarly, when relating the two models to geopolitical and economic spaces, the analysis turns into a superficial distinction between a contractual core Europe and a liberal Atlantic area. This juxtaposition of a contractual and a liberal model does not reflect the extent to which all western European countries after 1945, including Britain (Milward and Brennan 1996) and Scandinavia (Sørensen 2001), faced a similar dilemma between continued economic regulation to assure employment in the short run and gradual liberalization nationally and internationally to facilitate growth, employment and welfare in the long run. Nor does this juxtaposition chime with existing literature on neo-corporatist and welfare state models. In this literature, core Europe is typically split into different models based on different sets of relations between the state and economic interests and varying types of welfare systems. Thus, the Benelux countries and Germany are normally considered to share a 'Rhenish', largely neo-corporatist model, whereas France is characterized as a protectionist state interventionist model (Zysman 1977). Discussing economic elites and European integration in relation to this and other broader literature, including the Milwardian school, would have allowed this research team to refine their thesis about a predominately contractual core Europe. As it stands, the project has important merits, but is perhaps informed by a somewhat narrow and predominantly French perspective, and its overarching thesis remains rudimentary and of limited value.

New directions in the economic history of European integration

Having explored the major interpretations of the economic history of European integration, this section focuses on new directions in the literature. By addressing some of the weaknesses of the established interpretations recent publications on the formation of European public policies of a primarily economic nature and on the role of business and firms have significantly transformed the research agenda.

To study European public policies is an essential task for historians of European integration for several reasons. Firstly, inspired by historical institutionalist theory, recent research has demonstrated that key decisions taken in the origins of these policies have had strong 'path-dependent' effects on how they evolved in the decades that followed. Both the CAP (Knudsen 2009) and competition policy (Leucht and Seidel 2008; Hambloch 2009) are excellent examples of the long-term consequences of initial decisions. Thus, the CAP's price support mechanism adopted in 1962 continued to haunt the later (attempted)

CAP reforms. Similarly, the ordo-liberal design of the EEC competition policy embedded in Regulation 17/1962 had a major effect on the way competition policy was administered by the Commission in the framework of the internal market in the late 1980s and the 1990s. As these examples show, such long-term effects make historical studies of policy fields all the more important to other disciplines studying contemporary Europe and the EU.

Secondly, studies of public policies require not only a sophisticated understanding of the functioning of European politics. Crucially, this research has also contributed to a better understanding of political processes in the EEC as an emerging polity. These new insights are essential to enable economic historians to go beyond the state-centric approach. At present historical research on the most important European public policies is characterized by a mix between state-centric research and, recently, a few more sophisticated studies. Thus, historical research on the early plans for monetary cooperation and the establishment of EMU have focused on the diplomacy by respectively France and Germany in the period from 1968 to 1973 (for example, Frank 1995; Wilkens 1999). However, few publications have dealt with the role of the Commission and the national central banks (Curli 2000; Maes 2004). In contrast, recent political science studies of the history of EMU, including a collection of sources dating back to the 1920s (Dyson and Quaglia 2010), have demonstrated the need to go beyond the analysis of governmental policy-making and include transnational networks in particular of national bankers (Verdun 2002) and the role played by monetary and economic policy paradigms (Marcussen 2000). Compared with historical research on EMU, recent historical studies of the CAP (Knudsen 2009) and competition policy (Hambloch 2009) have gone much further in utilizing innovative conceptualizations and providing new empirical insights into the functioning of European politics.

Analysing the most important European public policy in historical perspective, the CAP, Knudsen has sketched European policy-making in a way that differs somewhat from the assumptions of the state-centric approach. In fact, the Commission played a key role in the political process that led to the establishment of the CAP, instigating and cultivating the transnational organization of agricultural interests, developing policy proposals, and functioning as a broker. Moreover, member states did not behave as unitary actors and often failed to articulate a 'national interest' in the sense of a calculated utility-maximizing position behind which the entire government was united. This more nuanced understanding of how member states conducted their

European policy-making does not imply that the relative trading positions in agriculture were unimportant to the negotiations. At the more fundamental level, the negotiations over the CAP were not (as traditionally portrayed) a simple bargain between France and Germany supposed to balance the gains of German industries from the common market for industrial goods. Instead, all six governments shared a common set of values about the necessity of placing the 'farmers on welfare'. Although the reality of subsidies was different and large farms and companies arguably profited more in the end, it was the joint defence of the mythical 'family farm' against volatile international markets to secure the long-term food supply that shaped the CAP with its price support regime (Knudsen 2009, 304–17).

The book by Sibylle Hambloch (2009) on the establishment of EEC competition policy confirms many of the insights of Knudsen's study of the CAP. As in the case of the CAP, the Commission also played a crucial role in the establishment of EEC competition policy. The Commission applied different methods to influence policy-making, including the systematic consultation of national experts in numerous expert committees. These were often officials from national administrations or came from interest groups with a stake in the decisions. Not only did these experts provide the Commission with technical knowhow beyond what the small administration in Brussels could muster, but expert input also legitimized the Commission proposals. Over time these experts were socialized by their common European experience, as Katja Seidel (2010) has also shown. In addition, the Commission gave transnational associations of interest organizations a stake in competition policy in order both to gauge their position and to legitimize the final proposal and decision. Hambloch also demonstrates the important role played by the ECJ and European law in the field of competition policy. Not least, the ECJ's jurisdiction influenced the way member states conducted policy-making, keeping certain elements of competition policy not originally included in the EEC treaty outside the Community framework. Hambloch concludes that as a consequence of the 'Empty Chair' crisis of 1965–66, when France boycotted the Council of Ministers for six months, government control over decision-making in the field of competition was tightened considerably.

What Knudsen and Hambloch have shown is just how complex European policy-making already was in the core Europe of only six member states in the 1960s. Any historian who wants to embark on the writing of a political economy analysis of European public policies has to take this into account. It is obviously not enough to assume that national governments aggregate socio-economic interests and then defend them in Brussels. Instead, societal interests that sought to have a say in the formulation of agricultural policy and competition policy at the European level already acted both at the national and European level of decision-making. Moreover, it is evident that the establishment of European institutions and public policies created a new political space in addition to the national arena, which firms and other types of economic actors had to take into account when defending their interests. In fact, it is precisely the field of business and firms in European integration which has seen significant new research in recent years.

The analysis of the role of business and firms could be revealing because it focuses attention on the micro level of economic integration. For example, relatively little is known about the economic and political consequences of the establishment of the common market, both in terms of its macroeconomic impact and local responses by firms to the new challenges. Firms not only had to consider the direct economic impact of integration, especially in terms of mostly reduced tariffs barriers, but also the consequences of the EEC's legislation in fields like company and competition law. So far the historiography of European integration has not fully addressed these and other research questions. As discussed above, several studies have looked into the formation of European identities among economic elites. Several studies have also analysed national business associations and transnational business networks (for example, Rhenisch 1999; Rollings and Kipping 2004). However, only few industrial sectors have been analysed in detail, primarily the coal and steel sector (Schwabe 1988; Wilkens 2004) and the agricultural sector (Noël 1988; Noël 1995). Few studies of single firms exist, but this state of affairs is quickly changing. Thus, Marine Moguen-Toursel (2007) has edited a book that focuses on firm strategies and public policies in Europe from 1950 to 1980, and two excellent new books by Neil Rollings (2008) and Sigfrido Ramírez (2010) demonstrate the importance of business history for a broader economic history of European integration.

Rolling's monograph on British business in the formative years of European integration until 1973 is an example of how rich a conceptually and empirically strong business history can be. One of his major conclusions is that research needs to extend below peak organizations and analyse business at the level of individual companies. The complexity of the consequences of European integration was such that opinions varied greatly between branches and even between similar firms, depending on their own perception. To understand the full range of consequences of European integration, even for British business outside of the Community until 1973, one has to look beyond tariffs, preferences and protection. Thus, foreign direct investment and joint ventures increasingly became a response by British firms to maintain and improve competitiveness as they were confronted with the rapid trade expansion in core Europe in the 1950s and the formation of the common market in the 1960s. In addition, British business was fully aware of the regulatory elements of the common market, including competition policy and the (largely futile) attempts at harmonizing taxation and company law. Rollings also demonstrates that the British government did not act in a unitary manner domestically. Rather, business in varying degrees played a policy-making role in close cooperation with particular sections of the changing governments and the administration. One important asset business possessed in this relationship was its access to information that even British diplomacy could not secure, which derived from its participation in various transnational European business networks.

Ramírez (2010) similarly contributes to improving our understanding of how firms responded to European integration by studying the Italian and French automotive industries from 1945 to 1958. He even goes beyond the scope of Rolling's study and explores in great detail how multinational automotive firms influenced the national strategies of industrialization, and as a consequence, also the connections between these strategies and European integration. His study confirms Rolling's findings concerning the sheer complexity of different factors that combined to inform the often negative attitudes of companies towards European integration. Thus, the French and Italian automotive industry opposed liberalization beyond a very narrow French-Italian customs union in the late 1940s for fear of competition from German and American firms. The fear of American multinationals continued during the 1950s and led to the rejection of wider schemes of liberalization in the OEEC, in the form of the British proposal for a free trade area or in the global General Agreement on Tariffs and Trade. This fear played a key role for the Italian and French decision in favour of the EEC as a neo-protectionist bloc, at least with regard to trade in cars. Nevertheless, private automotive companies from both countries still rejected the EEC at the outset, while state-owned Renault backed the French government's decision to join. At no point were the business elites of the French and Italian car industries European-minded. Rather, they were highly sceptical about the benefits of integration.

Together, these two studies bring out the sheer complexity of the economic and political consequences of European integration and the interconnected nature of integration and national industrial modernization strategies. In fact, none of the major macro level interpretations of the economics of integration discussed in this chapter is entirely confirmed when analysing single firms. Milward's state-centric analysis does not capture the nuanced ways in which business acted both nationally and transnationally already in the 1950s, or the effects of the common market on individual firms. Likewise, Ramírez' study of the automotive industry does not confirm the notion that private business necessarily developed a European identity during the twentieth century. Thus, by exploring companies as a new category of actors, Rollings and Ramírez have made an important contribution towards better understanding the economic and political dynamics of integration.

Conclusion

The historiography of the economic dimension of European integration has focused on economic policy-making by states and European institutions, the mentality and identity of economic actors, as well as the role played by business and firms. Other classical fields of economic history, for example macroeconomic analysis of the economic consequences of integration, have been neglected. Initially, economic historians of European integration led by Milward focused on exploring state archives, which became accessible for the first post-war decade during the 1980s. As a result, they wrote heavily state-centric histories of national economic and commercial policies, attempting to understand these in their proper domestic context. Formulating his own integration 'theory', Milward proposed that the choice of European integration resulted from its strengthening of national policies of modernization and welfare. Unrelated to the works of Milward and his disciples, Girault, Bussière and Dumoulin launched a project which fundamentally broke with the state-centric perspective of diplomatic history and the Milwardian school. Exploring the emerging European identities of economic actors in particular in continental Europe, but without linking this to policy-making processes, this project was limited in scope, however. Recent contributions have developed in two directions, but with similar results. New studies of the public policies of an economic nature established by the EEC in the 1960s have contributed to an improved understanding of how crucial policies such as the CAP and competition policy were formed, and they have provided new insights into how European politics have functioned. Together with new micro studies of business and single firms and their role in integration, a more differentiated view of the new European polity emerges, which gradually developed from 1952 onwards.

Several lessons can be learned from the evolution of historical research on economic dimensions of integration. In order to write a political economy history of European integration, economic historians need to abandon the simplistic conceptualization of states as acting out of calculated 'national interests' in a unitary manner, representing the economic and commercial interests of domestic interest organizations and the electorate. Instead, they should embrace a much more complex conceptualization of European politics as that of an emerging European polity. Not only did the Commission and the ECJ play a role in the Community's policy- and decision-making processes, but member states also acted much less as unitary actors and often could not even articulate 'national interests' coherently. Furthermore, business and single firms, often with transnational contacts inside and outside of the ECSC/EEC, began to orientate themselves towards the new European institutions and European policy-making, especially as the common market developed from 1958 onwards, trying to take its impact into account for their business strategies. To understand the socio-economic dynamics behind the choice for integration, economic historians thus have to trace these dynamics in all of these different processes and actors of the emerging European polity.

Unfortunately, too many other historians of European integration have largely ignored economic history. Ironically, Milward's impact has been more pronounced outside the sub-field of integration history. Fortunately, however, much of the more recent economic historiography has moved beyond the state-centric paradigm developed by Milward and towards a more conceptually refined approach to analysing the socio-economic and political dimensions of European integration. The recent contributions discussed in the last section of this chapter link up nicely with a broader research agenda for the history of European integration, namely that of reconceptualizing the history of the present-day EU as that of a slowly emerging European polity (Kaiser, Leucht and Rasmussen 2009). In this way a new generation of historians, bridging old dividing lines within the sub-field, can integrate a new economic history into this broader agenda. To do so would not only address important gaps in the literature. For example, the complex consequences of established public policies such as the CAP on the socio-economic and political structures of European societies largely remain unexplored, as Lorenzo Mechi also argues in his chapter. Instead – a larger point also made by Kaiser in his chapter on cross-disciplinary cooperation in European Studies – the broader research agenda would link the economic history of integration to research in the social sciences, which appears to become more sensitive once more towards its historical evolution.

8
Formation of a European Society? Exploring Social and Cultural Dimensions

Lorenzo Mechi

Society is a complex subject of historical research, characterized by fragmentation and marked differences between countries and historical periods. As a consequence, a strongly differentiated historiography has developed on the subject, as regards the object of study, methodology and interpretative lines. This is particularly visible in studies on the interaction between society and European integration, the latter an extremely complex phenomenon in itself, with two particularly relevant characteristics. The first of these is that the most important milestones of European integration have depended on formal acts by governments or Community institutions, be they the signing of treaties or the enactment of legislation. This does not mean that non-state actors, such as political parties or trade unions, have not played a role, with specific actions at a national or transnational level. But theirs was a role that often consisted of lobbying activities with limited public visibility, which was also due to an institutional order that has largely left decision-making powers in the hands of governments. As a consequence, these activities have had hardly any measurable political impact. The second characteristic concerns the restricted sphere of action that was a feature of the Communities until the late 1960s, which focused on the coal and steel sectors, the construction of the common market and agricultural policy, and with only a limited attention for strictly social aspects. All this has contributed to the fragmentation of historiographical perspectives, resulting in research and publications based on varied approaches and sources that defy easy classification under a common heading.

For these reasons, a purely chronological exposition of works on the social history of integration would have raised several problems of thematic coherence, entailing a parallel discussion of approaches that are essentially disconnected from each other. The choice made here is rather to classify different works on the basis of their perspective and the object of analysis – a choice that leads to the identification of three groups, albeit with relatively fluid boundaries, which the chapter's three sections will explore in sequence.

The first section considers works that study society as a whole and the impact of the integration process on it; and, more specifically, whether or not this process encouraged the formation of a more homogeneous European society. This is the broadest and most diverse category of the three, particularly because it includes topics which may not be classified as social history proper – above all those of a largely cultural nature, connected to the definition of European identity, its social base and its symbolic dimensions.

The next section deals with the interaction between European integration and political parties, trade unions, employers' associations and other expressions of civil society. It therefore includes studies which analyse this relationship both from the bottom up – the role played by elites in the integration process – and from the top down – the influence exercised by integration on their cultures and organizational structures, mainly by acting as a stimulus for the creation of increasingly strong and active transnational networks. If, therefore, the works considered in the first section deal with the Europeanization of societies in general, those discussed in the second part address the Europeanization of elites.

Finally, the third section takes into consideration works that investigate the objectives and social impact of Community policies. This includes social policies in a strict sense as well as the social dimension of other 'first generation' policies, that is those conceived during the first 25 years of integration, such as the Common Agricultural Policy (CAP) or Regional Policy. This is a choice dictated by the availability of archival sources that, on the basis of the 30-year rule, have so far allowed a consistent historiography to emerge only for these themes.

Reference to some of the policies launched in the 1980s will be made in all three sections, but only when strictly necessary to explain general concepts or historiographical interpretations. One exception will be made to this rule. The topic of social policies has close ties with that of the European social model, a particularly debated matter during the first decade of the new century, which also touches upon issues outlined in the first section, on convergence and European social identity. For this reason, it will be the subject of some final reflections, inspired by current trends in the social sciences, but which also opens up interesting perspectives for historical research.

Indeed, within the framework described by Wolfram Kaiser in his chapter, where the low level of interdisciplinarity is seen as one of the main limits of European Studies, the historiography on social aspects is perhaps a partial exception. Partly to cover the widest possible time-frame, thus overcoming the restrictions imposed by the 30-year rule, and partly as a stimulus to solve analytical and interpretative problems, social historians have sometimes adopted concepts and methodological tools from other disciplines, occasionally entering into some of the most animated debates amongst social scientists. In this regard, it is worth noting how the historiography discussed in each of the three sections has tight connections with specific disciplines. In the first section, on most issues there is a lively dialogue with sociology. As regards the themes discussed in the second section, historical research has been more influenced by political science, from which the most recent historiography has borrowed a number of concepts and tools. Finally, the aspects covered in the last section are often also treated by scholars of a number of other disciplines, including not only sociology and political science, but also economics and law.

European society and its general characteristics

In recent decades several works have tried to evaluate the degree of homogeneity of European societies and to identify possible convergence trends. This aspect, with its evident ties to the question of European identity, is deeply rooted within the intellectual history of the continent, but has also received new stimulus from the deepening of integration from the Maastricht Treaty in 1992–93 to the Lisbon Treaty in 2008–09. The official adoption of economic and social cohesion as a primary objective of the European Union (EU), for instance, has certainly contributed to revive the interest of social scientists in such themes. The fall of eastern European regimes has strengthened this interest, opening up the prospect of EU enlargement, which, by increasing its internal diversity, has further amplified the problems of cohesion, both on an economic and socio-cultural level.

The result is several books, mainly by sociologists, that analyse the constitutive elements of national societies in a pan-European perspective. Thus, aspects such as family structures, industrial relations systems or the organization of welfare states are used as indicators to measure homogeneity and convergence between European societies, usually accompanied by comparisons with other regions, first of all the United States (US) (Bailey 1998; Crouch 1999; Bettin Lattes and Recchi 2005). Although with a variety of nuances, the idea of social convergence seems to be generally accepted. Much more controversial is the question of its causes, and particularly the role played by European integration. Colin Crouch (1999, 408–9), for instance, credits it only with a secondary role and identifies long-term economic trends, such as globalization, as the primary causes of convergence. While not overlooking the existence of EU policies oriented towards homogenization, such as the Stability and Growth Pact, he emphasizes how some of them could actually lead to the opposite outcome when applied to very different national contexts.

Taking a markedly different position is Hartmut Kaelble, the only historian who has paid systematic attention to such themes. In his works, Kaelble has regularly stressed convergence, which, in this view, accelerated after World War II. If this evaluation has remained substantially unchanged, his view of the role of European integration has evolved. In his book *Social History of Western Europe* published in 1989 he identified industrialization and, to a lesser extent, the post-war economic boom as the main causes of social convergence. In this framework he assigned European integration only a marginal role, even if he did not neglect its function as a deterrent against possible centrifugal trends in times of crisis (Kaelble 1989, especially 141–9). In his most recent works his interpretation has changed. Although Kaelble still identifies long-term factors as primary causes of convergence, he now stresses that European integration has also induced further homogenization. First of all integration has encouraged the harmonization of social protection and education systems, as shown by the increasingly similar proportion of the population covered by welfare state provisions and 'of young people completing an academic secondary school or studying at university' in European countries (Kaelble 2004, 293–4). Secondly, it has increased the mobility of EU citizens, with the abolition of frontiers, exchange programmes for students and teachers and the promotion of widespread knowledge of foreign languages, all of which have favoured more intense exchanges of experiences and lifestyles. Finally, the process of integration has substantially contributed to the consolidation of democracy and cooperation in Europe, which represent the basic framework that makes all other social transformations possible (Kaelble 2004, 293–8; 2005b, 185–92).

Kaelble's analyses have been criticized for not being sufficiently rigorous. Referring to Kaelble's first book, for instance, Crouch (1999, 396) pointed out the excessive generalization of partial data, only 'limited to Germany, France and/or Britain', to the whole of Europe. In fact, the chosen time-frames also created the impression of somewhat teleological interpretations. Thus, in Kaelble's first book the adoption of 1880 as a starting point seems aimed at stressing the role played by industrialization. Similarly, in *Sozialgeschichte Europas* published in 2007 the limitation to the post-World War II period contributes to stressing the influence of the integration process. However, the author seems to have responded to Crouch's criticism by extending the analysis to a wider number of national cases, thus offering a more solid European outline (Kaelble 2007). In his latest works, moreover, Kaelble has constantly stressed the 1980s as a turning point characterized by the strengthening of the Community's institutions and the greatly increased scope of its legislation (Kaelble 2005b, 111–17, 186–7). Developments like the internal market programme, the significance of which could not be completely grasped in the late 1980s, would explain the new importance accorded to European integration. Kaelble supports this argument by referring to its facilitating of citizens' mobility, its contribution to democratic consolidation and other phenomena that became more evident only from the 1990s onwards. Only time and new studies will confirm or refute Kaelble's interpretation. In the meantime, his works remain an essential reference point for any research on the social history of contemporary Europe and the integration process, not the least because Kaelble considers several other aspects closely intertwined with the discourse on European society, some of which are tightly connected with the theme of European identity.

The issue of European identity is particularly thorny and mostly of a cultural nature. Historians have dedicated several studies to understanding the evolution of European identity. Alfredo Canavero and Jean-Dominique Durand's studies on the religious factor in European integration are one example. The authors have paid attention to both philosophical matters (like Judaism or Christianity and the idea of Europe) and politico-cultural aspects (such as the attitude of the church during specific phases of integration) (Canavero and Durand 1999, 25–103, 105–230). But religion is only one element of a European cultural identity which was progressively fashioned over the centuries, and which most authors accept as given. In fact, as Robert Frank has argued, a European identity largely preceded national identities; it was of a cultural nature and mainly developed in delineation to other civilizations

(Frank 2004, 30–2). Thus, several works have aimed at identifying and analysing its constitutive elements, focusing on the examination of single philosophical components, such as rationality, liberty or pluralism (Joas and Wiegandt 2008), or on more political concepts like nation or citizenship (Passerini 1998; Maas 2007). In any case, a cultural identity does not automatically result in a meaningful political identity or, for that matter, in the formation of a European society. 'In spite of its age', Frank (2004, 33–6) continues, 'European identity remains elitist and cultural in character, while national identities, born of cultural specificities, too, also acquire a political dimension.'

This also explains why the Community's institutions have tried to encourage a sense of belonging in European citizens, through the promotion of cultural policies and the adoption of European symbols. Symbols are regarded as extremely important by several authors. Luisa Passerini (2003, 21–33) has stressed the necessity to 'overcome the so-called symbolic deficit, which results in part from a construction based on economic and financial considerations'. Gérard Bossuat (1999, 58–9, 64–6) has defined fundamental criteria for choosing the symbolic moments of a united Europe: they must not have been used as national symbols, that is, represent symbols of a divided Europe such as 14 July, the French national holiday, and they must be generally known, or at least easily understandable.

From a historical perspective, however, it seems to be of even greater relevance how symbols have emerged or have been officially adopted during the integration process, and what their actual capacity is for becoming popular. Tobias Theiler, for example, depicts as a failure the cultural and symbolic policies activated by the Community in the 1980s, regularly undermined by 'shifting alliances of national governments'. In the 'continued determination of national elites to protect their near-monopoly over the tools of political identity creation from supranational interference', Theiler (2005, 1–7) sees a sign 'of the possible limits of European integration as a political and institutional project', an assessment apparently confirmed by events such as the removal of references to the European hymn and flag from the Lisbon Treaty signed in 2007.

At the same time, these very dynamics seem to justify more positive conclusions when considered in a longer-term historical perspective. Thus, Kaelble regards the dynamics of identity politics as new evidence of an emerging European society. Indeed, by comparing the symbols chosen in the 1950s and 1960s by the federalist movements but still practically unknown, and those adopted by the Community in the

1980s, he concludes that European symbols have grown in importance and now have a much more concrete meaning, having shifted from vague mentions of a distant European past to direct references to current political events (Kaelble 2003, 58–60).

The question of European identity is also connected to that of the popularity, or lack thereof, of the EU. This was a matter regarded as so sensitive by European political leaders that in 1973 they created the Eurobarometer, an instrument to monitor the evolution of public opinion. Since its establishment, the Eurobarometer has produced a huge quantity of data that historians have also begun to use. A book by Anne Dulphy and Christine Manigand, for instance, has brought together chapters on the oscillations of European public opinion towards the integration process from 1973 to 1993. The results do not demonstrate a great degree of European convergence, given that the element that seems to mark most clearly the rift in public opinion is still nationality (Dulphy and Manigand 2004, 15–17). This conclusion, however, might have been influenced by the very structure of the book, composed of chapters by scholars of different nationalities, each treating their respective home country.

In fact, other works, which consider longer periods and more diverse points of view, advance more differentiated evaluations. A book edited by Marie-Thérèse Bitsch, Wilfried Loth and Charles Barthel, for instance, identifies the historical phase of each state's accession to the present-day EU as the key element in determining citizens' sympathy towards European integration. This interpretation does not deny the primacy of the national dimension, but puts it into perspective by emphasizing the long-term evolution of integration. The same volume also points out the emergence of transversal and transnational political cultures, within national and European institutions and administrations, but also in civil society (Bitsch, Loth and Barthel 2007, 1–4; Frank 2007, 467–74).

Here, in line with his general argument, Kaelble assumes the existence of a European public sphere, although with an elite character that differentiates it from national public spheres. He argues that in the early stages after World War II, a European civil society composed of international institutions and transnational organizations and interest groups began to emerge. But only with the widening of the Community's competences in the 1980s did a European public sphere begin to take a clearer shape. That a growing number of matters have been decided in Brussels from then onwards greatly increased public attention to

European themes, which have henceforth increasingly permeated the domestic political debates of member states. Countering those who deny the existence of such a public sphere with arguments such as the lack of a common language and genuinely European media, Kaelble argues that the European public sphere has its peculiarities, such as multilingualism and the absence of a pan-European media system, and that therefore it cannot be measured with the same criteria applied to national public spheres (Kaelble 2002, 9–23; 2005b, 142–60). The alleged incomparability between national and European public spheres is perhaps one of the weakest points of Kaelble's thesis. Even if supported by several other authors (Delanty and Rumford 2005, 102–4; Schulz-Forberg 2007, 183–200), some of whom apply the same analytical logic to conceptualizing European identity (Kohli 2000, 113–37), Kaelble's approach seems to be substantially self-referential. This is in fact what other scholars have alleged, seeing the idea of a European public sphere and identity as an artificial invention of the Commission's press service and Eurobarometer (Baisnée 2007).

Clearly, the controversies outlined above will only be clarified by more empirical research. Thus, Jan-Henrik Meyer's study of the attitude of the press and of interaction between different national information milieus in the context of European summits from 1969 to 1992 has made an interesting contribution (Meyer 2010). However, by restricting the analysis to a few major newspapers from only three member states, Meyer risks obtaining only partial and perhaps not particularly relevant results. The danger is at the same time to consider only the most educated part of public opinion and to exclude many of the various European interest groups that emerged at the beginning of the integration process, which have been defined as 'the most advanced part of the European public sphere' (Kaelble 2002, 20–1). Indeed, despite otherwise diverging views, there has been general agreement that the scope of the European public sphere has been relatively limited (Kaelble 2002, 19; Baisnée 2007). Those who follow European politics and maybe try to influence it, are first of all the interest groups in sectors of EU competence, which until the 1980s were still few. This is also why, alongside the study of the national press, which treated European themes at length only in a few core episodes of integration, more systematic research on local and sectoral newspapers and other media could offer the best chance to understand the changing European public sphere, its breadth and, above all, its evolution over time.

Transnational networks and the social integration of elites

European integration has been an elite-driven phenomenon. What is less clear, however, is the precise role of particular social groups from various countries or professional environments, and with different political and cultural inclinations, in this process. Beginning with research on the federalist movements discussed by Daniele Pasquinucci in his chapter, historians have studied different elites who have played a role in integration. Given that the most publicly visible historical moments were marked by government decisions – from French Foreign Minister Robert Schuman's declaration of 1950 to the treaty establishing the European Economic Community (EEC) signed in 1957, the Treaty on European Union (TEU) in 1992 and the Lisbon Treaty – attention paid to political parties has always been significant. This included not only the 'founding fathers' like Schuman, German Federal Chancellor Konrad Adenauer and Italian Prime Minister Alcide De Gasperi, for example, but also their respective parties and other political forces that sought to influence the integration process. This research has resulted in studies such as Nicholas Crowson's (2007) that uses a variety of sources from different party levels and geographical regions to reconstruct the history of the relationship between the British Conservative Party and European integration since 1945. Other books compare national parties of the same political family, such as the studies on European socialists by Richard Griffiths (1993) and Kevin Featherstone (1988), the former focused on early integration and the latter on the entire period since World War II.

While not entirely neglecting international interactions of parties, these books focus primarily on the national dimension and are based on the implicit idea of an absolute centrality of the state. This perspective has long dominated the historiography of European integration. However, with subsequent enlargements, the strengthening of EU competences, and the growth of new forms of transnational civil society, the heavily state-centric view has been strongly contested. Hence, new approaches that pay more attention to the activities of social groups beyond national frontiers have come to the fore. This new orientation has been particularly marked among political scientists, and has resulted in several volumes on the transnational organization of political parties, with some analysing the impact of political forces solidly organized at EU level – such as the Party of European Socialists, on the Community's decision-making process (Lightfoot 2005); others studying the coordinating efforts of less well-organized groups such as the radical left-wing parties (Dunphy 2004); still others presenting general outlines of the major European political groups (Delwit, Külahci and Van de Valle 2001; Hanley 2008). While organized in different ways, these works share the same assumptions about the importance of the transnational dimension as the fundamental political environment for policy-making in the EU.

Over the last few years this approach has extended its influence to the historiography of integration, enriching it with new conceptual tools and opening up new vistas for research. Thus, Kaiser (2007) has analysed the role played by European Christian democratic networks in defining the characteristics of integration in the early years. He argues that the close ties between Christian democrat leaders facilitated mutual influence and resulted in the formation of a set of fairly homogeneous ideas about European reorganization, with a focus on the coal and steel sectors and 'the concept of core Europe with supranational features excluding Britain' (Kaiser 2007, 233). Their cooperation facilitated socialization and stimulated the formation of a shared political culture and policy ideas, especially concerning European integration.

In the 1990s historiography explored transnational networks and focused especially on economic and social issues, in works such as Michel Dumoulin and Anne-Myriam Dutrieue's study (1993) of the European League for Economic Cooperation and Patrick Pasture's (1995) and Andrea Ciampani's (1995) chapters on trade union cooperation. But, stimulated by numerous works by political scientists on economic interest associations in the era of Commission President Jacques Delors (for example, van Apeldoorn 2002), later historians developed a keen interest in informal relations and networks. One book edited by Eric Bussière, Dumoulin and Sylvain Schirmann (2007) is an interesting example. It comprises, inter alia, several chapters on semi-informal networks such as the European Round Table of Industrialists or the Association pour l'Union monétaire de l'Europe.

In fact, the same approach has been applied to earlier periods of European integration. Dumoulin's edited book *Réseaux économiques et construction européenne* (2004), for instance, contains several chapters examining how transnational business networks contributed to shape the European architecture in the 1950s and 1960s. Neil Rollings and Matthias Kipping (2004, 280) discuss the role played by the Council of European Industrial Federations since its inception, as a pressure group but above all as an arena 'where industry representatives could meet, exchange ideas and develop more far reaching initiatives' in a climate of growing reciprocal trust (see also Rollings and Kipping

2008). Jerome Wilson reconstructs the action of the informal Bellagio Group in promoting a common policy culture and preferences in the field of monetary policy. Created by leading economists in the mid-1960s, this group had a strong influence on state institutions, and thus contributed to paving the way for the monetary projects launched a few years later at the summit of The Hague in 1969 (Wilson 2004, 391–410).

More recently, Kaiser, Brigitte Leucht and Morten Rasmussen have set this phenomenon within a coherent theoretical framework. Referring to concepts typically used by political scientists, they have identified, for the first 20 years of integration, the outlines of a European polity and political system in the making – a political system constituted not only of the official relations between national and supranational institutions, but also characterized by the presence of 'an incipient transnational political society of intense networking and informal political co-ordination and governance' (Kaiser, Leucht and Rasmussen 2009, 1–11). These authors see networks, with their functions of fostering socialization and cultural convergence, as a key element for explaining the interaction between the politico-institutional dimension and social dynamics, their reciprocal influence and their evolution over time (Kaiser 2009a, 2009d, 12–20). In essence, this approach was proposed by some other authors somewhat earlier (for example, Dwan 1998), but is now supported by a solid theoretical framework and more recent research results (Kaiser 2007; Kaiser and Leucht 2008; Gehler, Kaiser and Leucht 2009). It provides a new key to understanding the dynamics of the elites' social interaction and integration, thus also opening up new research perspectives for revisiting the better known earlier phases of integration.

Historians need to avoid two potential risks in this context, however. The first is to underestimate the transatlantic dimension, which undoubtedly played a crucial role in influencing and shaping many networks during the initial decades of the integration process. Indeed, this dimension is clearly identified and articulated by Leucht (2009a), for example. The second risk is, more generally, to overestimate the scope of the transnational civil society of early post-war decades, a historical phase dominated by Keynesian policies, the building of welfare systems and the centrality of the nation-state. This phase was also characterized by a high level of mass political participation, which surely contributed to keeping the primary attention of political and union leaders concentrated on the domestic objectives of full employment and social justice.

The social dimension of common policies

Researching the relationship between European integration and society necessarily also involves studying common policies. The fact that most of these were conceived and activated only after 1970 has forced historians to deal mainly with 'first generation' policies, such as the CAP and social policy in its infancy. In spite of a huge social science literature, the 30-year rule for the opening of state archival sources has only allowed historians to begin analysing the origins and evolution of other policies with strong social impact, like environment and regional policy in the new century. Laura Scichilone (2008), for example, has published a first history of EU environmental policy, which reconstructs its evolution from the early debates to the end of the 1990s. Largely based on archival sources, the book traces all fundamental developments of that policy, highlighting the main turning points and stressing the influence of different forces and actors involved, thus paving the way for more in-depth research in future.

The case of regional policy is more complex. Initiated with the activation of the European Regional Development Fund in 1975, its roots lie in the more distant past. In fact, ever since the time of the negotiations leading up to the creation of the EEC, the Italian government pressed for the establishment of a regional policy aimed at addressing the most pressing traditional Italian social problem, namely unemployment and poverty in the south, the Mezzogiorno. Antonio Varsori (2007b) has discussed this issue. More recently, Lorenzo Mechi (2008, 2009) has analysed the vicissitudes that prevented the structural funds from ameliorating social conditions in southern Italy. Apart from this, the social impact of the regional fund remains unexplored, but could be studied with the progressively greater availability of archival sources. One possible object of research could be its effects on popular perceptions of the EEC, especially in regions where it has been economically and socially most influential, such as Ireland and some Spanish regions. But there are also other socially relevant aspects of regional policy, such as the urban question in European integration discussed by Laura Grazi (2006). This issue emerged since the first analyses of regional imbalances, in the 1960s, and became more relevant as a result of the new cultural sensitivity towards the environment and life quality issues. Later on, the Commission has started several programmes and invested growing resources into addressing related problems.

As the first important common policy, the CAP has already inspired several historical works, which have increasingly stressed the importance of its social dimension. Guido Thiemeyer (2007, 201), for example, has shown how, between 1880 and the early 1950s, national agricultural policies 'had become a form of social policy', with the aim 'no longer to secure the supply of food, but to secure the incomes of a still large part of the working population'. According to him, the CAP for some countries was a way of sharing the financial burden of supporting their agricultural communities. Gilbert Noël (2006) has described how social dimensions of the CAP were acknowledged early on by Community decision-makers, and accompanied by projects of wider structural reforms. All of this is largely confirmed by Ann-Christina Knudsen (2001, 425), who centres her interpretation of the CAP as 'founded on the logic of welfare state provisions' on its social dimensions. In her works she reconstructs the early years of the CAP with its deep socio-economic roots and its ideological and cultural dimensions, thus providing a complex explanation of the widespread consensus on the creation of the CAP 'in the shape of a redistributive policy with a distinct social purpose' (Knudsen 2001, 427; 2009). Knudsen's approach suggests several new directions for future research, in particular concerning the CAP's concrete social impact. This impact is not to be measured in terms of quantitative data on employment rates or life conditions in agriculture, which has been done, but rather in terms of the evolution of family structures and the social status of farmers. It could thus be verified to what degree and for how long the CAP really achieved its original ideological objective of defending the traditional values of agricultural life.

Academic attention to social policies proper has increased in the last 20 years since the reforms of the Delors era, when the Community's social dimension became more prominent in Community discourse and in European law. In the 1990s, a great number of books were published by lawyers, political scientists and sociologists dealing in general with European social policy or focusing on specific aspects such as the 1989 Social Charter, codifying fundamental social rights for workers, the Social Protocol annexed to the TEU, or the European Employment Strategy launched in 1997 by the Amsterdam Treaty, aimed at coordinating the member states' employment policies. In line with the respective traditions of these disciplines, most of these works concentrate on current affairs and deal with the historical dimension only in short introductory chapters. A notable exception is Stefano Giubboni's *Social Rights and Market Freedom* (2006), a detailed reconstruction of Community social law since the European Coal and Steel Community (ECSC) treaty. Without betraying the legal nature of his analysis,

Giubboni extensively uses the historical and political science literature on European integration for his interpretation of the evolution of social policy as a continuous attempt at 'embedding' the liberalism promoted by the creation of the European common market. From this perspective his book is most interesting for historians too, and, alongside the publication by Kaiser, Leucht and Rasmussen, represents another excellent example of interdisciplinarity.

A second relevant exception to the general 'presentist' bias of the social science and legal literature are the volumes published by the European Trade Unions Institute, which are mainly focused on industrial relations in the last 20 years, but often characterized by a solid narrative dimension. For example, Jon Erik Dølvik's (1999) study on Euro-corporatism analyses the progressive involvement of trade unions in the EU decision-making process. In his view, this process provided an answer to a dual need increasingly perceived by the unions: to stimulate a European social dimension to compensate for diminishing national welfare competences and provisions, and to secure a permanent channel for interacting with EU institutions. Other scholars, like Corinne Gobin (1997, 133–42), see this process more negatively, as a means to 'domesticate' the workers' movement through its increasing subordination to the socially conservative and fundamentally anti-democratic rationales of European integration. The European Trade Unions Institute has also published Jean Degimbe's *La politique sociale européenne* (1999), the only work that describes in detail the evolution of all aspects of the social dimension from the 1950s to the Amsterdam Treaty. Unfortunately, the lack of archival sources, together with the author's non-academic background as a former senior official of the Commission, results in a relatively poor historical contextualization and interpretative sophistication.

As far as the historical literature is concerned, most publications to date have concentrated on the period before the mid-1970s. A few exceptions, often based on sources from private archives, have interesting foci on topics that will probably be studied in greater depth over the coming years, such as French President François Mitterrand's project for a social Europe or the social policy initiatives of the Delors Commission (Saunier 2003; Didry and Mias 2005). In contrast, the phase from the creation of the ECSC to the launch of the first EEC Programme of Social Action in 1974 is relatively well understood. Mechi (2004) has shown, for example, how political reasons led to the involvement of the social partners in the ECSC negotiations in 1950, and how this resulted in a marked social dimension in the activities of the ECSC once set up. Since its early years the ECSC High Authority showed a strong sensitivity to the working and living conditions of manpower and implemented measures such as the financing of housing for workers, strict rules for health and safety at work, and, most of all, the creation of a fund aimed at facilitating the reintegration of unemployed workers into the labour market. The Adaptation Fund, which financed retraining and reinstallation, was widely utilized throughout the 50-year existence of the ECSC, and represented its main instrument to soften the social effects of the crisis in the coal and, later, the steel industry.

So far the social dimension of the EEC has been treated mainly through focusing on single issues. Thus, Mechi (2006) has reconstructed the history of the first European Social Fund, which operated until 1972, and explained the reasons why, although modelled on the ECSC fund, it had much more limited effects. Varsori, in turn, has dealt with the Economic and Social Committee (ESC), the institution originally intended as the primary place for discussions on social issues. After focusing on the difficulties of its creation resulting from different conflicting concepts and interests, Varsori has shown how these also characterized the following years, causing the paralysis of the ESC (Varsori 2000, 3–23). The same author has discussed vocational training, an issue largely ignored by historians, but which in effect represented an important element in the construction of the common market. Indeed, in spite of sharp disputes about the harmonization of national training systems, its importance was stressed by European institutions right from the early years. Since the 1970s its centrality has become even more marked, leading to the creation of specific Community institutions and policies and the progressive extension of European policy-making to the larger field of education (Varsori 2006a; Paoli 2007). Finally, Maria Eleonora Guasconi (2003) has analysed the dynamics that led to a stronger involvement of trade unions in the decision-making process, through the promotion of the first tripartite conference and the creation of a special committee on employment problems, in the early 1970s.

Varsori and Josefina Cuesta Bustillo have also proposed the first historical reconstruction of European social policy from its origins to the present day. In this context, they have attempted to highlight both normative developments and the roles played by the various actors, such as governments, socio-economic actors and, last but not least, the Community's institutional environment (Varsori 2007c, 2009; Cuesta Bustillo 2009). From this last point of view, a book about Lionello Levi Sandri, the European commissioner for social affairs in the 1960s, has addressed the role of personalities, emphasizing the importance of individual initiative and political culture in shaping the early European social policies (Varsori and Mechi 2008).

Such broad coverage of social themes does not mean, of course, that there is no space for new research. Apart from the countless possibilities of archive-based more in-depth investigations on all the topics discussed here, perhaps the most promising opportunities concern the developments of the 1970s, with many innovations and the strengthening of the Community social action to face the economic crisis. For example, an evaluation of the impact of the ECSC Adaptation Fund and EEC Social Fund in specific sectors would be particularly interesting, especially if focused on their influence on choices by individuals, such as changes in job or residence. Other important aspects include the measures aimed at favouring the employment of disadvantaged minorities, such as young people or long-term unemployed, the cultural influences in this debate and the role of the main actors in shaping the guidelines of Community legislation.

All such research would contribute to shedding new light on one of the most important phases in the history of EU social policy, when the guidelines inspiring currently existing policies were developed. Thus, historians could make a relevant contribution to one of the most compelling issues of our times, namely the debate about a European social model. This term indicates specific characteristics of European society, usually identified as a high level of solidarity, attention to the quality of life, and strong welfare states. Literature on this model usually emphasizes its different character compared to the more competition-inspired US model. Not surprisingly, during the presidency of George W. Bush in particular, a great number of works on differences between the EU and the US were published, all of which saw the diverging social models as central elements. Alberto Alesina and Edward Glaeser (2004) have explained the different sensitivities to social issues, particularly visible in the scope of policies of redistribution, as the result of historical and cultural factors, such as the higher ethnic fragmentation of the US and their institutional architecture as particularly favourable to political conservatism. The American left-wing author Jeremy Rifkin (2004) favours the European model, claiming that Europe's better quality of life will lead, in the long term, to higher economic productivity and social mobility.

But the European social model is also an integral part of the EU's own political discourse, which pursues its rescue and strengthening, aiming at combining greater market liberalization with continued social solidarity. Indeed, the Lisbon Strategy, adopted by the European Council in March

2000, aims at diverting resources from traditional welfare state policies to invest them in research, education and training, in an attempt to create a more efficient economy and flexible labour market and, at the same time, offer citizens the opportunity to be constantly competitive. Such a difficult and contested challenge could give rise to acute social tensions and, precisely for this reason, calls for the support of social partners.

Thus, training, flexibility and social dialogue are presented as the ingredients of the 'new' European social model. As we have seen, all these elements have been present since the start of the integration process, but have become progressively more central in the emerging European economic culture. This is where historians can offer a relevant contribution, more particularly by tracing the history of the rise of each ingredient of the European social model to strategic importance. Such an analysis should not be limited to the dynamics of the Community's decision-making process, national governments and European institutions, but also consider, as much as possible, more informal aspects, such as the role and influence of social forces and pressure groups, or the cultural background and references of the principal actors. As far as vocational training is concerned, for example, the works by Varsori represent a useful starting point, and need only to be extended to encompass the wider socio-cultural dimension. On social dialogue a more abundant literature exists including the works by Dolvik (1999) and Gobin (1997) but also, for example, a co-authored book on the evolution of social partnership in several European countries over the last century (Davids, Davos and Pasture 2007). Finally, as far as flexibility is concerned, besides several works on the freedom of movement in the common market, an interesting book edited by Bo Stråth (2000) focuses on the shift in the economic culture of several European countries from the full employment imperative to the logic of flexibility. Even if it is not discussed directly, the influence of the EU and its policies is clearly visible throughout book, so that it can form a suitable basis for further research. Such research would cover political, economic, social and cultural dimensions, and possibly extend to the origins preceding the integration process itself, such as the studies carried out in the International Labour Organization in the 1920s. In short, such research would aim to make an important contribution to the debate about European identity.

Conclusion

European integration has an important social dimension that historians have studied from different perspectives. The heterogeneity of the

literature has not prevented shared interpretative lines from emerging, which represent a solid starting point for further research. There
is, first of all, general agreement on a trend of convergence between
European societies. This trend is partially due to long-term factors, but
in part directly stimulated by the integration process. In particular, several reforms launched from the mid-1980s onwards, including a certain harmonization of the education systems, the growing mobility of
European citizens and the spreading knowledge of foreign languages
may have acted as powerful homogenizing agents. More disputed is the
question whether such elements have also brought about cultural convergence, and whether they have favoured the birth of a transnational
public sphere that represents the core of a true European society. This
is a question that cannot be measured with quantitative data only, and
that needs more exhaustive research to be answered satisfactorily in
historical perspective.

Concerning these and other themes of social and cultural integration,
historians can now make an important contribution to larger debates.
Studies of the coverage of European issues by some major national newspapers, their interaction and mutual influence, could be beneficial. It
would, however, seem desirable to extend this research to other media,
in order to trace the perception of European politics within national
societies since the early post-war years. The analysis of the local and
sectoral press, especially from those regions and sectors that have been
most directly touched by European policies, could be very fruitful, for
example. Indeed, an appraisal of the breadth of the European public
sphere must not disregard the perception of Community politics and
policies by the most involved citizens, who in the early phases of the
integration were substantially the workers of certain sectors and the
inhabitants of certain areas. It is also useful to recall that in the 1950s and
1960s associations of a political or other kind played a crucial mediating
role between politics and society. In Italy, for example, the formation of
public opinion occurred partially in milieus such as Catholic parishes
or *case del popolo* (community centres tied to left-wing parties), which
filtered political events and contributed to the emergence of a common
perception. An in-depth study of the European public sphere in the early
phases of the integration process should not neglect these dimensions.
For instance, research on different associations, their pamphlets and
political or cultural publications aimed at assessing their perception of
European politics and policies could bring about interesting insights.

Such an approach would be perfectly in line with more recent historiographical trends that, at a 'macro' level, identify cultural factors
as the key to explaining political dynamics. From this perspective,

transnational networks of a political, economic or different nature have played a central role in European integration. They have favoured the socialization of individuals and groups from diverse countries and the establishing of shared views and preferences and common culture. In other words, formal and informal networks have represented a fundamental means for the transnational social integration of elites, and thus, have widely contributed to shaping the entire integration process. This is why more in-depth research on networks is desirable, in order to obtain a key to reinterpret the history of integration from a new perspective, less centred on the role of governments and more attentive to the socio-cultural dimension. Of course, such research should avoid ascribing undue significance to relatively irrelevant dynamics, or overly reducing the importance of nation-states at the very moment of their apogee, that is during the first 20 years of European integration.

Finally, as far as the social dimension of common policies is concerned, historians have already made relevant contributions, especially on the policies conceived before 1970, such as CAP, regional policies and, naturally, the early social policies proper. This research will no doubt evolve with the progressive availability of new archival sources. It should also be broadened to new policy fields. Once more, however, the greatest innovation could result from a more in-depth study of the socio-economic aspects of two possible research fields. The first is strictly connected with research on associations and local press proposed above, and concerns the concrete impact of common policies on the lives of citizens in terms of their influence on professional or residential choices, on changes of social status for workers of specific sectors or the attractiveness of residential areas. The second is related to the European social model and its components like education and training, flexibility, and social dialogue. Reconstructing their historical roots, the debate on their inclusion in the treaties and their later rise as pillars of what could be called the EU's economic culture could make a major contribution to understanding not only the historical evolution of European integration but also its current status.

9
Partners and Rivals: Assessing the American Role

Mark Gilbert

History writing on the role played by the United States (US) in the gene-
sis and development of European integration has taken place within the
boundaries imposed by two overlapping interpretative debates. The first
of these is the debate over the post-war American motivation in pressing
for European integration (as it indisputably did). The earliest generation
of practitioners – diplomats, politicians and political commentators –
presented a very benign picture of the US' actions and purpose. Ernst
van der Beugel (1966, 393), a Dutch diplomat-turned-historian, is typical: 'Since 1947, the constant element in United States foreign policy
has been to consider European co-operation and integration as a vital
contribution to the strength of the Atlantic world and the interests of
the United States. American support for European integration in general was based upon the conviction that the medium-sized nation-state
in Europe was obsolete in relation to the solution of basic political, military and economic problems. It was inspired by the genuine and almost
missionary belief that the United States should use its power to trans-
plant the blessings of its own federal system and of its own continental
size to the countries of Europe, with which it felt itself so emotionally
linked.'

Few scholars would nowadays be quite so unambiguous in their
Atlanticism. Nevertheless, for the most part, historians of transatlantic political and economic history have broadly presented the US as a
hegemonic power whose influence on the countries of western Europe
(and the process of integration) was both profound and beneficial. Most
historians that have occupied themselves with the American role have
concluded (by implication, if not explicitly) that the pervasive presence
and encouragement of the US was decisive for the unprecedented degree
of cooperation shown by Europe's principal states after 1945.

The second major debate that has agitated historians of the transatlantic dimension to European integration is: why did the relationship sour? That the transatlantic relationship ceased to be a harmonious one in the 1960s and has known several prolonged periods of intense disagreement since (most notably in 1973–74, in the early 1980s and in 2002–04) is a fact. Tracing the causes of this decline into greater disharmony has already become a subject of importance for historians. Is the responsibility chiefly due to American anxiety about Europe's growing strength? Has there been, as Geir Lundestad (2003) suggests, a 'transatlantic drift' in values which has made friction inevitable? Or is there reason to believe, as many pundits have suggested, that now Europe is more able to play an equal part in world politics, relations may potentially improve, making the period since the late 1960s seem no more than a troubled parenthesis? Much of this latter debate belongs to the category of speculation. Yet such speculations do at least provide future historians with a map for their research; one which they will in future fill with detail and perhaps alter in some of its main features, but which will nevertheless serve as a guide through the archival maze.

This chapter addresses these questions in the following way. It begins by depicting the contribution of specialists of the transatlantic relationship to the American role in the period from 1945 to 1958. As other chapters in this book show in detail, these scholars' depiction is not necessarily shared by other historians who have worked predominately in the European archives. As E. H. Carr (2001 [1961], 18) famously contended, in history where you fish determines what fish you catch. The first two sections of this chapter are hence primarily concerned with surveying what historians trawling through American archives have managed to catch.

The third section addresses the second question posed above. Is it right to depict the US as a supporter (and guarantor) of the European project even after the creation of the European Economic Community (EEC) in 1958, or as an insecure hegemon, anxious to constrain its protégées? And should we present the present-day European Union (EU) as a victim of the Americans' mean-spiritedness, or as free riders anxious for parity of prestige but not parity of contribution? Here, the jury is out, still unsure of the tendency of the evidence, with some scholars insisting on the fundamental continuity of the US' attitude towards Europe and others contending that, under the presidencies of John F. Kennedy first and especially under Richard Nixon, it saw 'Europe' – in its own way as much a construction of US foreign policy analysis as 'the communist bloc' or the 'free world' – as a potential rival that had to be monitored and checked. As archive access expands to include the presidencies of Jimmy Carter and Ronald Reagan, it will be interesting to see how the debate evolves – for evolve it will. The many strong views held about the changing character of the US and the equally debated issue of the nature of the EU guarantees that. This chapter concludes by examining recent attempts to chart and predict the main tendency of transatlantic relations.

Child of the Cold War

Reading the work of the principal historians who have occupied them-selves specifically with the transatlantic dimension of the construction of 'Europe' after World War II, one realizes quite soon that they are mostly telling a story that stresses the indispensability of the US' inter-vention into the domestic politics of western Europe. Intervention was congenial to the post-war generation of American leaders. They were confident of the democratic values and efficiency of the US system of government, granite-like in their opposition to communism, and deeply conscious of the immense economic and military power of the US government, which had proved during the war that it was capable of stimulating unheard-of levels of economic productivity. America stood across the world like a colossus, and to its leaders it was obvious that defeated Europe should follow its lead.

As the American scholar Michael Hogan (1987, 427) has argued, motivating the US administration's efforts was a 'policy synthesis' incorporating a 'vision' of an 'integrated Western European economy very much like the large internal market that had taken shape in the United States after the Constitution of 1787'. To achieve this objective: 'Marshall Planners blended ... free traders' and planners' approaches. They aimed to reduce barriers to the free flow of goods, services and capital, put intra-European trade and payments on a multi-lateral basis, and permit market mechanisms to promote a rational integration. But they also sought to organize European institutions with the power to transcend sovereignties and coordinate policies so that normal market forces could operate. If led by qualified experts and civil servants of international status, institutions of this sort could help to depoliticize divisive issues, discipline the selfish pursuit of national interests, and weld once rival states into an organic unit of economic and political power' (Hogan 1987, 428).

American policy-makers saw these efforts as part and parcel of their wider plans to contain Soviet communism. By uniting, the Europeans would become partners in the wider struggle. Equally important, European unity was seen as a means by which the newly established Federal Republic could be rehabilitated as a sovereign state – a step necessary for defence reasons but which inspired alarm among Germany's neighbours, especially France. European integration was, in short, the economic and political concomitant of the 1949 Atlantic Pact and the creation of the North Atlantic Treaty Organization (NATO), although this does not mean, Hogan asserts, that the policy-making elite 'manipulated the rhetoric of unification to entangle the United States in the defence of Europe'. US planners were too pragmatic to permit the translation into institutional fact of the federalists' 'enthusiastic eruptions' (Hogan 1987, 430). US policy, in short, was based upon both a realistic assessment of European strength and a deep-rooted sense of America's historical mission as the world's most advanced industrial democracy to export the lessons it had learned to the old continent.

The 'enthusiastic eruptions' were a genuine force, however – on both sides of the Atlantic. It is still instructive to read an article published by Armin Rappaport (1981) in *Diplomatic History*, to get a sense of the widespread pressure exercised on the Harry S. Truman administration in the American press, civil society and Congress on behalf of European federation. Commentators such as Walter Lippmann, the most influential journalist of the day, strongly argued for European federation. Senator William J. Fulbright of Arkansas and Representative Hale Boggs of Louisiana, among many others, took up the cause in Congress.

Given the volume of vocal support within the US for federation, some historians hint that American policy-makers, especially in the State Department, were too sensitive to European (especially British) sensibilities. Had the US pressed for the construction of a western European Union, they might have provided the stimulus necessary to break down residual attachments to national sovereignty. Klaus Schwabe (1995, 119) has depicted the debate thus: 'Americans seemed to believe that the Europeans could be pressured by the United States into forming a union overnight. The State Department did not share that illusion ... A European shot-gun marriage ... would have been counter-productive as it would [have] provide[d] grist to the mill of communist propaganda ... In the final analysis one could argue that the State Department's reluctance to put more than rhetorical pressure on the Europeans may even have contributed to the setbacks that the process of European integration suffered in the 1950s.'

Nevertheless, as Schwabe stresses, the State Department was a crucial sponsor in 1949–50 of the event that decisively launched European integration along its current path: the Schuman Plan. Instead of pressing for a broad western European organization led by Britain, the US 'concentrated its efforts on persuading France to assume the leadership in European integration, even if this meant Britain's temporary exclusion from an integrated Europe' (Schwabe 1998, 43). According to this view, this pressure led directly to Schuman's bold move, since the French were acutely aware both of the Americans' desire for progress towards European unity and their intention to consolidate the role of the new German democracy on their eastern borders.

The US welcomed the Schuman Plan with enthusiasm. Here, at last, was a European initiative on a scale to gladden American hearts. The role played by US diplomats in ironing out the details of the treaty creating the European Coal and Steel Community (ECSC) is emphatically asserted in historians' accounts of the negotiations, which were conducted primarily between France and Germany, with the high-ranking French civil servant Jean Monnet as a 'ringmaster' who cracked the whip of American pressure in order to keep the talks on track (Gillingham 2003, 25). Without the active participation of the US High Commissioner for Germany, John J. McCloy, it is quite possible that France and Germany would not have found the crucial compromise whereby Germany, in exchange for France's abandonment of a demand for a cap on the steel production of any individual German firm, committed itself to reorganizing its steel industry and to limiting the amount of coal production any single German steel maker could control. Recently, Brigitte Leucht has crafted several layers of thick description on to this picture of the negotiation of the crucial antitrust provisions of the ECSC treaty. She shows that the involvement in the negotiation of transatlantic 'policy networks' of key advisors (lawyers, economists and diplomats) enabled Monnet 'to transfer his efforts to break with French cartel traditions to the core European level'; enabled, in other words, the drafting of the treaty more consonant with American free market preferences (Leucht 2009a, 69).

The Schuman Plan, in short, 'though not the by-product of American initiative' was nevertheless 'inspired in part by American policy and brought to fruition with the help of American intervention' (Hogan 1987, 378). The same point is made by many other scholars. The leading American historian of the Schuman Plan, John Gillingham, stresses the role of what he calls 'American monnetism' in bringing the negotiations to a successful conclusion. By 'monnetism', Gillingham means that many of the leading policy-makers in the State Department, and some other influential branches of the US government, were enthralled by Monnet's vision of a united Europe, and by Monnet personally: they were far more committed to supranationalist ideals than many Europeans. This was even more the case once European policy was in the hands of the 'genuinely europhile team' led by the incoming US President, Dwight D. Eisenhower (Vaicbourdt 2002, 33). The work of Pascaline Winand, in particular, has charted in impressive detail just how intimately Monnet was integrated into US policy-making towards western Europe during the Eisenhower and Kennedy administrations (Winand 1993, 1997). Eisenhower himself, John Foster Dulles, Monnet's close friend since 1919 and a long-time committed advocate of European unity, US Ambassador David Bruce, one of Monnet's most devout acolytes who became Dulles' special representative in Paris, and Robert Bowie, the director of the State Department's Policy Planning Staff, were all convinced believers in the construction of a federal state in western Europe (Warner 1993; Görtemaker 1994).

The Europhilia of the Eisenhower administration, in particular its powerful support for the idea of a European Defence Community (EDC), has generated a substantial historical literature. In American eyes, the EDC promised to unite Europe, bolster defence against the Soviets under US leadership at low cost and integrate Germany into the democratic community of nations, thus minimizing the risk that German policy would take a revanchist turn. Marc Trachtenberg, in his book *A Constructed Peace: The Making of the European Settlement, 1945–1963*, goes further and suggests that Eisenhower wanted the western European bloc to become 'a third great power bloc' in world affairs (1999, 147): to become a political entity capable of sharing more of the burden of its own defence and allow the US forces present to withdraw. The EDC seemed a step in the right direction: '[T]he EDC would pave the way towards the political unification of Europe, and since a unified Europe was by far the best solution to the strategic problem, the EDC could not be allowed to fail' (Trachtenberg 1999, 122).

For this reason, the Eisenhower administration pushed for the EDC with intense, even disconcerting energy. Pierre Mélandri (1980, 488) talks of the 'blind enthusiasm' shown by the Americans for the EDC. Schwabe (2001, 26) says that the US, once 'won over' to the EDC adopted it 'lock, stock and barrel' for the very good reason that it was seen as the 'panacea that ensured a continued double containment of the Soviet Union and Germany ... In the long run it promised the founding of a European Federal Union closely allied to the United States.' The US government's leverage was limited, however. On 30 August 1954, amid scenes of nationalist fervour and the full-throated singing of the 'Marseillaise', the French National Assembly sank the treaty.

According to Mélandri (1980, 488), with the defeat of the EDC, 'it was as if something had broken' between the US and the European project. Lundestad (1998, 1) agrees: 'The United States promoted the integration of western Europe rather strongly until the 1950s, less strongly after that.' The Suez crisis (July–November 1956), which culminated in America's disavowal of its British and French allies before the United Nations, only worsened things. Winand and Mélandri make the identical ironic joke that Dulles, by opposing French foreign policy so vigorously at Suez, achieved more for European unity than he had in years of advocacy for the European cause (Mélandri 1975, 119; Winand 1993, 93). Suez arguably brought home to the French government that it was powerless against the Americans, and convinced its policy-makers of the need to bring about an independent European construction able to stand up to the Americans. Other scholars, however, insist that Suez did not significantly change the course of events.

Despite its frayed relationship with France, historians concur that the US did not obstruct the negotiating process that began at Messina on 2 June 1955 and that led, by various troubled stages, to the signature of the Treaties of Rome establishing the EEC and the European Atomic Energy Community (Euratom) in March 1957. Scholars have ascertained that this was in part because the Eisenhower doctrine on these matters – that all European efforts to achieve unity should be supported as worthwhile in themselves – still held true. It was also because Euratom was the brainchild of Monnet and offered the prospect of a welcome centralization of European activity in this hyper-delicate field. However, as both Mélandri and the Italian scholar Federico Romero (1993) have underlined, there was a particularly favourable conjuncture in US foreign economic policy that made the creation of the EEC acceptable to the powers that be in Washington.

Between June 1955 and March 1957, the US continued to regard itself as being substantially unaffected by the Europeans' rising economic strength. The American economy was booming, domestic incomes were rising and the US enjoyed a surplus in its balance of payments with the six ECSC countries (1,463 million US dollars in 1956; 1,636 million in 1957). In this favourable climate, the US government regarded itself as being 'strong enough to withstand without great difficulty the additional discrimination inherent in the foundation of the EEC', and considered that the gap separating 'a prosperous and allied Europe from a Europe that was too powerful and too keen on independence' was still too wide to be worth worrying about (Mélandri 1975, 201, 124). As Romero (1993, 168–9) has pointed out '[a]s long as the American economy remained buoyant, and foreign trade growing, the positive U.S. attitude towards European integration was not vulnerable to domestic pressures for an assertion of the USA's immediate commercial interest.' Dulles still saw European integration as a reinforcement of the West in the broader strategic struggle against the Soviet peril and the policy-making consensus as a whole was content to accept that the EEC represented a staging post on the journey to freer trade at international level. Significantly, the US did not give its backing for the British plan (1956–58) to construct a free trade area in western Europe which could have encompassed the EEC. Subsequently, however, the Americans would 'regret the liberalism with which they had facilitated the construction of an economic bloc that was prosperous, but too protectionist for their taste' (Mélandri 1975, 201).

Indeed, almost as soon as the ink was dry on the EEC treaty, the US suffered a sharp setback in its trade balance, to a point where its traditional surplus in manufactured exports, which until 1957 had broadly covered imports and the substantial costs of maintaining its military commitments overseas, could no longer hide the dollar outflow. The principal cause of this about-turn was the outstanding export performance of the EEC states, which were shipping goods on a large scale to the American market. Once the EEC treaty was signed, moreover, the would-be common market, whose joint output was about one-third of that of the US, but growing much more rapidly, seemed a lucrative opportunity for American firms. After March 1957, dollars flowed to the EEC in the form of direct investment in factories and new plants and, to a lesser extent, into stocks and shares. By 1958, when currency convertibility was introduced, the six EEC member states possessed dollar reserves much greater than the gold hoard of the US Treasury – a point of potential importance, since paper dollars could be exchanged for gold at a fixed exchange rate of 35 US dollars per ounce. Romero (1993, 176) shows convincingly that this situation aroused great disquiet among US policy-makers: the 'era of U.S. commercial sacrifices for the sake of European growth and stability was over'. He concludes (1993, 179): 'In 1958 the first big drop in the U.S. trade surplus, the worsening of its payments deficit, and the convertibility of European currencies into the dollar suddenly brought the post-war world to an end. Interdependence had grown far beyond what U.S. policy makers had envisioned a few years earlier ... The defence of the United States' commercial and financial position took centre stage. Thus timing was crucial: if it [the trade slump] had come about just two years later the Common Market would have certainly received very different treatment in Washington.'

Benign guardians?

From the perspective of general American historiography, the transatlantic relationship from 1945 to 1958 was essentially a paternalistic one. As Stephen Ambrose and Douglas Brinkley (1997, 101) put it: 'The Marshall Plan, followed by NATO, began in earnest an era of American military, political and economic dominance in Europe.' Robert D. Schulzinger's (2002, 12) take is essentially similar: 'The United States used its wealth and military might to gain influence. It entered the two world wars, revived the economies of Europe with the Marshall Plan, created the North Atlantic Treaty Organization, and looked with approval on the formation of the EEC as a sort of embryonic United States of Europe.'

As we have seen from the survey above, the specialist historiography on US foreign policy essentially concurs in this diagnosis. While nobody would seriously claim that European integration was a direct product of US foreign policy, it is broadly agreed that the US created the conditions that made it possible and supported it almost without qualm. As the chapters in this book by Antonio Varsori, Daniele Pasquinucci, Morten Rasmussen and Lorenzo Mechi show, however, much of the literature focused on western European economics and politics does not rate the American impact on post-war reconstruction and integration nearly so high. Indeed, the role of the US in the post-war construction is a sensitive issue since there used to be a tendency to denote as 'Americanization' the broad process of rapid modernization that enabled countries such as Italy to take their place as a leading industrial nation in the 1950s (Ellwood 1992).

In this regard, Alan S. Milward's work on the reconstruction of the western European economy, which is discussed from a different vantage point by Rasmussen in this volume, is of key importance as a precursor for revisionist studies in this field. In *The Reconstruction of Western Europe, 1945–1951* (1984) Milward portrays the period as one in which the Europeans essentially decided their economic and political arrangements for themselves, with the Americans taking on the role of an over-zealous rich uncle, full of good, general advice that was not always applicable to the concrete situation the Europeans found themselves in or heeded by them.

Milward's account breathes an understanding of the almost haphaz-ard way major shifts in world politics actually occur. His story is one of many actors, but no benevolent *deus ex machina*. He begins by calling into question the significance of the Marshall Plan, which did not – or so he plausibly avers – save western Europe from penury, but merely filled the dollar gap created by the sheer pace with which Europe was rebuild-ing. Western Europe urgently needed tractors, trucks, trains, factory lathes and raw materials. Germany, the pre-Nazi supplier of industrial equipment, was not yet able to meet demand. European nation-states hence imported them from the US, 'fatalistically' assuming that the US government would as a matter of its own political and economic interest find a way to let them have the dollars (Milward 1984, 50–1). In hindsight, the risk they ran was colossal. The US might easily have said 'no' and unwittingly provoked a calamity of 1930s proportions, but at the time western European governments felt they had no choice. Their peoples would not have accepted a post-war world without work and welfare, merely for the sake of balancing the national budgets.

The US administration subsequently hoped to use the Marshall Plan as a way of transforming the Organization for European Economic Cooperation into a customs union and, eventually, a federal European state. But 'Marshall Aid was not in fact important enough to give the United States sufficient leverage to reconstruct western Europe accord-ing to its own wishes', according to Milward (1984, 469). The Europeans, especially the British and the French, proved un-malleable clay in the American sculptor's hands. Anglo-French obstinacy 'thwarted' American plans for a federal future. Britain's economic difficulties, which culminated in the shock devaluation of 18 September 1949, when the exchange rate against the dollar was cut by over 30 per cent, left France as the United States' main interlocutor in western Europe. But the French were not exactly enthusiasts for the free trading European order envisaged by the State Department's ideologues. By the end of 1949, far from being lordly masters of western Europe's fate, 'America was no longer in a position to object to any French initiative, no mat-ter how limited in geographical scope or how protectionist, unless the whole idea of European integration was to be given up altogether, which was too drastic a reduction to contemplate' (Milward 1984, 474). Almost by default, France found herself in the European driving seat and seized the opportunity to take a fork in the road she found convenient. The Schuman Plan was undeniably an initiative of great significance, but it bore little resemblance to American blueprints for Europe's future: 'In place of a liberal unified Europe came a closely regulated little European common market whose twin purposes were to provide French national security by containing West Germany and to permit its members to continue to pursue a very limited range of common economic policies in a few specific sectors of the economy ...' (Milward 1984, 476).

Milward's argument is a useful corrective to any kind of narrative that perceives European integration as part and parcel of the planned expansion of American power. The western European nations were anything but bystanders in a wider Atlantic order ruled by the US. The French rejection of the EDC was only the most dramatic instance of frank European defiance of American wishes in the period from 1945 to 1958, but one need not rely on such an extreme example to make the general case. All the principal steps to greater economic integration were taken by the European countries at moments of their own choosing. The US surely encouraged an ideology of free trade and mutual interdependence, but were pushing at an open door since leading European policy-makers, all of whom had vivid memories of the 1930s, had an almost 'exaggerated' conviction of the necessity of free trade to stimulate economic growth and the provision of welfare (Milward et al. 1993, 8); European policy-makers in the national governments, most of whom were Christian democrats, were anything but beholden to the American model of European federalism, or to American society and ideology in general, but were rather 'frankly hostile' to a way of life that they regarded as being too 'marked by Protestant individualism and materialism' and were determined to carve out their own independence (Kaiser 2003, 65; see also Kaiser 2007). The US, had it been dictating events, would not have been so accommodating to the British preference to stay outside the process but would have compelled Britain to take a leading role.

Lundestad's reiterated argument that post-war Europe became 'an empire by invitation' – certainly one of the most important contributions to the literature in this field – underestimates the autonomy and creativity shown by western European leaders after World War II. That the Europeans invited the Americans to defend them and accepted their dollars with enthusiasm is not in doubt. The pejorative term 'empire', however, implies that the Europeans were somehow subjugated to an alien form of rule, which is not true – and, indeed, Lundestad himself, who writes from an Atlanticist standpoint, is emphatic that it is not true (Lundestad 1986, 1998).

In his subsequent book *'Empire' by Integration*, however, Lundestad (1998) has the merit of laying out a hypothesis that has perhaps been taken for granted in the mainstream historiography on the transatlantic dimension to European integration. Was the fact of the American presence in post-war western European politics the decisive element that made European integration possible? Without American aid and encouragement would the Europeans, and especially the French and Germans, have fallen back into the same dank pit of nationalist rivalry that had ruined Europe since 1914? Lundestad dissents from Dulles, who had apparently wondered whether American intervention, via the Marshall Plan and NATO, might not paradoxically have *retarded* European unification (since in the face of the Soviet threat western Europe's nations would have had no choice but to federate had the US adopted an outright isolationist stance). In contrast, Lundestad (1998, 153) argues that 'history would have repeated itself, in the sense that the traditional rivalry among the West European states, especially Germany and France, would have continued. Integration was something dramatically new in European history.' Milward, by contrast, if only because he thinks it was in the interests of western European nation-states to work out common institutional arrangements that maximized economic benefits while retaining as much sovereignty as possible, is strongly implying that European states would have found a *modus vivendi* anyhow.

Of course, asking what would have happened had US policy taken an isolationist turn, leaving western Europe to its own devices, is to pose a bold counterfactual question. The received wisdom about counterfactual argument is that one's thought experiments should be limited to minimum rewrites of past events, to ensure that one only speculates about virtual histories that were genuinely possible futures at any given moment. It is not clear that positing American isolationism is a legitimate experiment to make. It *is* reasonable, however, to ask what would have happened if the Truman administration had pressed more insistently during 1948–50 for rapid progress to supranational political institutions. This was, after all, its preferred policy. Would less American deference to the principle that the Europeans themselves should choose their own pace of integration have fast-forwarded the history of European integration by 40 years? Or accelerated (perhaps in exacerbated form) the potential for nationalism shown by France in 1954? What would the domestic political impact of greater American assertiveness have been in countries like Italy, with its two million strong Communist Party? How would it have impacted on relations with Britain? Just to pose the questions shows that what we call the 'process' of European integration, by our choice of words implying something essentially predictable, was a highly contingent development (Gilbert 2008). Irrespective of whether the European states, especially France, were primarily responsible, or whether the Americans were benign guardians keeping Europe's nationalist instincts finally in check, both might very easily have choked the tender plant of European integration even before it gave its first timid blooms.

Partners or rivals?

The emergence of the EEC upset the existing order. As Romero pointed out, the creation of the EEC gave a fillip to the EEC's economic performance relative to the US and siphoned off American investment. The EEC's ability in the 1960s to negotiate on a par with the US during trade talks and stand up for its perceived interests (also discussed by Giuliano Garavini in his chapter) against the full weight of American pressure added some credibility to the notion that the EEC was at least potentially an international power that was greater than the sum of its constituent parts. As Piers Ludlow (2007, 364) says: 'The success of US-sponsored regional integration within Europe thus necessitated an altered American approach to global commercial arrangements.' The EEC states' dollar hoards were also a source of power. France, as Kennedy constantly fretted, swung the 'club' of selling off dollars for gold over American heads throughout the 1960s. Under Kennedy, both the US Treasury and the Pentagon favoured reducing the dollar outflow through troop withdrawals from Europe and pressed, with some presidential sympathy, for letting the Europeans stand on their own (Gavin 2002). The dollar was a perennial source of American weakness throughout the 1960s and one which French President Charles de Gaulle, the chief European thorn in the American side, exploited for his own political ends, with the argument that the US was abusing its position as the issuer of the chief reserve currency by paying for its overconsumption with the printing press (Zimmermann 2003, 132). These proofs of growing European economic power unquestionably shifted the American attitude to European integration. From something to be nurtured, it became something to be monitored – though never to be outright undermined.

When did this ambivalent American attitude begin? Under Kennedy, Lyndon B. Johnson or Nixon? Kennedy's policy towards the EEC – his so-called 'Grand Design' – was to urge British entry to the EEC; obtain from Congress, via the 1962 Trade Expansion Act, presidential power to negotiate a liberal new trade regime that would strengthen the economic ties between the US and an enlarged EEC in a broad 'Atlantic Community'; to seek, even, to meet the EEC states' desire to have greater autonomy in the defence field by inventing the concept of the multilateral force, an 'essentially political cause' (Giauque 2002, 115), which would have placed a 'small flotilla' of surface vessels armed with tactical nuclear weapons in the hands of crews from European states (albeit with an American finger on the trigger). Was this strategy actuated from the desire to enhance Europe's role as a partner, as Kennedy's rhetoric promised, or keep it under the US' thumb? The German scholar Eckart Conze and the American diplomatic historian Frank Costigliola have both suggested that the Grand Design, far from being a way of raising Europe up to partnership was actually a way of perpetuating American hegemony over western Europe at as low a cost as possible.

As Conze sees it, de Gaulle's articulation between 1958 and 1961 of a clear preference for a small, core Europe, dominated by France, spurred the Kennedy administration's *Gesamtkonzept* (master plan) of seeking 'hegemony through integration' of the EEC into the wider Atlantic world (Conze 1995, 328). Costigliola says bluntly that '[T]he Kennedy administration ... valued European integration as the way to contain West Germany and build a broader market for American products. Consequently, it talked about equal partnership with a united Europe. Yet like its predecessors, this administration had difficulty practising partnership on other than American terms' (Costigliola 1984, 228). The French historian Denise Artaud anticipated the same argument in the early 1980s by suggesting that the 'Grand Dessein' was a 'consciously planned project' whose goal was 'preventing, through Atlantic partnership, a Europe proceeding towards unification from deviating towards a destination different from that of America'. She adds that it is important to notice that the plan is 'preventive, even pre-emptive'. A political union was still unborn; the common market 'still had not harmed American economic interests'. In her view, the Americans reasoned that 'it is always better to prevent than to cure' (Artaud 1982, 263). Such views are a clear echo of de Gaulle's concern, most clearly expressed in his press conference rejecting Britain's membership application in January 1963, that US policy was working to undermine the 'European construction' that was France's goal.

Most scholars are inclined by contrast to cut the Kennedy administration some slack by portraying the Grand Design as a genuine attempt to achieve greater equality. It might have worked had politicians and diplomats on both sides of the Atlantic been more open to compromise. A recent study insists that the Atlantic Community concept was taken 'very seriously' both in Washington and the main European capitals (Giauque 2002, 99). Nevertheless, Winand (1993, 252) admits that the

Kennedy administration was not prepared to contemplate the EEC as anything more than a 'junior partner'. Giauque (2002, 124) concurs, arguing that the Americans were sincere but ultimately too fearful that 'without strong American leadership a uniting Europe might forsake America's interests'. As a result they failed to 'offer the Europeans an equal partnership'.

Kennedy's policy towards Europe, whatever his motives, has been the subject of a substantial historical literature. His successor, Johnson, by contrast, has not had his policy examined in the same detail. Nevertheless, recent historiography has moved on from the view that, preoccupied as he was by Vietnam, Johnson displayed 'a complete lack of interest' for the complex questions posed by western Europe during his presidency (Ellwood 1993, 524). Johnson, who was subjected to a good deal of patronizing transatlantic criticism when he took office, seemingly did offer the major European states parity of a practical sort by treating relations with France, Germany and Britain as bargaining sessions with moderately powerful allies who had legitimate interests to defend, just like the parish-pump Congressmen with whom Johnson had been accustomed to deal. Johnson may well have been, as de Gaulle patronizingly thought, incapable of strategic thought, but he prided himself on his understanding of power and possessed both a shrewd grasp of how much power actually lay in European leaders' hands and a patient determination to put up with the Europeans' frequent fits of self-importance in order to ensure the long-term goal of mutual coop- eration. Such, at any rate, is the core argument of Thomas A. Schwartz's short book *Lyndon Johnson and Europe: In the Shadow of Vietnam* (2003), which makes a cogent case for favourably assessing the success of Johnson's policy towards the key European states that Schwartz inci- dentally treats as largely identical with the EEC.

Schwartz's book is complemented by Massimiliano Guderzo's *Interesse nazionale e responsabilità globale: Gli Stati Uniti, L'alleanza atlantica e l'integrazione europea negli anni di Johnson, 1963–1968* (2000), which con- centrates much more on Johnson's attitude to the European project, and which is equally positive in assessing the president's record. If the 1960s were something of a 'lost decade' for the European project, Guderzo con- tends, this was the fault of the political elites in the EEC states, not of their citizens, or of the administration in Washington. The US did eve- rything within its power to raise Europe up to American levels, or close to them. As Guderzo says in his book's peroration, during Johnson's five-year presidency, '[t]here was no occasion where the Americans missed an opportunity to give a verbal promise or concrete sign of their openness to European progress towards unification. Sometimes, unintentionally, they mixed up the cards on the table, confusing such distinct concepts as integration and construction, unity and unification, community, confederation and federation: but always they did so in good faith, in the conviction that the new destiny of the Europeans, after the suicide of World War II, would be realized in the *summa* of their enormous energies, not in conflict; and in the persuasion that this *summa* should be harnessed by any means possible to serve the common running of the western camp. It was obvious who commanded in this camp: the United States ... but ... [the Americans'] long-term objective was joint responsibility for the running of the West. The pay-off for the Americans lay in their understanding that the national interest of the United States partly coincided with European integration' (Guderzo 2000, 567).

There appears to be a growing consensus among historians of the transatlantic relationship that during the subsequent Nixon administrations from 1969 to August 1974, the second of which was cut short by the president's threatened impeachment and resignation over Watergate, this pay-off grew less enticing, at any rate in economic terms, and American policy-makers shifted with remarkable rapidity and even unscrupulousness to an 'America First' policy that was designed to reassert hegemony over its allies. Lucia Coppolaro (2008a, 136), tongue in cheek, has called this position 'hostile support'. Wolfram Hanrieder's *Germany, America, Europe: Forty Years of German Foreign Policy*, which despite its title is an acute reading of the post-war role of the US in western European, not just German, politics, argues that under Nixon (and Gerald Ford and Carter), the US government 'signalled the abrogation of the post-war transatlantic economic compact ... [whereby] ... the United States, based upon its hegemonic and monetary position, would be willing to make economic sacrifices in return for political privileges' (Hanrieder 1989, 306).

What provoked this abrogation? Francis Gavin (2007, 198) has underlined one root cause: 'As countries like France, West Germany, Japan, and others accumulated ... deficit dollars, a sense of economic insecurity and vulnerability – not hegemony – developed among top U.S. policy makers.' By the time Nixon became president in 1969, it had became more and more difficult for the US government, engaged as it was on an expensive war in Vietnam and on vast new social spending programmes launched by Johnson, to finance its costly military commitments around the world. The US ran a consistent deficit on its balance of payments between the late 1950s and early 1970s, as a booming

American economy, boosted by higher public spending on defence and social welfare, sucked in imports. Transfers of American wealth to fund US military commitments overseas and private capital investment, which poured into western Europe and Japan throughout this period, just compounded the problem.

The US government should, in theory, have eliminated this problem by deflating, that is, by raising taxes or restricting credit. Nixon, who had no desire to restrain demand in the year before the presidential election due in 1972, chose instead to abandon gold convertibility for the dollar and to introduce temporary import surcharges. These decisions set off a lengthy bout of currency turmoil and, because of asymmetries in EEC currencies' appreciation against the dollar, subverted the European common market. David W. Ellwood's (1993, 547) comment that '[t]he widespread upheaval of the international system, determined by the end of the post-war monetary order between 1971 and 1973, was a disaster for America's prestige and authority comparable in scope to that inflicted by Vietnam', may be an exaggeration. However, there is no doubt that this sudden American decision to 'put the domestic economy first and let the international chips fall where they might' was a watershed in transatlantic relations and had a powerful spillover effect upon the process of European integration (Kunz 1997, 218).

With hindsight, Nixon ushered in a four-decade period of loose American fiscal policy and gaping trade deficits, which together have flooded the world with a sea of dollars. Although the EEC governments began to discuss European monetary cooperation before the end of the Bretton Woods system, the international monetary regime established after World War II, the Euro and the single market can be seen, up to a point, as two of the long-term consequences of Nixon's action: by trading together more and reducing currency fluctuations between national currencies Europeans have managed to construct an island of relative stability from the dollar ocean's swells and tides (Calleo 2001, 218–20). The island has nevertheless been swept by heavy waves on more than one occasion. We still lack, however, a historian of comparable stature to Milward able to trace the full complexity of the effects, intended and unintended, of this epochal shift in US policy on the process of European integration.

By contrast, the Nixon administration's other moment of discord with the Community can seem somewhat ephemeral, though it is one that has already generated a flourishing empirical literature. This is Henry Kissinger's 'Year of Europe' in 1973, when the US Secretary of State demanded a greater EC role in world affairs. Arguably the least edifying moment in post-war transatlantic relations, at any rate until the Iraq conflict, the Community came close during 1973 to defining its new foreign policy in overtly anti-American terms – and if the French had had their way it would have (Hamilton 2006). Ellwood (1993, 549) has contended that the 'Year of Europe' idea was characterized by 'superficiality and opportunism' and 'finished in a disaster'. Certainly the historiographical trend seems to be to depict Kissinger's move as a calculating attempt to ensure that the Community did not achieve its goal, first set out in the Community summit in Paris in October 1972, of becoming a 'distinct entity' in international affairs. Claudia Hiepel (2007, 296) says, for instance that 'the Year of Europe was considered a shrewd device to give the US a say in EC matters and to incorporate Europe into a US-controlled structure' and it is plain that she concurs with this assessment.

Playing devil's advocate, it might be argued that this conclusion is one wide open for future revisionism at the hands of a scholar willing to write a broad, synoptic history of the US' role in European integration from, say, 1958 through to the onset of the Reagan administration. The Europeans have got off lightly in existing scholarship. It is at least thinkable that the Bretton Woods system could have survived, had the EEC states been willing to make greater sacrifices for it. Throughout the 1960s and 1970s, the Europeans wanted to be treated as equals, but not to bear equal burdens. Had the newly rich Europeans contributed much more to their own defence, as American policy-makers urged them, the US might have been more willing to take them more seriously.

Alan P. Dobson and Steve Marsh's remark that western Europe's key states were 'disturbingly prone' to 'regard the Cold War as an important but secondary issue next to defending their established interests, adjusting to a post-war world and contending with economic globalization' has a ring of truth to it. It is at least arguable, though the argument is certainly not emphasized in the historiography of the subject, that in these years, Europeans 'came to bite the hand that fed them' (Dobson and Marsh 2006, 67). Certainly, as Garavini also argues in his chapter, both de Gaulle in the mid-1960s and the trio of Willy Brandt, Edward Heath and Georges Pompidou in the early 1970s seemed determined to lead the unfulfilled entity known as 'Europe' down a path to greater cohesion and influence, even if this injured relations with the all-too-present American ally.

Conclusion

The history of the American connection since the late 1970s is obviously still to be written and the history of the post-1958 relationship, as suggested in the preceding paragraphs, is in any case likely to be revised in coming years. It is interesting to speculate what the predominant interpretative approach to the post-1958 period will be in future narratives. The purpose of this chapter's diachronic structure has been to underline that there is a disjuncture in the literature of the transatlantic dimension to European integration. Before 1958, the interpretative consensus among the literature that focuses on explaining US policy towards Europe overwhelmingly concludes that the US was enthusiastically in favour of European integration and did everything possible to encourage its progress. This consensus appears unlikely to be overturned. To what extent US policy actually mattered has been a much more controversial question among contemporary historians of European integration, though, Milward apart, their critiques have remained in the realm of specialist historiography, and have not influenced the way Americans themselves interpret their own post-war role.

For the period after 1958, by contrast, the interpretative consensus is still unsettled. Will future emphasis be on the US' reiterated support for European integration and on the capacity of the two sides of the Atlantic to find agreement on the major issues? Or will the interpretative consensus stress that crisis, rather than cooperation and common values, have been the keynote of the relationship between the US and western Europe (Del Pero and Romero 2007)? This underlying debate will in all probability intensify in coming years as historians study the interaction of the Carter, Reagan and George Bush I administrations with the Community and its member states and ascertain the extent to which certain choices made by the present-day EU, above all monetary union, were consciously aimed at counter-balancing American economic hegemony. In fact, Antonio Varsori (2007a, 38–39) has suggested that, if 'in the late 1960s/early 1970s the integration process had been also the western European response to U.S. moral decline and in the mid-1970s to U.S. political weakness, from the mid-1980s the integration process was the European response to the challenge posed by a new U.S. hegemony.'

These words imply a huge research agenda. Such an agenda will obviously be based upon archival research and documents discovered, compared and analysed. It is mistaken to think that historical interpretations cannot emerge from the 'bottom up' as the outcome of historians' wrestling with their source material and trying to make sense of it. But they will also depend upon perceptions of the trend of the relationship between Europe and the US. Since the end of the Cold War, and in particular since the George Bush II administration's adoption of a neo-conservative foreign policy, this question of 'whither transatlantic relations' has generated an interpretative literature of vast proportions and mixed quality in all the major European languages. Nevertheless – at any rate in the literature in English – a clear divide has emerged from this exercise in trend-spotting. On the one hand, there is a reading of events that subscribes to the view that 'transatlantic drift' has taken place over the last 30 or so years; a second major interpretation sees the decisive development as being the rise to effective parity of Europe with the US, which is seen as hopeful both for the future of Euro-American relations and for the world as a whole.

The principal exponent of the first of these interpretations is Lundestad, who identifies eight 'primary reasons of concern' for the future of the transatlantic relationship (Lundestad 2003, 281). The gist of Lundestad's argument is that generational, cultural and demographic changes on both sides of the Atlantic explain the increasingly fractious relations between Europe and the US, as epitomized by the genuine crisis over the Iraq war in 2002–04. Americans have become more 'southern', religious and nationalist. Europeans have developed a different frame of reference to judge America. Vietnam and out-of-control consumerism now weigh more heavily on the European mind than the Marshall Plan and friendly, gum-chewing American soldiers; Europeans have also evolved a strong conviction of the superiority of their own social model (Romero 2007). Americans are 'increasingly blamed by Europeans not for what they do, but for who they are' (Lundestad 2003, 290). Since there are also plenty of policy areas, such as trade, Russia and the Middle East, where Europe and America have different opinions and divergent interests, the likelihood is that the drift will continue, even accelerate, though a dive into outright enmity is improbable in Lundestad's judgment. This argument that Europe and America have basically become too different to get along is certainly buttressed by a reading of neo-conservative thinkers like Robert Kagan (2004) who consider that Europe, by pressing ahead with integration, has opted out of history and has chosen to dwell in a 'Kantian' paradise whose existence is guaranteed by the force of American arms; and by progressive European philosophers who urge Europe, on explicitly culturalist grounds, to 'throw its weight on to the scales at international level ... in order to counter-balance the hegemonic unilateralism of the United States' (Habermas and Derrida 2006, 42).

The second interpretation's most eloquent exponents are probably Timothy Garton Ash, David Calleo and Robert Cooper (Cooper 2003). In essence, all three of these writers regard the evolution of the EU as an epochal shift in global politics that has been going on throughout the post-1945 period and has the potential to be an immense boon for humankind. The EU represents a new kind of power according to these writers: potentially, it is a 'formidable component of the free world' (Ash 2005, 210). The argument is that the European project has attracted nations to its sphere of prosperity, has disciplined such nations into accepting liberal and democratic values, and now is rippling ever-outwards, establishing a 'post-modern empire', to use Cooper's phrase, that will make it the point of reference for countries in Eurasia and Africa. If things go well Europe could become a political union of 650 million people and 35 states, with another 650 million people associated with it in a 'great arc of partnership' stretching from Marrakesh to Vladivostok (Ash 2005, 220). This vast Commonwealth would be able to act as a check on the US without necessarily entering into conflict with it. Such a Europe would not need to establish its own identity by demonizing the American 'Other' because it would not have any kind of inferiority complex towards the US. Rather, it might, if its leaders are up to the job, share global leadership with the US and persuade it to undertake a radical agenda of reforms including poverty relief, climate change control and the reinforcement of international law which would make the world a safer and happier place.

Such ideas are not historiography, but they are not alien to history writing either. Historians do not enter the archives with blank slates for minds. The notions of 'transatlantic drift' and what Calleo calls a 'western global partnership' (Calleo 2001, 372) are the two dominating paradigms characterizing the Atlantic relationship today. As historians begin the laborious task of writing the story of the transatlantic relationship since the mid-1970s, and revisiting the post-1958 story, such broad conceptions of history's direction will be present in their minds. These rich interpretative lodes, plus the sheer quantity of historical ore to be mined, seem certain to ensure that the transatlantic dimension to European integration will be one of the most exciting and rewarding sub-fields in international history over the next decade.

10
Foreign Policy beyond the Nation-State: Conceptualizing the External Dimension

Giuliano Garavini

In the current literature on the history of European integration little space is devoted to the external dimension of the present-day European Union (EU) – the principle reason being that, more or less explicitly, most authors share the idea that the main actors of foreign policy were, and remain, national governments. This is confirmed by the nature of the sources that historians of European integration have mainly used, until recently, to write their histories, namely the archives of national ministries of foreign affairs. The existing general histories of the EU contain no extensive accounts of how its formation and evolution affected international relations. Although some studies have been devoted to analysing the negotiations leading to the various enlargements of the European Communities (EC) and the vagaries of transatlantic relations, as discussed separately by Mark Gilbert in his chapter, John Gillingham (2003) does not even mention the association agreements with African countries and considers the EC's external dimension nonexistent up to the end of the 1970s.

As Wolfram Kaiser shows in his chapter, most general histories of contemporary Europe pay very little attention to European integration as a whole. They generally describe western Europe as a battlefield for struggles between national communities and ethnic groups or between the two superpowers (for example, Wasserstein 2007). Recently, Holger Nehring and Helge Pharo (2008) have argued in favour of discussing post-war Europe also in terms of its active peace-making capability, thus including European integration as an important factor. Still, if western European governments are viewed as mainly interested in reconstruction and the resolution of internal conflicts, there appears to be no need to deepen our understanding of the external dimension of the EU.

The historiography on Europe more generally admits an effective role of European institutions in foreign affairs only for the end of the 1980s, with the enlargement to encompass southern European countries and the approval of the Single European Act under the new President of the European Commission, Jacques Delors. To the extent that European institutions are considered to have played a role, this is mainly in setting a model for the enlargement to Greece, Portugal and Spain, and then to eastern Europe after the collapse of the Soviet Union (Judt 2005, 6–7) or in the necessity to cooperate effectively to compete in the new global economic environment (Mazower 1998, 402–11). These two points intuitively assess the new role acquired by the EC in the 1980s, but they remain nothing more than intuitions, since they are not backed up by research on the policies of European institutions, the interactions between 'Brussels' and the member state governments, and on the negotiations within international economic institutions such as the General Agreement on Tariffs and Trade (GATT), the International Monetary Fund (IMF) or the International Bank for Reconstruction and Development (IBRD, World Bank). Even though recent histories of Europe have been of a high quality in other respects, they have not yet fully considered, as Charles Maier (2000) has also stressed, the importance of the decline of the nation-state and of its territorial dimension during the 1960s and 1970s, and the fact that European integration has been strongly linked to this process.

For historians of international relations and the Cold War too, the EU seems to have played a role in world affairs only from the end of the 1980s. Interest in the role of European integration increases with the crisis of the Soviet Union (SU) in the second half of the 1980s because the EC undoubtedly represented a strong pole of attraction for economic and political reasons. The EC was attractive for both governments and ordinary citizens. Some historians even go as far as to argue that the magnetic force represented by the EC and the common market should be considered an important element in explaining the pace of the fall of communism in eastern Europe (Bozo et al. 2008).

While, for example, a traditional account of the foreign policy of the EU, such as that by Romain Yakemtchouk (2005), devotes only 35 out of a total of 470 pages to the period prior to the 1980s, this chapter will show that there is much to be said about the external dimension of the EC before the advent of Delors and before the crumbling of the Berlin Wall. Many efforts have been made to define the nature of this external dimension, which is multifaceted and primarily of an economic character, especially up to the 1980s (Bretherton and Vogler 2006, 12–36). To assess current historical knowledge of the EU's external dimension, this chapter will discuss the main spheres in which European integration has had a noticeable external impact on non-EC countries. These spheres are: trade policy, development policy and relations with Less Developed Countries (LDCs), association agreements and the EC enlargement process, East–West relations and, to a lesser extent, relations with Mediterranean countries, international monetary relations and participation and negotiation in international economic bodies such as the IMF or the World Bank. Due to the influence of the prevalent 30-year rule for the opening of state archives, this chapter will focus on existing literature on the period up to the late 1970s. The conclusion will highlight some of the challenges for future historical research on the external dimension of the EU in the period after the re-launch of European integration in the mid-1980s.

The ECSC and the limits of functional integration

The European Coal and Steel Community (ECSC) created in 1951, and the High Authority that governed it, were principally active in the international arena in the negotiations within the GATT. In this context the ECSC successfully negotiated a waiver for coal and steel. On the other hand, the High Authority did not succeed in developing special links with South America, as Dirk Spierenburg and Raymond Poidevin (1993, 299) have shown in their study of the ECSC. Thus, this kind of functional sectoral integration, while very important for Franco-German reconciliation and for creating a climate of growing confidence between European economies and business actors, can hardly be considered to have had a substantial direct external impact.

In contrast, the creation of a European Defence Community (EDC), which was eventually rejected by the French parliament in 1954, would have had a major impact on international politics. The reasons for the EDC's collapse are complex. Arguably, however, except for a minority of politicians with federalist inclinations and, to some extent, the Italian government led by Alcide De Gasperi (Ballini and Varsori 2004), few within the six ECSC member states were prepared to invest much into a single European foreign policy. Not surprisingly, as Daniele Pasquinucci also shows in his chapter, it is mainly Italian federalist historians who have enquired into what they regard as the 'tragedy' of the failure to create a common European army and to build a European Political

Community to coordinate it, at this early formative stage of integration. Federalist historians view the failure of the EDC as a lost opportunity that only presented itself again in similar form at the time of the Maastricht Treaty on European Union in 1991 (Preda 1994). Raymond Poidevin (1986, 375–6) has connected the failure of the EDC with the French defeat in Indochina. However, most historians of European integration writing about the EDC have ignored the growing literature on decolonization, and the fact that according to this literature the 1950s were a period dominated by what has been called a 'late-colonial shift', that is, the attempt by European nation-states to revive the colonial state (Shipway 2008, 14). In other words, this was hardly a policy environment in which shared foreign policy-making by western European governments could have thrived.

It was only the setting up of the European Economic Community (EEC) in 1957–58, and the resulting creation of a common external tariff and trade policy, which prompted western European leaders to discuss in greater depth the links of this new regional economic area with the rest of the world. One of the options debated at the time was the concept of what came to be known in French as *Eurafrique*: that is, a structured institutionalized link between Europe and Africa, especially francophone western Africa, as a key contribution to the reform of empire and its economic vitality and a means for strengthening western Europe's role in world politics. Emphasizing this particular regional dimension of European global interests, the concept of *Eurafrique* has, not surprisingly, mainly attracted interest from French historians. At the conference *L'Europe unie et l'Afrique* (Bitsch and Bossuat 2005), the participating historians agreed that the project of common institutions between Europe and Africa failed decisively with the Yaoundé Association between the EEC and francophone African countries in 1963 and with the creation of the Organization of African Unity in the same year (Migani 2008a). Until 1963 several western European countries feared that the setting up of the EEC could harm their economies by separating them from those of their (former) colonial empires. This was especially true of France and Britain, which applied for EEC membership for the first time in 1961, but to a more limited extent also for Italy and the Netherlands.

From the creation of the EEC to the summit at The Hague

As the determined Soviet opposition to its creation demonstrates (Rey 2005), the setting up of the EEC in 1957–58 had important implications and consequences for the rest of the world, not only resulting from the sheer size of the national economies involved, but also due to the much greater ambition of this project compared with that of the ECSC, namely to move decisively beyond limited sector integration.

Most historians of European integration so far have been mainly interested in the internal developments of the present-day EU, especially its politics in the period when Charles de Gaulle was French President from 1958 to 1969. Although there has been much debate about de Gaulle's project for an independent 'European Europe', as he called it, the Fouchet Plan (named after Christian Fouchet, French Ambassador to Denmark and chairman of the intergovernmental committee established to draw up a plan for European political union), which aimed to establish some form of intergovernmental foreign policy coordination among the EEC states, failed in 1962. It failed because it excluded European institutions from decision-making, Britain from participation before its EEC accession, which de Gaulle was intent on thwarting, and also because outside of France decision-makers did not feel an urgent need for a common European foreign policy that could be at odds with the policies of the United States (US) in the North Atlantic Treaty Organization (NATO) (Gerbet 1989; Soutou 1999; Vanke 2001). Arguably, the Atlantic links and NATO remained the key reference points for the foreign policies of France's partners in the EEC throughout the 1960s. The growing literature on transatlantic elites and organizations also discussed by Gilbert in his chapter tends to confirm this dominance of the NATO framework for foreign and security policy (Nehring 2004). At the same time, attempts by the EEC states at strengthening their links with Latin America as envisaged for example by the Brazilian government in 1960 failed while the US reinforced its influence over the continent, not least with its regional policy entitled Alliance for Progress.

Yet the EEC did have a large degree of autonomy in foreign economic policy, as the formation of a common commercial policy was a legal requirement of the customs union. This autonomy led to many economic conflicts with the US. According to Gérard Bossuat, in his edited book *L'Europe et la mondialisation* (2006), the EEC affected other nations in three main areas during the 1960s: as a very important actor in the GATT negotiations alongside the US; through its role in agricultural trade; and in the relations with the LDCs.

Historians who have written about the GATT and its Kennedy Round, which lasted from 1963 to 1967, agree that the EEC managed to remain a cohesive actor in trade policy at an extremely delicate moment for the Community, the 'Empty Chair' crisis during 1965–66, successfully defending its evolving Common Agricultural Policy (CAP) and also over-coming the challenge from the European Free Trade Association (EFTA) formed under British leadership in 1959–60. In particular, EFTA failed in its main objective of imposing on the EEC a pan-western European free trade area in industrial goods (Kaiser 1997). Although EFTA con-tinued to exist and actually managed to abolish its internal tariffs one and a half years before the EEC, it turned into a holding operation fol-lowing the unsuccessful EEC applications by its member states Britain, Denmark and Norway as well as Ireland in 1961–62. Subsequently, the EEC became by far the most important partner and adversary of the US in international trade negotiations.

The main dispute among historians appears to concentrate on whether the Kennedy Round ended with US or EEC success (Winand 2006). As Lucia Coppolaro (2008b, 127) has argued, 'the United States proved unable to sway the Six. Washington discovered that the EEC was just as mercantilist as the United States; the EEC would not agree to participate in a new round unless its regional policies were preserved and unless the agreement held the prospect of increasing its own exports. As the Six saw it, solutions to the U.S. payments problem had to be sought elsewhere.' If the government in Washington, under serious stress due to its overseas expenditure, especially in Vietnam, had imagined the Kennedy Round as a way to improve its balance of payments, the Kennedy Round did nothing to ameliorate the situation: the US balance of payments problem continued until the collapse of Bretton Woods, the international monetary regime established after World War II, and the floating of the US dollar in 1971.

The domestic policies of the EEC also had significant external impact, however. Concerning the CAP in particular, there is something of a paradox. When this was set up in the 1960s, scholars debated its nega-tive impact on LDCs in terms of the likely reduction of their agricul-tural exports to the EEC. At the time, they even saw this as one of the main reasons for advancing the Mansholt Plan – named after Dutch Commissioner for Agriculture Sicco Mansholt – to reform the CAP of December 1968, which was subsequently aborted. In contrast, histori-ans have predominately considered the CAP in terms of the struggles within the EEC over setting it up (Ludlow 2005b; Thiemeyer 2007). In 1970 Adrian Zeller (1970) criticized the CAP sharply for forcing some third country economies, such as Algerian wine production, to recon-vert their agricultural production at incredible domestic social costs, and for stimulating the overproduction in Europe of some commodities such as sugar while actually bargaining for an even further increase of

its international quota. In 1971, Pierre Uri (1971, 20), the French economist and long-standing and high-ranking civil servant at the European
level, summed up some of the contradictions of the CAP: 'With their
agricultural policies, industrialized countries are being drawn into a
vicious cycle: while contributing to the crash of world market prices,
they are forced to protect themselves against this development.' Ann-
Christina Knudsen (2001) has shown that in the Uruguay Round of the
GATT, concluded in 1994, international negotiations for the first time
precipitated a reform of the CAP to reduce overproduction and liberal-
ize somewhat international agricultural trade (see also Bianchi 2006).
In his autobiography, Edgar Pisani, the French minister of agriculture
from 1961 to 1966 and one of the main builders of the CAP, makes
no references whatsoever to the CAP's adverse impact on LDCs in the
1960s and 1970s (Pisani 2004). Pisani was subsequently a member of
the Brandt Commission – named after the former German federal chancellor Willy Brandt – which worked between 1977 and 1981, and he
became deeply involved in trying to redistribute wealth towards LCDs.
But researchers should not replicate the short-sighted view of the politicians at the time of the setting up of the CAP and analyse more fully the
external impact of the CAP and the resulting image of the EEC amongst
those most negatively affected by it.

Despite the negative impact of the CAP on third countries, not least
in Africa, the Community did create a development policy of sorts in
the 1960s. However, most authors see this policy from a normative perspective, implicitly or explicitly, as a kind of 'embryo' and precursor to
a more fully fledged European foreign policy. As such, it can only have
been a 'good thing'. Both Marie-Thérèse Bitsch in her introduction and
Anjo Harryvan and Jan van der Harst (2005, 319) in their contribution
to the book that resulted from the conference, *L'Europe unie et l'Afrique*,
argue that the failure of the colonial idea of *Eurafrique*, and the decision
by the EEC to sign the Yaoundé Association with some African countries in 1963, were 'the starting point of the fully-fledged development
policy of the present-day European Union'. Bossuat (2009a) has made
the same point about the alleged continuity between Yaoundé and the
later development policy. However, as Guido Thiemeyer (2005, 285) has
argued forcefully, 'All in all, European politicians in the second half of
1950 were still convinced of the superiority of Europe in relation to the
African continent. Moral arguments, which would come into politics
with the Foreign Assistance policy in the late 1960s, did not yet come
into plate.' In fact, the Yaoundé Association had little to do with development policy and the needs of the poor countries, and everything to do

with French national power, as demonstrated by Frédéric Turpin (2007), although his contribution still suffers from some confusion between Yaoundé and the Community's later relationship with the LDCs. Having said this, the debate on the continuity, if any, between Yaoundé and the later agreements of Lomé (1975–2000), reflect in interesting ways the transformation of European integration and its interpretation. Those authors who highlight the continuity in the Community's development policy are normally keen to attribute more importance to its institutional framework than the substance of the policy and its position relative to other policies. Yet, if historians were to examine trade and development policy in the 1960s in conjunction, as they should do, they would probably agree on the predominately mercantile nature of European integration in this decade.

There is in fact little evidence to suggest that, in the 1960s, the EEC as a whole or the Commission as an institution had any clear development policy towards LDCs. The concrete effects of the Yaoundé Association inside the African associated countries have not been sufficiently explored, not least due to great difficulties with accessing local archival sources. Overall, however, the evidence suggests that 'European' development policy was mainly a French policy, closely linked to French geo-political interests and only reluctantly accepted by its EEC partners, in particular Germany and the Netherlands, in order to avoid communist expansion in Africa and safeguard the common market politically. Indeed, the whole 'development' and 'aid' policies of western European countries in the 1960s were independent from one another. They were mostly of a bilateral nature and guided by national political and commercial interests (Schmidt and Pharo 2003; Calandri 2006).

Similarly, so far only limited research has been done on the perception of the role of the EEC in forums such as the United Nations Conference for Trade and Development (1964), where questions of trade and aid were discussed at length, the GATT, or the IMF during the debate over the reform the international monetary system and the possible introduction of Special Drawing Rights (Caviglia and Garavini 2009). Although all the EEC member states had to abandon their more or less developed 'imperial illusion' at the beginning of the 1960s and eventually came to argue in favour of ending every colonial experiment (with the exception of the EFTA member state Portugal), in nearly all international arenas the EEC was invariably seen by LDCs as the main conservative international actor – far more conservative in fact than the US (Vietnam notwithstanding), or the SU. As an Indian expert (Singh 1962, 265) put it in the early 1960s, '[if] countries like India feel apprehensive, it is not because they are fundamentally opposed to the idea of European integration, but because they feel that certain aspects of the arrangements for European integration suggest an inadequate appreciation of the needs of developing countries like India for higher export earning for financing their development plans'. This fact is rarely acknowledged by historians, who seem to forget the larger dimension of the North–South confrontation when analysing the Yaoundé Asscoiation and the complicated machinery of western European development policy (Garavini 2007).

The search for a common European identity after 1968

Few of the existing publications on the various external dimensions of European integration conceptualize the importance of the changing political and cultural climate around 1968 and the resulting weakening of the nation-state. However, Antonio Varsori (2007, 11–12) has stressed that the social and cultural turmoil of 1968, with the challenge it posed to the authority of the nation-state and nationalist ideology such as de Gaulle's, was probably one of the most important factors in initiating a substantial change of pace in European integration. The summit at The Hague in December 1969 was not just another summit of EEC leaders, and was not only a necessity stemming from the completion of the common market the year before. Instead, it implied the prospect of a new, more 'political' and 'cultural' form of European integration. Some authors discuss important transformations of the EC's external dimension after The Hague, especially concentrating on the enlargement to include Britain in 1972–73 and its symbolic significance as marking the end of a Gaullist Europe. Van der Harst (2003, 7) seems rather dismissive of the summit results concerning foreign policy, more particularly the European Political Cooperation (EPC), which resulted from the work of the Davignon committee – named after its chairman, the Director of Political Affairs in the Belgian Foreign Ministry, Etienne Davignon: 'The EPC ... turned into a low-key forum for co-ordination of foreign policies and never developed into a credible player in the global arena.'

On the contrary, the first half of the 1970s actually marked the period during which the EC, in particular through the actions of the new leaders of France (Georges Pompidou), Germany (Brandt) and Britain (Edward Heath), actually launched its most ambitious attempt to become a global actor, also actively trying to set new rules for the international economy. According to Daniel Möckli (2008, 1) this period of foreign policy activism in western Europe started in 1969, with the advent to power of the new political leaders, and it ended in 1974 when the EC states realigned themselves with the foreign policy preferences of the US: 'By 1973, the Europeans were already the single most effective actor group in the [Commission on Security and Cooperation in Europe] CSCE. They also became involved in the search for peace in the Middle East, negotiated with the US on a reorganization of the West and a new European-American bilateralism, issued a declaration on their common identity, and even discussed European defence cooperation.' However, as Möckli concludes, 'much of this proved unsustainable. Europe's quest for a distinct foreign policy provoked a sharp American reaction, with the severe transatlantic crisis of 1973/74'.

Not surprisingly, the definition by François Duchêne (1973) of the EC as 'civilian actor' dates back to 1972 at the height of its new foreign policy ambitions. At this time, too, the Soviet Union could no longer afford aggressive opposition to the EC and, albeit reluctantly, had to acknowledge the latter's existence (Yamamoto 2007). From this perspective, historians will find it hard to agree to American political scientist Stanley Hoffmann's recent restatement (2000, 200) of the empty contemporary idea of the 1970s as a period of 'Eurosclerosis': 'In the period that followed de Gaulle's resignation, some steps were taken toward a common diplomatic approach on some issues (especially the Arab-Israeli conflict), but they remained timid, limited to declarations, declamations and deplorations.'

The creation of the EPC in fact marked an effort by the member states to cooperate outside the Community legal framework in the field of foreign policy. Most authors argue that several motives combined to bring about the formation of the EPC: the weakening of the American model, the Federal Republic's need to counterbalance its new *Ostpolitik*, the effort by the Brandt government to normalize relations with eastern Europe and at the same time gain more freedom to manoeuvre in the Third World, with a stronger western European engagement, the prospect of the enlargement of the EC and its becoming the world's largest trading block (Möckli 2007; Zampoli 2007). Once set up, the EPC's main focus was firstly, to foster East–West dialogue in the context of the CSCE process from 1972 to 1975. Secondly, the EC states were keen to instigate a mutually beneficial economic and political dialogue in the Mediterranean region and the Middle East. Historians argue (Romano 2009) that coordination by the nine EC states in the context of the CSCE was a resounding success. Some even go as far as to argue that the EC states exercised the strongest influence over the negotiations.

After all, they managed to insert the reference to human rights into the Helsinki Final Act of 1975 – an accomplishment that would eventually make it easier for the opposition to the communist regimes in eastern Europe to articulate their demands by drawing upon this international legal framework. In fact, the Commission also played a bigger role during the negotiations than originally anticipated, when its representation was to be limited to partaking in the negotiation of trade-related issues. Indirectly, the Soviet Union also recognized the Community, not just the nine member states, as a partner in the negotiations. At the same time, although the western Europeans were far keener than the US to debate human rights in the CSCE, they were also extremely prudent after 1975 in their use of the human rights clauses to attack the Soviet Union, which could have endangered the much craved for détente.

So far historians have done much less research on the EC states' cooperation with Mediterranean countries, although by 1971 the EC actually had agreements with all but three of the 17 countries along its shores. In fact, at the Paris summit of 1972 the nine EC states openly declared their ambition to build what they called a Global Mediterranean Policy. Subsequently, the EC concluded seven cooperation agreements with Mediterranean countries between 1975 and 1977. Arguably, these agreements at least amounted to Global Mediterranean Policy on a smaller scale. However, it is not clear who was the driving force, whether it was the Commission, negotiating 'on behalf of the member states' on trade issue, or the EPC, and indeed if the Community as a whole had any strategy at all. As part of its approach to the Mediterranean, the EC also fostered the so-called Euro-Arab dialogue after the 1973 oil crisis. Various studies, most of them by political scientists, not historians, agree that the Arab League was more interested in political dialogue, while the EC, due to internal differences and violent American opposition to what the administration in Washington saw as the EC's pro-Palestinian attitude, had to limit itself to economic dialogue. This dialogue produced several declarations in favour of the rights of the Palestinians, but the EC and other western European countries had to leave the peace-making process in the region entirely to the US (Bourrinet 1979; Allen 2008).

The Community also deepened its relations with LDCs after the summit at The Hague. The intensification of relations resulted from internal pressures within the EC, from shifting public opinion concerning the so-called Third World and its dire problems, but also from the increasing radicalization of the LDCs, which western Europe saw as a threat during the Cold War. In the first half of the 1970s the EC developed its regional dimensions, developing further its existing links with African and, to a lesser extent, Mediterranean countries, and the global dimension of its development policy, launching for the first time what became known as the Global Development Policy. Jean-Marie Palayret has demonstrated the crucial influence of LDCs and of the debate over a New International Economic Order (NIEO) in the negotiating process leading up to the signing of the Lomé Convention between 1974 and 1975. At the time, many in Europe thought of Lomé as a revolution. In fact, Commission President François-Xavier Ortoli called it a 'turning point in history', which had not been the perception of the previous Yaoundé Association. Indeed, the Lomé Convention differed markedly from previous agreements in that it created a mixed group of francophone and anglophone African Caribbean and Pacific (ACP) countries bargaining together with the EC. It also abolished inverse preferences, created the so-called STABEX mechanism to stabilize export earnings of ACP countries from the sale of raw materials, and saw the Commission play a new and central role in the negotiations (Palayret 2006; Migani 2008b). To date, however, historians have not done much research on the creation of the System of Generalized Preferences in1971, which helped the EC to create a preferential trade system with the LDCs. In any case, the debate within the Community between 'regionalists' and 'globalists' after the Lomé Convention seems to have shifted slightly in favour of the globalist vision, which was also reflected in the creation in 1977 of a development policy for countries not associated with the Community (Calandri 2009). Yet much research remains to be done in particular on the shift in the second half of the 1970s from mainly bilateral development and aid policies to much stronger reliance on multilateral economic institutions such as the World Bank and the IMF.

After the oil shock in 1973 western Europe saw a heated debate among political scientists, policy experts and politicians over the challenge posed by a common front of oil producing and developing countries in their battle for a NIEO (Wessels 1977). Research on the NIEO was conducted by social scientists at the time, but has been neglected by historians. Understanding the failure of a NIEO in the 1970s is crucial, however, for conceptualizing the re-launch of globalization in the 1980s, which was mainly driven by neo-liberal economic policies, and also of the re-launching of European institutions. In the 1970s, the EC states were at the forefront of the debates about transforming the global economic order. Their leaders saw the Community as a strategic tool for a European way out of the international economic crisis of the 1970s. The Tindemans Report of 1975, named after Belgian Prime Minister Leo Tindemans, also considered a common European position on the

North–South confrontation as indispensable. In fact, the EC organized a joint representation at the Conference for International Economic Cooperation (CIEC) between 1975 and 1977, also called North–South Dialogue (Garavini 2009a). From 1977 onwards the Commission also represented the Community, alongside the member states Germany, France, Britain and Italy, at the G7 summits of the most industrialized countries created in 1975 (Garavini 2006). Indeed, the EC was at the centre of every attempt to reform international economic institutions and increase expenditure on LDCs. In the end, however, it failed to achieve a more comprehensive reform of the international monetary system, and eventually had to withdraw to the regional project of the European Monetary System (EMS) created in 1978–79. In fact, the EMS was at the same time an effort to save the common market from protectionist tendencies and monetary turmoil and reflected that the Europeans were now calculating with floating currencies and long-term financial instability at a global level. Up to now none of the studies of the origins of the EMS has analysed this important international dimension of the European solution to monetary instability.

Nearer to home, the Community increasingly also had to develop a strategy for its enlargement. British accession in 1973 changed the EC, but how and to what extent is not clear, no more than how much it changed Britain. As Johnny Laursen (2009a, 290) has recently argued, '[t]he consequences of enlargement on the Community are fairly well described in broad syntheses on development of the EC, but hardly based on a critical mass of empirical research. Too little is simply still known on the adaptation of the Community institutions to the broader number of members.' The first enlargement established a model for future negotiations (for example, Poggiolini 2004). However, the degree to which EC membership actually 'Europeanized' Britain, for example by strengthening demands for decentralization that eventually happened with devolution after 1997, requires much more research on long-term change (Kaiser 1998).

The second EC enlargement to include the southern European countries Greece (1981) and Spain and Portugal (1986) clearly had a much more substantial impact on these new economically underdeveloped member states that had only emerged from dictatorships in 1974–75 (Tsoukalis 1981; Morlino 1998; Costa Pinto and Teixeira 2002). Politically, the study of the transformations in southern Europe remains a delicate matter as long as some Spanish and Portuguese historians still fear that analysing the European dimensions of these processes could call into question the idea of 'national revolutions'. Nevertheless, historians have begun to study the transition, democratization and EC accession process, addressing the role of the EC institutions and member states and the more informal transnational politics of European political parties and leaders, emphasizing especially the role of European socialists in facilitating the eventual election of socialist governments in Spain in 1982 and in Portugal and Greece in 1983 (Trouvé 2008). However, until the beginning of the 1970s the EC and its member states did not strongly support democratization in Spain and Portugal. The majority of European leaders were quite satisfied to negotiate and make trade arrangements with the strongly anti-communist authoritarian regimes of the Iberian peninsula. The initiative to provide massive support for the democratic parties, which existed in Spain before 1974–75, but not in Portugal, was a late decision stemming from the speed of the collapse of the Portuguese regime and the need to minimize the danger of a communist takeover in the region (Muñoz-Sánchez 2009).

All in all, the role of the EC and of its institutions, especially the Commission, in external relations, was significantly strengthened in the 1970s, and the former French opposition to supranational decision-making on international economic issues virtually disappeared. Progress on foreign policy cooperation was much more limited, however. It is true that the EC and its member states played a crucial role in the CSCE process. The Community also sought to activate the new EPC to create the Euro-Arab dialogue. The EC came under less fire for its alleged policy of neo-colonialism than in the 1960s, but its perception in third countries, especially outside of Europe, has not been studied by historians. Arguably, the years between 1975 and 1977 could be considered as the high point for the Community's external representation. In 1975 it participated in the signing of the Lomé Convention and the Helsinki Final Act, and the EC also spoke with one voice in the CIEC in Paris. In 1977, finally, it became fully included in the G7, which reflected its ambition to be much more than an international organization and to play a direct role in international economic relations and politics. By the end of the 1970s, however, the EPC looked quite weak, especially in relation to the much greater ambitions of European leaders after the summit at The Hague.

New research on the external dimension of the EU

Until recently most historians have focused on the member states, the ministries for foreign affairs and to some extent, the role of the European Commission in the evolving external relations of the present-day EU.

Just as in the case of the domestic development of the Community, however, limiting the analysis to policy-making by diplomats and officials in Brussels does not allow a broader conceptualization of the transformations and policy developments discussed above. In particular, historians need to study further the role of new political, social and economic actors. Without a better understanding of the role of these new actors, even in the field of foreign relations, it will be impossible to assess appropriately the shifts that took place in the EC's external policies. For example, historians would have to explore the changing ideology and policy preferences of European political parties and trade unions and the shifts in public opinion, influenced to a certain extent by the 'Third-Worldism' of the 1968 student movements, to explain satisfactorily the declaration at the end of the summit in Paris in 1972 that the EC should become 'the developing countries'' most understanding partner'. Like the EC's internal developments, its external policies cannot be explained as a technical aspect of European integration. Instead, as other authors like Kaiser, Morten Rasmussen and Lorenzo Mechi also argue in their chapters in this book, it has to be understood in the context of the political, socio-economic and cultural history of contemporary Europe more generally.

Especially in the first half of the 1970s trade unions and their international organizations exerted a strong influence over national governments whose survival to some extent hinged on avoiding too much disruption and pressure from strike action, as British Conservative Prime Minister Heath found when he lost two national elections in 1974. The trade unions managed in particular to influence the opening towards the demands from LDCs before 1973 and later, the emphasis on regional socio-economic development in the context of the single market programme. As is also discussed by Mechi in his chapter, historians have begun to study the role of the International Confederation of Free Trade Unions (Ciampani 2000), but more research should be done on the role of the European Trade Unions Confederation officially formed in 1974, whose foreign policy programme and initiatives (Dølvik 1999) were not necessarily ineffective only because the organization was internally fragmented.

Similarly, historians will find it difficult to conceptualize adequately the evolving transatlantic relationship or the EC's policies towards the LDCs without understanding the history and preferences of the main political party groups in Europe. Significant research has been done on Christian democratic parties and their networks (Lamberts 1997; Kaiser 2007), although it is mostly not focused specifically on their non-European foreign policies (but see, for example, Kaiser 2003). Research on the networks of European socialist parties is less developed for the time being (Devin 1993; Sassoon 1997). In a book about the 'globalization' of Christian democracy and socialism up to 1965, however, Peter Van Kemseke (2006) has shown, for example, why the EEC member states could not have devised a serious European development policy by the early 1960s. At the time, socialist thinking evolved around Walt Rostow's ideas in *The Stages of Economic Growth* (1960). Socialists were mainly interested in productivity and growth, not global redistribution. Similarly, the Christian democrats were preoccupied with the integration of the European economy and the battle against communism. Think-tanks linked to, or even created by political parties played an increasingly important role in foreign policy formulation. One excellent case in point is the German Friedrich Ebert Foundation linked to the German social democrats and its influence on German and European foreign policy in the 1970s. This foundation developed initiatives ranging from polices towards the LDCs to how to deal with the aftermath of the energy crisis in 1973 and supporting and influencing socialist parties in the democratic transition in Spain and Portugal (Kaiser and Salm 2009).

While research on the growing role of the Commission in the EC's external relations has grown, historians should arguably pay more attention to the role of leading individuals as policy entrepreneurs, something that social science research in the 1970s neglected completely. Some research has been done on the first Commission President, Walter Hallstein (Loth, Wallace and Wessels 1998), and also on Delors, who led the Commission from 1985 to 1995. However, very little is known about other presidents of the Commission or single commissioners, in this case especially those with responsibility for foreign relations. The book on the European Commission between 1958 and 1972 edited by Michel Dumoulin (2007) brings out the crucial role played by Commissioners like Franco Maria Malfatti and Mansholt in international economic politics. The proposal by US President Richard Nixon to call the GATT negotiations following the Kennedy Round the Malfatti Round might have been intended as a provocation, but it also reflects the growing role of the Commission in the EC's foreign relations, especially in trade policy. Similarly, the French Commissioner Claude Cheysson played a leading role in the North–South dialogue, which is central to our understanding of this policy field, as is that of the British Commission President Roy Jenkins in the battle to obtain a seat for the EC at the table of the G7 countries (Adonis and Thomas 2004).

Alongside research on the role of trade unions, political parties and individual actors in European institutions in the EC's foreign relations, historians will also have to conceptualize the influence of the new social movements, especially the student and worker movements in 1968, and their impact on the search for a European international as well as domestic identity that would be very different from the American and Soviet models. More recently, the EU's Marie Curie programme has funded a large-scale research network entitled *European Protest Movements since the Cold War. The Rise of a (Trans-)national Civil Society and the Transformation of the Public Sphere after 1945*, with several conferences and publications, but minor involvement of historians. From the limited research that has been done, however, it seems that the direct and indirect impact of the new social movements on European integration and the evolution of new policies, also in the field of the EC's external relations, has been underestimated, not least due to the lack of knowledge of the present-day EU among most of those social scientists who have dominated social movement research since the 1970s.

Arguably, public opinion also had an increasing influence on foreign relations from the 1970s onwards, as foreign policy became somewhat less elite-dominated in most western European countries and increasingly hotly debated, whether concerning North–South issues or the nuclear arms race, for example. Historical research could aim to assess how shifts in public opinion might have confined the options open to EC foreign policy-making elites and their diplomacy. As a useful starting point Brunello Vigezzi (1985) compiled a book in which historians, especially of international relations, took up the challenge of studying cultural dimensions and public opinion, and how they relate to and influence (foreign) policy-making. Henk Wesseling (1985) has shown just how difficult it was for Dutch citizens to abandon resentment over the loss of the colonies and how little colonialism and its evils were debated there well into the 1960s. This in turn clearly had an impact on the prevailing thinking about development issues. This and similar types of research could in future embed the study of the Community's foreign relations much more in broader socio-economic and cultural trends than traditional diplomatic studies have done, which rely exclusively on state and foreign ministry sources.

Conclusion

From its origins in 1957–58, the present-day EU had a distinctive external dimension, which has developed in parallel and was intertwined with the foreign policies of its member states. Unfortunately, since it is especially indispensable for historians of foreign relations to consult the archives of EC institutions and member states, which generally operate a 30-year rule for access to sources, most historical research on the external relations of the EC has been limited to the period up to the late 1970s. As time goes by, historians will begin to address other issues which played such an important role in the 1980s and 1990s, including the EU's policy towards the transformation and collapse of the Soviet bloc and its attractiveness for the formerly communist Europe and its citizens; the process of Eastern enlargement; the EU's contribution to globalization and the management of the international institutions that govern it; and the impact of the Euro on the international economic environment (Nuttal 2000).

Together with these and other thematic challenges, the future also holds several dangers for historical research on the EU's external relations, especially for the period after the Maastricht Treaty came into force in 1993. The most serious of these is the normative danger of falling into the trap of considering European integration as a positive outcome in itself, and thus to view everything it has produced or encouraged, as civilized, peaceful and positive for the rest of the world. In fact, a fairly consistent body of literature mostly written by social scientists exists already, very much welcome in Brussels policy-making circles and dangerously appealing even to historians, which considers the EU with very positive connotations as a 'dream' (Rifkin 2004), 'civilian power' (Telò 2006), 'normative power' (Padoa Schioppa 2007), 'model of constitutional patriotism' (Habermas 2001) fit for export or even, as the 'power that will run the 21st century' (Leonard 2005). However, Mark Mazower (2008) has recently warned against considering or recommending Europe and the EU as a model for the rest of the world. While there may be some truth in the conceptualizations of the EU and its external role listed above, they need to be thoroughly tested against the EU's actual external policies and their local effects, not used to fit the politically desired projection. Any serious study of the EU's external dimension needs to compare the EU's ambitions and rhetoric with its image abroad and the positions of other countries and people, including, for example, the views of African immigrants of the Schengen Agreement – originally signed in 1985 by five of the then ten EC member states to provide for the abolition of border controls – and their impact on immigration policy; the perception of the impact of the CAP in countries like Brazil or India; Serb views of the EU's role in the Balkan region; and other regions' attitudes to the EU's policy of exporting its model of regional integration to the rest of the word (Lucarelli 2007). Contradictions between the EU's ambitions and rhetoric and the reality of its international impact are routinely overlooked, but will have to be fully integrated into any historical narrative of the EU's external dimension. During the 1980s a network of European think-tanks stressed what they believed was the growing role of economics and the decreasing role of politics in the contemporary world, and the re-launching of European integration with the Single Market Programme seemed to be a case in point. In reality, however, the single market and subsequently, the transformation of the EC into the EU with the Maastricht Treaty were intrinsically political projects that generated economic winners and losers inside and outside Europe.

While historians are devoting increasing attention to the external dimension of European integration, their research still has some shortcomings. Arguably, their main achievement to date is to have shown that writing about the foreign policy of western European nation-states from the 1960s, without fully taking into account the context of European integration and the EEC and its institutions, is futile and will produce highly misleading narratives. At the same time, however, as the example of historical research on European development policy demonstrates very well, historians tend to underestimate discontinuities such as, for example, between the Yaoundé Association and the Lomé Conventions. So far most research has also not yet adequately taken into account the broader international context in which EC policies evolved and in which its own progressive enlargements took place. In particular, it should be evident that no serious narrative of the EC's external relations up to the 1980s is possible without organic reference to the Cold War and to the North–South conflict between developed countries and the LDCs (Garavini 2009b). Moreover, not even those external policies that appear to be of a predominantly 'technical' character like trade and monetary policy, can be adequately understood without understanding more fully political and cultural shifts and changing public opinion within the member states and in the EU as a whole.

It is clear from the above that research on the EC's external dimension will often have to take the form of collaborative work to do justice to all of these crucial interlinked dimensions. Ultimately, however, no account, however sophisticated, will be able to fully explain western European foreign policy in its entirety – not only because the member states continued to have their national priorities and policies, but also because they have participated separately in important international organizations such as NATO, the World Bank or the IMF on which historical research is arguably lagging behind that on European integration (Dülffer 2009).

Bibliography

Abelshauser, Werner (1995). The Re-entry of West Germany into the International Economy and Early European Integration, in Clemens Wurm (ed.), *Western Europe and Germany. The Beginnings of European integration 1945–1960*, Oxford: Berg, 27–53.

Adonis, Andrew and Keith Thomas (eds) (2004). *Roy Jenkins. A Retrospective*, Oxford: OUP.

Affinito, Michele, Guia Migani and Christian Wenkel (eds) (2009). *Les deux Europes*, Brussels and Berne: PIE-Peter Lang.

Albertini, Mario (2007a [1959]). *Tutti gli scritti*, vol. 3, *1958–1961*, ed. Nicoletta Mosconi, Bologna: Il Mulino.

Albertini, Mario (2007b [1964]). *Tutti gli scritti*, vol. 4, *1962–1964*, ed. Nicoletta Mosconi, Bologna: Il Mulino.

Alesina, Alberto and Edward Glaeser (2004). *Fighting Poverty in the US and Europe. A World of Difference*, Oxford: OUP.

Allen, David (2008). The Euro-Arab Dialogue, *Journal of Common Market Studies*, vol. 16, no. 4, 323–42.

Ambrose, Stephen E. and Douglas G. Brinkley (1997). *Rise to Globalism. American Foreign Policy since 1938*, New York: Penguin.

Anderson, Benedict (1983). *Imagined Communities. Reflections on the Origin and Spread of Nationalism*, London: Verso.

Andresen-Leitao, Nicolau (2001). Portugal's European Integration Policy, 1945–72, *Journal of European Integration History*, vol. 7, no. 1, 25–36.

Angerer, Thomas (1998). Exklusivität und Selbstausschließung. Integrationsgeschichtliche Überlegungen zur Erweiterungsfrage am Beispiel Frankreichs und Österreichs, *Revue d'Europe Centrale*, vol. 6, no. 1, 25–54.

Angerer, Thomas (2001). Gegenwärtiges Zeitalter – gegenwärtiges Menschenalter. Neuzeit und Zeitgeschichte im begriffsgeschichtlichen Zusammenhang, *Wiener Zeitschrift zur Geschichte der Neuzeit*, vol. 1, no. 1, 114–33.

Apeldoorn, Bastiaan van (2002). *Transnational Capitalism and the Struggle over European Integration*, London: Routledge.

Arfè, Gaetano (1989). *L'integrazione europea nella storiografia italiana del dopoguerra*, in Valerio Grementieri and Antonio Papisca (eds), *Europa 1992: le sfide per la ricerca e l'Università*, Milan: Giuffré, 245–62.

Artaud, Denise (1982). Le Grand Dessein de J. F. Kennedy: proposition mythique ou occasion manquée, *Revue d'Histoire Moderne et Contemporaine*, vol. 29, no. 2, 235–66.

Ash, Timothy Garton (2005). *Free World*, London: Penguin.

Audland, Christopher (2007). The Historical Archives of the European Union. Their Opening to the Public, Management and Accessibility, *Journal of the Society of Archivists*, vol. 28, no. 2, 177–92.

Badel, Laurence (1994). Le Quai d'Orsay, les associations privées et l'Europe, in Gérard Bossuat and René Girault (eds), *Europe brisée, Europe retrouvée: nouvelles réflexions sur l'unité européenne au XXè siècle*, Paris: Publications de la Sorbonne, 109–32.

Badel, Laurence (1998). *Un milieu liberal et européen. Le grand commerce français 1925–1948*, Paris: Comité pour l'histoire économique et financière.

Badel, Laurence et al. (2004). Cercles et milieux économiques, in Robert Frank (ed.), *Les identités européennes au XXe siècle*, Paris: Publications de la Sorbonne, 13–46.

Badel, Laurence, Stanislas Jeannesson, and N. Piers Ludlow (eds) (2005). *Les administrations nationales et la construction européenne. Une approche historique (1919–1975)*, Brussels: PIE-Peter Lang.

Bailey, Joe (ed.) (1998). *Social Europe*, London and New York: Longman.

Baisnée, Olivier (2007). The European Public Sphere Does Not Exist (At Least It's Worth Wondering...), *European Journal of Communication*, vol. 22, no. 4, 493–503.

Bajon, Philip (2009). The European Commissioners and the Empty Chair Crisis of 1965–66, *Journal of European Integration History*, vol. 15, no. 2, 105–25.

Ballini, Pier Luigi and Antonio Varsori (eds) (2004). *L'Italia e l'Europa (1947–1979)*, vol. 1, Soveria Mannelli: Rubbettino.

Bauerkämper, Arnd and Hartmut Kaelble (eds) (2010). *Die Europäische Union und ihre Gesellschaft*, Stuttgart: Franz Steiner.

Becker, Josef and Franz Knipping (eds) (1986). *Power in Europe?*, vol. 1, *Great Britain, France, Italy and Germany in a Postwar World 1945–1950*, Berlin and New York: W. De Gruyter.

Bellier, Irène and Thomas M. Wilson (eds) (2000). *An Anthropology of the European Union. Building, Imagining and Experiencing the New Europe*, Oxford: Berg.

Benz, Wolfgang (1990). Kurt Schumachers Europakonzeption, in Ludolf Herbst, Werner Bührer and Hanno Sowade (eds), *Vom Marshallplan zur EWG. Die Eingliederung der Bundesrepublik Deutschland in die westliche Welt*, Munich: Oldenbourg, 47–61.

Benzoni, Mathilde and Brunello Vigezzi (eds) (2001). *Storia e storici d'Europa nel XX secolo*, Milan: Unicopli.

Berstein, Serge, Pierre Milza and Jean-Louis Bianco (eds) (2001). *Les années Mitterrand, les années du changement*, Paris: Perrin.

Bettin Lattes, Gianfranco and Ettore Recchi (eds) (2005). *Comparing European Societies. Towards a Sociology of the EU*, Bologna: Monduzzi.

Beugel, Ernst van der (1966). *From Marshall Aid to Atlantic Partnership. European Integration as a Concern of American Foreign Policy*, Amsterdam: Elsevier.

Bianchi, Daniela (2006). *La PAC toute la PAC, rien d'autre que la PAC!*, Brussels: Bruylant.

Bitsch, Marie-Thérèse (1986). Le rôle de la France dans la naissance du Conseil de l'Europe, in Raymond Poidevin (ed.), *Origins of the European Integration, March 1948–May 1950*, Brussels: Bruylant, 165–98.

Bitsch, Marie-Thérèse (2001). *Le couple France-Allemagne et les institutions européennes: une postérité pour le plan Schuman?*, Brussels: Bruylant.

Bitsch, Marie-Thérèse (2005), Introduction, in eadem and Gérard Bossuat (eds), *L'Europe unie et l'Afrique. De l'idée d'Eurafrique à la Convention de Lomé I*, Brussels: Bruylant, 1–6.

Bitsch, Marie-Thérèse (2008). *Histoire de la construction européenne de 1945 à nos jours*, Brussels: Ed. Complexe.

Bitsch, Marie-Thérèse and Gérard Bossuat (eds) (2005). *L'Europe unie et l'Afrique. De l'idée d'Euroafrique à la convention de Lomé I*, Brussels: Bruylant.

Bitsch, Marie-Thérèse, Wilfried Loth and Charles Barthel (eds) (2007). *Cultures politiques, opinion publiques et intégration européenne*, Brussels: Bruylant.

Bitsch, Marie-Thérèse, Wilfried Loth and Raymond Poidevin (eds) (1998). *Institutions européennes et identités européennes*, Brussels: Bruylant.

Boerger-De Smedt, Anne (1996). Aux origines de l'union européenne. La genèse des institutions communautaires (CECA, CED, CEE et Euratom) un équilibre fragile entre l'idéal européen et les intérêts nationaux, PhD, Liège: University of Liège.

Boerger-De Smedt, Anne (2007). Derrière la valse des chiffres. Retour sur les origines de la composition de l'exécutif européen, *Journal of European Integration History*, vol. 13, no. 1, 25–48.

Bosco, Andrea (1989). *Lord Lothian. Un pioniere del federalismo, 1882–1940*, Milan: Jaca Book.

Bossuat, Gérard (1988). La politique française de libération des échanges en Europe et le Plan Schuman (1950–1951), in Klaus Schwabe (ed.), *The Beginnings of the Schuman-Plan 1950/51*, Baden-Baden: Nomos, 319–32.

Bossuat, Gérard (1992). *La France, l'aide américaine et la construction européenne 1944–1954*, Paris: Ministère de l'Économie et des Finances.

Bossuat, Gérard (1993). La vraie nature de la politique européenne de la France (1950–1957), in Gilbert Trausch (ed.), *The European Integration from the Schuman-Plan to the Treaties of Rome*, Baden-Baden: Nomos, 191–230.

Bossuat, Gérard (1999). Des lieux de mémoire pour l'Europe unie, *Vingtième Siècle. Revue d'histoire*, vol. 61, no. 1, 56–69.

Bossuat, Gérard (2001a). *Les fondateurs de l'Europe unie*, Paris: Belin.

Bossuat, Gérard (2001b). De Gaulle et la seconde candidature britannique aux Communautés européennes (1966–1969), in Wilfried Loth (ed.), *Crises and Compromises. The European Project 1963–1969*, Baden-Baden: Nomos, 511–38.

Bossuat, Gérard (2005). *Faire l'Europe sans défaire la France. 60 ans de politique d'unité européenne des gouvernements et des présidents de la République française (1943–2003)*, Berne: Peter Lang.

Bossuat, Gérard (2006). La culture de l'unité européenne des élites françaises aux Communautés européennes, in Antonio Varsori (ed.), *Inside the European Community. Actors and Policies in the European Integration 1957–1972*, Baden-Baden: Nomos, 55–78.

Bossuat, Gérard (2009a). Europe as an International Actor. Origins and Development of the External Personality of the European Community, in Wilfried Loth (ed.), *Experiencing Europe. 50 Years of European Construction 1957–2007*, Baden-Baden: Nomos, 217–54.

Bossuat, Gérard (2009b). Face à l'histoire! Les décideurs politiques français et la naissance des traités de Rome, in Michael Gehler (ed.), *Vom gemeinsamen Markt zur europäischen Unionsbildung. 50 Jahre Römische Verträge 1957–2007*, Vienna, Cologne and Weimar: Böhlau, 147–68.

Bossuat, Gérard (ed.) (2006). *L'Europe et la mondialisation*, Paris: Editions Soleb.

Bourrinet, Jacques (ed.) (1979). *Le dialogue euro-arabe*, Paris: Economica.

Bozo, Frédéric et al. (eds) (2008). *Europe and the End of the Cold War. A Reappraisal*, London: Routledge.

Braga, Antonella (2007). *Un federalista giacobino. Ernesto Rossi pioniere degli Stati Uniti d'Europa*, Bologna: Il Mulino.

Branner, Hans (1993). På vagt eller på spring? Danmark og europæisk Integration 1948–1953, in Birgit Nüchel Thomsen (ed.), *The Odd Man Out? Danmark og den europæiske integration 1948–1992*, Odense: Odense Universitetsforlag, 29–64.

Brenke, Gabriele (1994). Europakonzeptionen im Widerstreit. Die Freihandelszonen-Verhandlungen 1956–1958, *Vierteljahrshefte für Zeitgeschichte*, vol. 42, no. 4, 595–633.

Bretherton, Charlotte and John Vogler (2006). *The European Union as a Global Actor*, London: Routledge.

Bruck, Elke (2003). *François Mitterrands Deutschlandbild. Perzeption und Politik im Spannungsfeld deutschland-, europa- und sicherheitspolitischer Entscheidungen 1989–1992*, Frankfurt am Main: Peter Lang.

Brugmans, Henri (1970). *L'idée européenne 1920–1970*, Bruges: De Tempel.

Brusse, Wendy Asbeek (1997). *Tariffs, Trade and European Integration, 1947–1957. From Study Group to Common Market*, London: Macmillan.

Bühlbäcker, Bernd (2007). *Europa im Aufbruch. Personal und Personalpolitik deutscher Parteien und Verbände in der Montanunion 1949–1958*, Essen: Klartext.

Bührer, Werner (1995). German Industry and European Integration in the 1950s, in Clemens Wurm (ed.), *Western Europe and Germany. The Beginnings of European Integration 1945–1960*, Oxford: Berg, 87–114.

Bührer, Werner (1997). *Westdeutschland in der OEEC. Eingliederung, Krise, Bewährung 1947–1961*, Munich: Oldenbourg.

Bührer, Werner (1999). Dirigismus und europäische Integration. Jean Monnet aus der Sicht der deutschen Industrie, in Andreas Wilkens (ed.), *Interessen verbinden. Jean Monnet und die europäische Integration der Bundesrepublik Deutschland*, Bonn: Bouvier, 205–24.

Bullen, Roger (1988). The British Government and the Schuman Plan May 1950 – March 1951, in Klaus Schwabe (ed.), *The Beginnings of the Schuman-Plan 1950/51*, Baden-Baden: Nomos, 199–210.

Bullen, Roger (1989). Great Britain and the Treaty of Rome, in Enrico Serra (ed.), *The Relaunching of Europe and the Treaties of Rome*, Brussels: Bruylant, 315–38.

Buller, Jim (2000). *National Statecraft and European Integration. The Conservative Government and the European Union, 1979–1997*, London: Pinter.

Bulmer, Simon (1983). Domestic Politics and European Community Policy-making, *Journal of Common Market Studies*, vol. 21, no. 4, 349–63.

Burgess, Michael (1995). *The British Tradition of Federalism*, Leicester: Leicester UP.

Burgess, Michael (2000). *Federalism and European Union. The Building of Europe*, London: Routledge.

Burgess, Michael (2006). *Comparative Federalism. Theory and Practice*, London and New York: Routledge.

Bussière, Éric (1992). *La France, la Belgique et l'organisation économique de l'Europe 1918–1935*, Paris: Comité pour l'histoire économique et financière.

Bussière, Éric (1997). Les milieux économiques face à l'Europe au XXe siècle, *Journal of European Integration History*, vol. 3, no. 2, 5–21.

Bussière, Éric (2006). Conclusions, in Eric Bussière, Michel Dumoulin and Sylvain Schirmann (eds), *Europe organisée, Europe du libre-échange? Fin XIXe siècle – années 1960*, Brussels: Peter Lang, 251–4.

Bussière, Éric, Michel Dumoulin and Sylvain Schirmann (eds) (2006a). *Europe organisée, Europe du libre-échange? Fin XIXe siècle – années 1960*, Brussels: Peter Lang.

Bussière, Eric, Michel Dumoulin and Sylvain Schirmann (eds) (2006b). *Milieux économiques et intégration européenne au 20 siècle. La crise des années 1970: de la conférence de la Haye è la veille de la relance des années 1980*, Berne and Brussels: PIE-Peter Lang.

Bussière, Éric, Michel Dumoulin and Sylvain Schirmann (eds) (2007). *Milieux économiques et intégration européenne au XXe siècle. La relance des années quatre-vingt (1979–1992)*, Paris: Comité pour l'Histoire Economique et Financière de la France.

Bussière, Éric, Michel Dumoulin and Silvain Schirmann (2009). The Development of Economic Integration, in Wilfried Loth (ed.), *Experiencing Europe. 50 Years of European Construction, 1957–2007*, Baden-Baden: Nomos, 45–101.

Calandri, Elena (1997). *Il mediterraneo e la difesa dell'occidente, 1947–1956. Eredità imperiali e logiche du guerre fredda*, Florence: Manent.

Calandri, Elena (2006). L'Italia e l'assistenza allo sviluppo dal neoatlantismo alla Conferenza di Cancun del 1981, in Federico Romero and Antonio Varsori (eds), *Nazione, interdipendenza, integrazione. Le relazioni internazionali dell'Italia (1917–1989)*, vol. 2, Rome: Carocci, 253–71.

Calandri, Elena (ed.) (2009). *Europa e intervento per lo sviluppo dal Trattato di Roma al dopo-Cotonou*, Milan: Franco Angeli.

Calleo, David (2001). *Rethinking Europe's Future*, Princeton, NJ: Princeton UP.

Campbell, Alan and Dennis Thompson (1962). *Common Market Law. Texts and Commentaries*, London: Stevens.

Camps, Miriam (1964). *Britain and the European Community 1955–1963*, Princeton, NJ: Princeton UP.

Canavero, Alfredo and Jean-Dominique Durand (eds) (1999). *Il fattore religioso nell'integrazione europea*, Milan: Unicopli.

Caraffini, Paolo (2008). *Costruire l'Europa dal basso. Il ruolo del Consiglio italiano del Movimento europeo (1948–1985)*, Bologna: Il Mulino.

Carr, E. H. (2001 [1961]). *What Is History?* 3rd edn, London: Palgrave.

Caviglia, Daniele and Giuliano Garavini (2009). Generosi ma non troppo. La Cee, i Paesi in via di sviluppo, e i negoziati sulla riforma del Sistema monetario internazionale (1958–1976), in Elena Calandri (ed.), *La Comunità europea e i Paesi in via di sviluppo*, Milan: Franco Angeli, 53–89.

Chiti Batelli, Andrea (1979). *Dalle elezioni dirette alla federazione europea*, Florence: Le Monnier.

Chiti Batelli, Andrea (1989). *L'idea d'Europa nel pensiero di Altiero Spinelli*, Manduria: Lacaita.

Ciampani, Andrea (1995). Il dilemma dell''Europa sindacale' tra cooperazi-one ed integrazione europea. L'Organizzazione Regionale Europea della 'Confederazione Internazionale dei Sindacati Liberi' (1950–1957), in idem (ed.), *L'altra via per l'Europa: forze sociali e organizzazione degli interessi nell'integrazione europea (1947–1957)*, Milan: Franco Angeli, 200–29.

Ciampani, Andrea (2000). La Cisl tra integrazione europea e mondializzazi-one. Profilo storico del 'sindacato nuovo' nelle relazioni internazionali: dalla Conferenza di Londra al Trattato di Amsterdam, Rome: Edizioni Lavoro.

Ciampani, Andrea (ed.) (1995). *L'altra via per l'Europa. Forze sociali e organizzazi-one degli interessi nell'integrazione europea (1947–1957)*, Milan: Franco Angeli.

Clark, Ian (1994). *Nuclear Diplomacy and the Special Relationship. Britain's Deterrent and America, 1957–62*, Oxford: OUP.

Commission Européenne – DG X Information, Communication, Culture, Audiovisuel (ed.) (1999). *40 ans des traités de Rome ou la capacité des traités d'assurer les avancées de la construction européenne*, Brussles: Bruylant.

Commission Européenne – Direction Générale de l'Education et de la Culture (1999). *Répertoire de l'Action Jean Monnet 1990–1999*, Luxembourg: OPOCE.

Commun, Patricia (2002). Von der deutschen Besatzung zur Europäischen Gemeinschaft für Kohle und Stahl? Lothringen und die deutsch-französische Handels- und Wirtschaftspolitik, 1931–1952, in Thomas Sandkühler (ed.), *Europäische Integration. Deutsche Hegemonialpolitik gegenüber Westeuropa 1920–1960*, Göttingen: Wallstein, 195–221.

Conrad, Yves and Michel Dumoulin (eds) (1992). *Répertoires des chercheurs et de la recherche en Histoire de la construction européenne*, Louvain-la-Neuve: Groupe de liaison des historiens près la Commission des Communautés Européennes.

Conze, Eckart (1995). Hegemonie durch Integration: Die amerikanische Europapolitik und de Gaulle, *Vierteljahrshefte für Zeitgeschichte*, vol. 45, no. 2, 297–340.

Conze, Eckhart (2001). Zauberwort 'Europa'. Die europäische Integration in Politik und Gesellschaft der Bundesrepublik Deutschland 1949–1999, in Marie-Luise Recker, Burkhard Jellonnek and Bernd Rauls (eds), *Bilanz. 50 Jahre Bundesrepublik Deutschland*, St. Ingberg: Röhrig, 151–68.

Cooper, Robert (2003). *The Breaking of Nations. Order and Chaos in the Twenty-first Century*, London: Atlantic.

Coppolaro, Lucia (2006a). Trade and Politics across the Atlantic: The European Economic Community (EEC) and the United States of America in the GATT Negotiations of the Kennedy Round (1962–1967), PhD, Florence: European University Institute.

Coppolaro, Lucia (2006b). The Empty Chair Crisis and the Kennedy Round of GATT Negotiations (1962–67), in Jean-Marie Palayret, Helen Wallace and Pascaline Winand (eds), *Visions, Votes, and Vetoes. The Empty Chair Crisis and the Luxembourg Compromise Forty Years on*, Brussels: Peter Lang, 219–39.

Coppolaro, Lucia (2006c). The European Economic Community in the GATT Negotiations of the Kennedy Round (1964–1967): Global and Regional Trade, in Antonio Varsori (ed.), *Inside the European Community. Actors and Policies in the European Integration 1957–1972*, Baden-Baden: Nomos, 347–68.

Coppolaro, Lucia (2008a). The United States and EEC Enlargement (1969–1973), in Jan van der Harst (ed.), *Beyond the Customs Union. The European Community's Quest for Deepening, Widening and Completion, 1969–1975*, Brussels: Bruylant, 135–62.

Coppolaro, Lucia (2008b). U.S. Payments Problems and the Kennedy Round of GATT Negotiations 1961–1967, in David M. Andrews (ed.), *Orderly Change. International Monetary Relations since Bretton Woods*, Ithaca, NY: Cornell UP, 120–38.

Costa Pinto, Antonio and Nuño Severiano Teixeira (eds) (2002). *Southern Europe and the Making of the European Union, 1945–1980s*, Boulder, CO: Westview Press.

Costigliola, Frank (1984). The Failed Design: Kennedy, de Gaulle and the Struggle for Europe, *Diplomatic History*, vol. 8, no. 3, 227–51.

Craveri, Piero (2007). *De Gasperi*, Bologna: Il Mulino.

Craveri, Piero and Antonio Varsori (2009). *L'Italia nella costruzione europea. Un bilancio storico (1957–2007)*, Milan: Franco Angeli.

Crouch, Colin (1999). *Social Change in Western Europe*, Oxford: OUP.

Crowson, Nicholas J. (2007). *The Conservative Party and European Integration since 1945*, London: Routledge.

Cuesta Bustillo, Josefina (2009). A Social Europe (1970–2006)?, in Wilfried Loth (ed.), *Experiencing Europe. 50 Years of European Construction, 1957–2007*, Baden Baden: Nomos, 193–216.

Curli, Barbara (2000). Il CES e le origini dell'unione monetaria, 1961–1964, in Antonio Varsori (ed.), *Il Comitato Economico e Sociale nelle costruzione europea*, Venice: Marsilio Editori, 66–76.

Daddow, Oliver (2003). *Harold Wilson and European Integration. Britain's Second Application to Join the EEC*, London: Frank Cass.

Daddow, Oliver (2004). *Britain and Europe since 1945. Historiographical Perspectives on Integration*, Manchester: MUP.

Davids, Karel, Greta Davos and Patrick Pasture (eds) (2007). *Changing Liaisons. The Dynamics of Social Partnership in 20th Century West-European Democracies*, Brussels: PIE-Peter Lang.

Dawson, Christopher (1939). *La formazione dell'unità europea dal secolo V al XI*, Turin: Einaudi.

Decleva, Enrico (1986). La sinistra democratica italiana fra Unione Europea e Communità Atlantica (1948–1950), in Raymond Poidevin (ed.), *Origins of the European Integration, March 1948–May 1950*, Brussels: Bruylant, 261–83.

Dedman, Martin J. (1996). *The Origins and Development of the European Union 1945–95. A History of European Integration*, London: Routledge.

Degimbe, Jean (1999). *La politique sociale européenne. Du Traité de Rome au Traité d'Amsterdam*, Brussels: ETUI.

Deighton, Anne (2001). The Second British Application for Membership of the EEC, in Wilfried Loth (ed.), *Crises and Compromises. The European Project 1963–1969*, Baden-Baden: Nomos, 391–405.

Deighton, Anne and Alan S. Milward (eds) (1999). *Widening, Deepening and Acceleration. The European Economic Community, 1957–1963*, Baden-Baden: Nomos.

Del Pero, Mario and Federico Romero (2007). *Le crisi transatlantiche. Continuità e trasformazioni*, Rome: Edizioni di storia e letteratura.

Delanty, Gerard (1995). *Inventing Europe. Idea, Identity, Reality*, London: Macmillan.

Delanty, Gerard and Chris Rumford (2005). *Rethinking Europe. Social Theory and the Implications of Europeanization*, New York: Routledge.

Dell, Edmund (1995). *The Schuman Plan and the British Abdication of Leadership in Europe*, Oxford: OUP.

Dell'Acqua, Stefano (2005). *Gli studi europei di Walter Lipgens a vent'anni dalla morte*, in Salvatore Aloisio and Cinzia Rognoni Vercelli (eds), *L'Europa nel nuovo ordine internazionale*, Bari: Cacucci, 147–58.

Dell'Acqua, Stefano (2006). Linee di una proposta storiografica: Alan S. Milward e la 'salvezza' dello Stato-nazione, in Federica Di Sarcina, Laura Grazi and Laura Schichilone (eds), *Europa in Progress. Idee, istituzioni e politiche nel processo di integrazione europea*, Milan: FrancoAngeli, 48–56.

Delors, Jacques (2004). *Mémoires*, Paris: Plon.
Delwit, Pascal, Erol Külahci and Cédric Van de Valle (eds) (2001). *Les fédérations européennes des partis. Organisation et influence*, Brussels: Editions de l'Université de Bruxelles.
Devin, Guillaume (1993). *L'Internationale socialiste. Histoire et sociologie du socialisme international*, Paris: Presse de la FNSP.
Di Nolfo, Ennio (ed.) (1992). *Power in Europe?*, vol. 2, *Great Britain, France, Germany and Italy and the Origins of the EEC 1952–1957*, Berlin and New York: W. De Gruyter.
Di Nolfo, Ennio and Pietro Pastorelli (eds) (2006). *Documenti diplomatici italiani*, serie 11, 1 gennaio–30 giugno 1949, vol. 2, Rome: Istituto Poligrafico e Zecca dello Stato.
Di Nolfo, Ennio, Romani H. Rainero and Brunello Vigezzi (eds) (1989). *L'Italia e la politica di potenza in Europa, 1945–1990*, Milan: Marzorati.
Didry, Claude and Arnaud Mias (2005). *Le moment Delors. Les syndicats au cœur de l'Europe sociale*, Brussels: Peter Lang.
Dimier, Véronique (2001). Leadership et institutionalisation au sein de la Commission Européenne: le cas de la Direction Générale Développement, 1958–1975, *Sciences de la Société*, vol. 53, 183–200.
Dimier, Véronique (2003). L'institutionnalisation de la Commission européenne (DG Developpement). Du rôle des leaders dans la construction d'une administration multinationale 1958–1975, *Revue Etudes Internationales*, vol. 34, no. 3, 401–28.
Dinan, Desmond (2004). *Europe Recast. A History of European Union*, Basingstoke: Palgrave.
Dobson, Alan P. and Steve Marsh (2006). *US Foreign Policy since 1945*, London: Routledge.
Dockrill, Michael (ed.) (1995). *Europe within the Global System 1938–1960. Great Britain, France, Italy and Germany. From Great Powers to Regional Powers*, Bochum: Brockmeyer.
Doering-Manteuffel, Anselm (1999). *Wie westlich sind die Deutschen? Amerikanisierung und Westernisierung im 20. Jahrhundert*, Göttingen: Vandenhoeck & Ruprecht.
Dølvik, Jon Erik (1999). *An Emerging Island? ETUC, Social Dialogue and the Europeanisation of the Trade Unions in the 1990s*, Brussels: ETUI.
Duchardt, Heinz et al. (eds) (2006–7). *Europa-Historiker. Ein biographisches Handbuch*, 3 vols, Göttingen: Vandenhoeck & Ruprecht.
Duchêne, François (1973). The European Community and the Uncertainties of Interdependence, in Max Kohnstamm and Wolfgang Hager (eds), *A Nation Writ Large? Foreign-Policy Problems before the European Community*, London: Macmillan, 1–21.
Duchêne, François (1994). *Jean Monnet. The First Statesman of Interdependence*, New York: Norton.
Duchenne, Geneviève and Michel Dumoulin (eds) (1999), *Répertoire des chercheurs et de la recherche en histoire de la construction européenne*, Louvain-la-Neuve: Groupe de liaison des historiens près la Commission Européenne.
Due-Nielsen, Carsten and Nikolaj Petersen (eds) (1995). *Adaptation and Activism: The Foreign Policy of Denmark 1967–1993*, Copenhagen: Jurist- og Økonomforbundets forlaget.

Dülffer, Jost (2009). The History of European Integration. From Integration History to the History of an Integrated Europe, in Wilfried Loth (ed.), *Experiencing Europe: 50 Years of European Construction 1957–2007*, Baden-Baden: Nomos, 17–32.

Dulphy, Anne and Christine Manigand (eds) (2004). *Les opinions publiques face à l'Europe communautaire. Entre cultures nationales et horizon européen*, Brussels: PIE-Peter Lang.

Dumoulin, Michel (ed.) (1995). *Wartime Plans for Postwar Europe, 1940–1947*, Brussels: Bruylant.

Dumoulin, Michel (ed.) (2004). *Réseaux économiques et construction européenne*, Brussels: PIE-Peter Lang.

Dumoulin, Michel (ed.) (2007). *The European Commission, 1958–72. History and Memories*, Luxembourg: OPOCE.

Dumoulin, Michel and Anne-Myriam Dutrieue (1993). *La Ligue européenne de Coopération Économique. Un groupe d'étude et de pression dans la construction européenne*, Berne: Peter Lang.

Dunphy, Richard (2004). *Contesting Capitalism? Left Parties and European Integration*, Manchester: MUP.

Duroselle, Jean-Baptiste (1990). *Europe. A History of its Peoples*, New York and London: Viking.

Dwan, Renata (1998). Un outil puissant: les théories de l'élite et l'étude de la construction européenne, in Elisabeth du Réau (ed.), *Europe des élites? Europe des peuples? La construction de l'espace européen 1945–1960*, Paris: Presses de la Sorbonne Nouvelle, 27–38.

Dyson, Kenneth and Lucia Quaglia (eds) (2010). *European Economic Governance and Policies. A Critical Commentary on Key Documents in Economic and Monetary Union*, Oxford: OUP.

Eichengreen, Barry (2007). *The European Economy since 1945. Coordinated Capitalism and Beyond*, Princeton, NJ: Princeton UP.

Ellison, James (2000). *Threatening Europe. Britain and the Creation of the European Community, 1955–1958*, Basingstoke: Macmillan.

Ellwood, David W. (1992). *Rebuilding Europe. Western Europe, the United States and Post-war Reconstruction*, London: Longman.

Ellwood, David W. (1993). L'integrazione europea e gli Stati Uniti, in Romain H. Rainero (ed.), *Storia dell'integrazione europea*, vol. 2, Milan: Marzorati, 523–71.

Enderle-Burcel, Gertrude et al. (eds) (2009). *Gaps in the Iron Curtain. Economic Relations Between Neutral and Socialist Countries in Cold War Europe*, Cracow: Jagiellonian UP.

European Commission – Directorate General for Education and Culture Jean Monnet Project (ed.) (2005). *Dialogue Between Peoples and Cultures. Actors in the Dialogue*, Luxembourg: OPOCE.

European Commission (ed.) (2006). *The History of European Cooperation in Education and Training. Europe in the Making – an Example*, Luxembourg: OPOCE.

Fauri, Francesca (2004). Italy's Industrial Forces and European Economic Integration (1950s–1960s), in Régine Perron (ed.), *The Stability of Europe. The Common Market: Towards European Integration of Industrial and Financial Markets? (1958–1968)*, Paris: Presses de l'Université de Paris-Sorbonne.

Favell, Adrian (2008). *Eurostars and Eurocities. Free Movement and Mobility in an Integrating Europe*, Oxford: Blackwell.

Featherstone, Kevin (1988). *Socialist Parties and European Integration. A Comparative History*, Manchester: MUP.

Fehrenbach, Elisabeth (1984). Nekrolog. Walter Lipgens 12.6.1925 – 29.4.1984, *Historische Zeitschrift*, vol. 239, no. 3, 757–9.

Fitzgerald, Maurice (2000). *Protectionism to Liberalisation. Ireland and the EEC, 1957 to 1966*, London: Ashgate.

Forsyth, Murray (1981). *Union of States. The Theory and Practice of Confederation*, Leicester: Leicester UP.

Foschepoth, Josef (1988). *Adenauer und die deutsche Frage*, Göttingen: Vandenhoeck & Ruprecht.

Frank, Robert (1995). Pompidou, le franc et l'Europe, in Association George Pompidou (ed.), *George Pompidou et l'Europe*, Paris: Edition Complexe, 339–70.

Frank, Robert (2004). Changement identitaires et difficultés de 'gouvernance' en Europe. Une approche historique, in Robert Frank and Rosalind Greenstein (eds), *Gouvernance et identités en Europe*, Brussels: Bruylant, 29–52.

Frank, Robert (2007). Conclusion, in Marie-Thérèse Bitsch, Wilfried Loth and Charles Barthel (eds), *Cultures politiques, opinions publiques et intégration européenne*, Brussels: Bruylant, 467–74.

Frank, Robert (ed.) (2004). *Les identités européennes au XXe siècle*, Paris: Publication de la Sorbonne.

Frank, Robert and Rosalind Greenstein (eds) (2005). *Gouvernance et identités en Europe*, Brussels: Bruylant.

Friedrich, Carl J. (1968). *Trends of Federalism in Theory and Practice*, London: Pall Mall.

Frøland, Hans Otto (2001). Choosing the Periphery. The Political Economy of Norway's European Integration Policy, 1948–73, *Journal of European Integration History*, vol. 7, no. 1, 77–103.

Garavini, Giuliano (2006). The Battle for the Participation of the Community in the G7 (1975–1977), *Journal of European Integration History*, vol. 12, no. 1, 141–59.

Garavini, Giuliano (2007). The Colonies Strike Back: The Impact of the Third World on Western Europe, 1968–1975, *Contemporary European History*, vol. 16, no. 3, 299–321.

Garavini, Giuliano (2009a). The Conference for International Economic Cooperation. A Diplomatic Reaction to the Oil Shock (1975–1977), in Ann-Christina L. Knudsen and Morten Rasmussen (eds), *The Road to a United Europe. Interpretations of the Process of European Integration*, Baden-Baden, Brussels: Peter Lang, 147–62.

Garavini, Giuliano (2009b). *Dopo gli imperi. L' Integrazione europea nello scontro Nord-Sud*, Florence: Le Monnier.

Gavin, Francis J. (2002). The Gold Battles within the Cold War: American Monetary Policy and the Defence of Europe, *Diplomatic History*, vol. 26, no. 1, 61–94.

Gavin, Francis J. (2007). *Gold, Dollars and Power. The Politics of International Monetary Relations, 1958–1971*, Chapel Hill, NC: University of North Carolina Press.

Gees, Thomas (2006). *Die Schweiz im Europäisierungsprozess. Wirtschafts- und gesellschaftspolitische Konzepte am Beispiel der Arbeitsmigrations-, Agrar- und Wissenschaftspolitik 1947–1974*, Zurich: Chronos-Verlag.

Gehler, Michael (1998). Klein- und Großeuropäer. Überlegungen zu einer vergleichenden Betrachtung der 'Six'- und 'Non-Six'-Staaten am Beispiel der Bundesrepublik Deutschland und Österreich, in Guido Müller (ed.), *Deutschland und der Westen. Internationale Beziehungen im 20. Jahrhundert*, Stuttgart: Steiner, 247–61.

Gehler, Michael (2001). *Zeitgeschichte im dynamischen Mehrebenensystem. Zwischen Regionalisierung, Nationalstaat, Europäisierung, internationaler Arena und Globalisierung*, Bochum: Winkler-Verlag.

Gehler, Michael (2002). *Der lange Weg nach Europa. Österreich vom Ende der Monarchie bis zur EU*, vol. 1, *Darstellung; Österreich von Paneuropa bis zum EU-Beitritt*, vol. 2, *Dokumente*, Innsbruck: Studien-Verlag.

Gehler, Michael (2006). *Vom Marshall-Plan zur Europäischen Union*, Innsbruck: Studien-Verlag.

Gehler, Michael (2009). *Österreichs Weg in die Europäische Union*, Innsbruck: Studien-Verlag.

Gehler, Michael and Hannes Schönner (2009). Transnationale christdemokratische Parteienkooperation in Europa 1965–1989. Der Beitrag österreichischer Ideen und Initiativen, *Demokratie und Geschichte*, vols 11–12, 271–318.

Gehler, Michael and Ingrid Böhler (eds) (2007). *Verschiedene europäische Wege im Vergleich. Österreich und die Bundesrepublik Deutschland 1945/49 bis zur Gegenwart*, Innsbruck: Studien-Verlag.

Gehler, Michael and Wolfram Kaiser (eds) (2004). *Transnationale Parteienkooperation der europäischen Christdemokraten. Dokumente 1945–1965 / Coopération transnationale des partis démocrates-chrétiens en Europe. Documents 1945–1965*, Munich: K.G. Saur.

Gehler, Michael et al. (eds) (1996). *Ungleiche Partner? Österreich und Deutschland in ihrer gegenseitigen Wahrnehmung. Historische Analysen und Vergleiche aus dem 19. und 20. Jahrhundert*, Stuttgart: Franz Steiner.

Gehler, Michael, Wolfram Kaiser and Brigitte Leucht (eds) (2009). *Netzwerke im europäischen Mehrebenensystem. Von 1945 bis zur Gegenwart*, Vienna, Cologne and Weimar: Böhlau.

George, Stephen (1992). *Britain and the European Community. The Politics of Semi-detachment*, Oxford: OUP.

Gerbet, Pierre (1989). The Fouchet Plan Negotiations 1960–2, in Roy Pryce (ed.), *The Dynamics of European Union*, London: Routledge, 105–29.

Geyer, Martin H. (2004). Im Schatten der NS-Zeit als Paradigma einer (bundes-) republikanischen Geschichtswissenschaft, in Alexander Nützenadel and Wolfgang Schieder (eds), *Zeitgeschichte als Problem. Nationale Traditionen und Perspektiven der Forschung in Europa*, Göttingen: Vandenhoeck & Ruprecht, 25–53.

Giauque, Jeffrey (2002). *Grand Designs and Visions of Unity. The Atlantic Powers and the Reorganization of Europe, 1955–1963*, Chapel Hill, NC: University of North Carolina Press.

Gilbert, Mark (2003). *Surpassing Realism. The Politics of European Integration since 1945*, Lanham, MD: Rowman & Littlefield.

Gilbert, Mark (2005). *Storia politica dell'integrazione europea*, Rome: Laterza.

Gilbert, Mark (2007). Delusions of Grandeur: New Perspectives on the History of the European Community, *Contemporary European History*, vol. 16, no. 4, 545–53.

Gilbert, Mark (2008). Narrating the Process. Questioning the Progressive Story of European Integration, *Journal of Common Market Studies*, vol. 63, no. 3, 641–62.

Gillingham, John (1988). Solving the Ruhr Problem. German Heavy Industry and the Schuman Plan, in Klaus Schwabe (ed.), *The Beginnings of the Schuman-Plan 1950/51*, Baden-Baden: Nomos, 399–436.

Gillingham, John (1998). National Policies to International Markets. Towards a New History of European Integration, in Guido Müller (ed.), *Deutschland und der Westen. Internationale Beziehungen im 20. Jahrhundert*, Stuttgart: Franz Steiner, 76–84.

Gillingham, John (2003). *European Integration 1950–2003. Superstate or New Market Economy?*, Cambridge: CUP.

Gillingham, John (2006). *Design for a New Europe*, Cambridge: CUP.

Girault, Réne (1982). Les relations économiques avec l'extérieur (1945–1975): mutations et permanences, in Fernand Braudel and Ernest Labrousse (eds), *Histoire économique et sociale de la France*, vol. 3, Paris: Presses Universitaires de France, 1379–426.

Girault, René (1989). La France entre l'Europe et l'Afrique, in Enrico Serra (ed.), *The Relaunching of Europe and the Treaties of Rome*, Brussels: Bruylant, 351–78.

Girault, René (1992). On the Power of Old and New Europe, in Ennio Di Nolfo (ed.), *Power in Europe?*, vol. 2, *Great Britain, France, Germany and Italy and the Origins of the EEC 1952–1957*, Berlin and New York: W. De Gruyter, 553–62.

Girault, René (ed.) (1994). *Identité et conscience européennes au XXe siècle*, Paris: Hachette.

Girault, René and Robert Frank (eds) (1984), *La puissance en Europe 1938–1940*, Paris: Publications de la Sorbonne.

Giubboni, Stefano (2006). *Social Rights and Market Freedom in the European Constitution. A Labour Law Perspective*, Cambridge: CUP [Italian 2003].

Gobin, Corinne (1997). *L'Europe syndicale entre désir et réalité. Essai sur le syndicalisme et la construction européenne à l'aube du XXIe siècle*, Brussels: Labor.

Görtemaker, Manfred (1994). John Foster Dulles und die Einigung Westeuropas, in Martin Greschat and Wilfried Loth (eds), *Die Christen und die Entstehung der Europäischen Gemeinschaft*, Stuttgart: Kohlhammer, 159–87.

Graglia, Piero (2001). *Il movimento federalista e la storia d'Europa*, in Maria Matilde Benzoni and Brunello Vigezzi (eds), *Storia e storici d'Europa nel XX secolo*, Milan: Unicopli, 115–35.

Graglia, Piero (2008). *Altiero Spinelli*, Bologna: Il Mulino.

Grazi, Laura (2006). *L'Europa e le città. La questione urbana nel processo di integrazione europea (1957–1999)*, Bologna: Il Mulino.

Greenwood, Sean (1998). Review of D. Baker and D. Seawright (eds), *Britain for and against Europe. British Politics and European Integration*, *Journal of Common Market Studies*, vol. 36, no. 4, 603–4.

Griffiths, Richard (ed.) (1993). *Socialist Parties and the Question of Europe in the 1950s*, Leiden: E. J. Brill.

Griffiths, Richard (ed.) (1997). *Explorations in OEEC History*, Paris: Organisation for Economic Cooperation and Development.

Griffiths, Richard and Brian Girvin (eds) (1995). *The Green Pool and the Origins of the Common Agricultural Policy*, London: Lothian Foundation Press.

Griffiths, Richard and Stuart Ward (eds) (1996). *Courting the Common Market. The First Attempt to Enlarge the European Community, 1961–1963*, London: Lothian Foundation Press.

Gruner, Wolf D. (1999). Der Platz Deutschlands in Europa nach dem Zweiten Weltkrieg aus der Sicht Jean Monnets (1940–1952), in Andreas Wilkens (ed.), *Interessen verbinden. Jean Monnet und die europäische Integration der Bundesrepublik Deutschland*, Bonn: Bouvier, 31–71.

Gruner, Wolf D. (2009). Die Bundesrepublik Deutschland und die Römischen Verträge in historischer Perspektive, in Michael Gehler (ed.), *Vom gemeinsamen Markt zur europäischen Unionsbildung. 50 Jahre Römische Verträge 1957–2007*, Vienna, Cologne and Weimar: Böhlau, 485–520.

Gstöhl, Sieglinde (2002). *Reluctant Europeans. Norway, Sweden and Switzerland in the Process of Integration*, Boulder, CO: Lynne Rienner.

Gualdesi, Marinelli N. (2004). *Il cuore a Bruxelles, la mente a Roma. Storia della partecipazione italiana alla construzione dell'unità europea*, Pisa: ETS.

Guasconi, Maria Eleonora (2003). Paving the Way for a European Social Dialogue. Italy and the Shaping of a European Social Policy after the Hague Conference of 1969, *Journal of European Integration History*, vol. 9, no. 1, 87–111.

Guasconi, Maria Eleonora (2004). *L'Europa tra continuità e cambiamento. Il vertice dell'Aja del 1969 e il rilancio della costruzione europea*, Florence: Polistampa.

Guderzo, Massimiliano (2000). *Interesse nazionale e responsabilità globale. Gli Stati Uniti, l'Alleanza atlantica e l'integrazione europea negli anni di Johnson 1963–1969*, Florence: Aida.

Guillen, Pierre (1989). La France et la négociation des traités de Rome. L'Euratom, in Enrico Serra (ed.), *The Relaunching of Europe and the Treaties of Rome*, Brussels: Bruylant, 513–24.

Guiotto, Maddalena (2006). Der Europagedanke in den christdemokratischen Parteien. CDU/CSU und DC in den fünfziger Jahren, in Gian Enrico Rusconi and Hans Woller (eds), *Parallele Geschichte? Italien und Deutschland 1945–2000*, Berlin: Duncker & Humblot, 175–202.

Guirao, Fernando (1998). *Spain and the Reconstruction of Western Europe, 1945–57. Challenge and Response*, London: Macmillan.

Haas, Ernst B. (2004 [1958]). *The Uniting of Europe. Political, Social and Economic Forces, 1950–1957*, Notre Dame, IN: Notre Dame UP.

Habermas, Jürgen (2001). *The Postnational Constellation. Political Essays*, New York: MIT Press.

Habermas, Jürgen, with Jacques Derrida (2006). February 15, or What Binds Europeans, in Jürgen Habermas, *The Divided West*, Cambridge: Polity Press, 39–48.

Hambloch, Sibylle (2009). *Europäische Integration und Wettbewerbspolitik. Die Frühphase der EWG*, Baden-Baden: Nomos

Hamilton, Keith (2006). Britain, France and America's Year of Europe, 1973, *Diplomacy & Statecraft*, vol. 17, no. 4, 871–95.

Hanley, David (2008). *Beyond the Nation State. Parties in the Era of European Integration*, Basingstoke: Palgrave.

Hanrieder, Wolfram F. (1989). *Germany, America, Europe. Forty Years of German Foreign Policy*, New Haven, CT: Yale UP.

Hansen, Peter (1969). Denmark and European Integration, *Cooperation and Conflict*, vol. 5, no. 1, 13–46.

Hansen, Peter, Melvin Small and Karen Siune (1973). The Structure of the Debate in the Danish EC Campaign. A Study of an Opinion-Policy Relationship, *Journal of Common Market Studies*, vol. 15, no. 2, 93–129.

Harrison, Reginald J. (1974). *Europe in Question. Theories of Regional International Integration*, London: Allen & Unwin.

Harryvan, Anjo G. and Jan van der Harst (eds) (2005). A Bumpy Road to Lomé. The Netherlands, Association and the Yaoundé Treaties, 1956–1969, in Marie-Thérèse Bitsch and Gérard Bossuat (eds), *L'Europe unie et l'Afrique. De l'idée d'Eurafrique à la convention de Lomé I*, Brussels: Bruylant, 319–34.

Harst, Jan van der (2003), Introduction, *Journal of European Integration History*, vol. 9, no. 2, 5–9.

Harst, Jan van der (ed.) (2007). *Beyond the Customs Union. The European Community's Quest for Deepening, Widening and Completion, 1969–1975*, Baden-Baden: Nomos.

Herbst, Ludolf (1986). Die zeitgenössische Integrationstheorie und die Anfänge der europäischen Einigung 1947–1950, *Vierteljahrshefte für Zeitgeschichte*, vol. 34, 167–205.

Hettlage, Robert and Hans-Peter Müller (eds) (2006). *Die europäische Gesellschaft*, Konstanz: UVK.

Heyen, Erk Volkmar (1992). *Die Anfänge der Verwaltung der Europäischen Gemeinschaft*, Baden-Baden: Nomos.

Hiepel, Claudia (2007). Kissinger's Year of Europe – A Challenge for the EC and the Franco-German Relationship, in Jan van der Harst (ed.), *Beyond the Customs Union. The European Community's Quest for Deepening, Widening and Completion, 1969–1975*, Brussels: Bruylant, 277–96.

Hirst, Paul (2000). Democracy and Governance, in Jon Pierre (ed.), *Debating Governance*, Oxford: OUP, 13–35.

Hitchcock, William (1998). *France Restored. Cold War Diplomacy and the Quest for Leadership in Europe, 1944–1954*, Chapel Hill, NC: University of North Carolina Press.

Hitchcock, William (2003). *The Struggle for Europe. The Turbulent History of a Divided Continent 1945–2002*, New York: Doubleday.

Hitchcock, William (2004). *The Struggle for Europe. The History of the Continent since 1945*, London: Profile Books.

Hoffmann, Stanley (2000). Towards a Common European Foreign and Security Policy?, *Journal of Common Market Studies*, vol. 38, no. 2, 189–98.

Hoffmann, Stanley (2006 [1966]). Obstinate or Obsolete? The Fate of the Nation-State and the Case of Western Europe, in Mette Eilstrup-Sangiovanni (ed.), *Debates on European Integration. A Reader*, Basingstoke: Palgrave, 134–59.

Hogan, Michael J. (1987). *The Marshall Plan. America, Britain, and the Reconstruction of Western Europe, 1947–1952*, Cambridge: CUP.

Hudemann, Rainer and Raymond Poidevin (eds) (1992). *Die Saar 1945–1955. Ein Problem der europäischen Geschichte*, Munich: Oldenbourg.

Jachtenfuchs, Markus (2002). *Die Konstruktion Europas. Verfassungsideen und institutionelle Entwicklung*, Baden-Baden: Nomos.

Jacobelli, Jader (ed.) (1988). *Il fascismo e gli storico oggi*, Rome: Laterza.

James, Harold (2003). *Europe Reborn. A History, 1914–2000*, Harlow: Longman.

Joas, Hans and Klaus Wiegandt (eds) (2008). *The Cultural Values of Europe*, Liverpool: LUP.

Judt, Tony (2005). *Postwar. A History of Europe since 1945*, London: Heinemann.

Kaelble, Hartmut (1988). *Vers une société européenne. Une histoire sociale de l'Europe 1880–1980*, Paris: Belin [German 1987].

Kaelble, Hartmut (1989). *A Social History of Western Europe, 1880–1980*, Dublin: Gill and Macmillan [German 1987].

Kaelble, Hartmut (2002). The Historical Rise of a European Public Sphere?, *Journal of European Integration History*, vol. 8, no. 2, 9–23.

Kaelble, Hartmut (2003). European Symbols, 1945–2000. Concept, Meaning and Historical Change, in Luisa Passerini (ed.), *Figures d'Europe. Images and Myths of Europe*, Brussels: PIE-Peter Lang, 47–61.

Kaelble, Hartmut (2005a). Eine europäische Gesellschaft?, in Gunnar F. Schuppert, Ingolf Pernice and Ulrich Haltern (eds), *Europawissenschaft*, Baden-Baden: Nomos, 299–330.

Kaelble, Hartmut (2005b). *Les chemins de la démocratie européenne*, Paris: Belin [German 2001].

Kaelble, Hartmut (2007). *Sozialgeschichte Europas. 1945 bis zur Gegenwart*, Munich: Beck.

Kaelble, Hartmut (ed.) (2004). *The European Way. European Societies during the Nineteenth and Twentieth Centuries*, New York: Berghahn.

Kagan, Robert (2004). *Paradise and Power. America and Europe in the New World Order*, London: Atlantic.

Kaiser, Wolfram (1995). The Bomb and Europe. Britain, France, and the EEC Entry Negotiations, 1961–63, *Journal of European Integration History*, vol. 1, no. 1, 65–85.

Kaiser, Wolfram (1996). *Using Europe, Abusing the Europeans. Britain and European Integration, 1945–1963*, London: Macmillan.

Kaiser, Wolfram (1997). Challenge to the Community. The Creation, Crisis and Consolidation of the European Free Trade Association, 1958–72, *Journal of European Integration History*, vol. 3, no. 1, 7–33.

Kaiser, Wolfram (1998). The Political Reform Debate in Britain since 1945. The European Dimension, *Contemporary British History*, vol. 12, no. 1, 48–76.

Kaiser, Wolfram (1999). *Using Europe, Abusing the Europeans. Britain and European Integration, 1945–63*, Basingstoke: Macmillan.

Kaiser, Wolfram (2001). Culturally Embedded and Path-Dependent. Peripheral Alternatives to ECSC/EEC 'core Europe' since 1945, *Journal of European Integration History*, vol. 7, no. 2, 11–36.

Kaiser, Wolfram (2002a). 'Überzeugter Katholik und CDU-Wähler'. Zur Historiographie der Integrationsgeschichte am Beispiel Walter Lipgens, *Journal of European Integration History*, vol. 8, no. 2, 119–28.

Kaiser, Wolfram (2002b). A Never-ending Story. Britain in Europe, *British Journal of Politics and International Relations*, vol. 4, no. 1, 152–65.

Kaiser, Wolfram (2003). Trigger-happy Protestant Materialists? The European Christian Democrats and the United States, in Marc Trachtenberg (ed.), *Between Empire and Alliance. America and Europe in the Cold War*, Lanham, MD: Rowman & Littlefield, 63–82.

Kaiser, Wolfram (2004). 'What Alternative is Open to us?': Britain, in idem. and Jürgen Elvert (eds), *European Union Enlargement. A Comparative History*, London: Routledge, 9–30.

Kaiser, Wolfram (2006). From State to Society? The Historiography of European Integration, in Angela Bourne and Michelle Cini (eds), *Palgrave Advances in European Union Studies*, Basingstoke: Palgrave, 190–208.

Kaiser, Wolfram (2007). *Christian Democracy and the Origins of European Union*, Cambridge: CUP.

Kaiser, Wolfram (2008). History Meets Politics. Overcoming the Interdisciplinary Volapük in Research on the EU, *Journal of European Public Policy*, vol. 15, no. 2, 300–13.

Kaiser, Wolfram (2009a). Bringing History back in to the Study of Transnational Networks in European Integration, *Journal of Public Policy*, vol. 29, no. 2, 223–39.

Kaiser, Wolfram (2009b). Bringing People and Ideas Back in. Historical Research on the European Union, in David Phinnemore and Alex Warleigh-Lack (eds), *Reflections on European Integration. 50 Years of the Treaty of Rome*, Basingstoke: Palgrave, 22–39.

Kaiser, Wolfram (2009c). Not Present at the Creation. Großbritannien und die Gründung der EWG, in Michael Gehler (ed.), *Vom gemeinsamen Markt zur europäischen Unionsbildung. 50 Jahre Römische Verträge 1957–2007*, Vienna, Cologne and Weimar: Böhlau, 225–42.

Kaiser, Wolfram (2009d). Transnational Networks in European Governance. The Informal Politics of Integration, in idem., Brigitte Leucht and Morten Rasmussen (eds), *The History of the European Union. Origins of a Trans- and Supranational Polity 1950–72*, London: Routledge, 12–33.

Kaiser, Wolfram and Brigitte Leucht (2008). Informal Politics of Integration: Christian Democratic and Transatlantic Networks in the Creation of ECSC core Europe, *Journal of European Integration History*, vol. 14, no. 1, 35–49.

Kaiser, Wolfram and Christian Salm (2009). Transition und Europäisierung in Spanien und Portugal. Sozial- und christdemokratische Netzwerke im Übergang von der Diktatur zur parlamentarischen Demokratie, *Archiv für Sozialgeschichte*, vol. 49, 259–82.

Kaiser, Wolfram and Jürgen Elvert (eds) (2004). *European Union Enlargement. A Comparative History*, London: Routledge.

Kaiser, Wolfram and Peter Starie (eds) (2005). *Transnational European Union. Towards a Common Political Space*, London and New York: Routledge.

Kaiser, Wolfram and Stefan Krankenhagen (2009). Europa ausstellen. Zur Konstruktion europäischer Integration und Identität im geplanten Musée de l'Europe in Brüssel, in Michael Gehler and Silvio Vietta (eds), *Europa – Europäisierung – Europäistik. Neue wissenschaftliche Ansätze, Methoden und Inhalte*, Vienna, Cologne and Weimar: Böhlau, 181–96.

Kaiser, Wolfram, Brigitte Leucht and Michael Gehler (eds) (2010). *Transnational Networks in Regional Integration. Governing Europe 1945–83*, Basingstoke: Palgrave.

Kaiser, Wolfram, Brigitte Leucht and Morten Rasmussen (eds) (2009). *The History of the European Union. Origins of a Trans- and Supranational Polity 1950–72*, London: Routledge.

Kauppi, Niilo (2005). *Democracy, Social Resources and Political Power in the European Union*, Manchester: MUP.

Kemseke, Peter Van (2006). *The Globalisation of Socialism and Christian Democracy, 1945–1965*, Leuven: Leuven UP.

Kipping, Matthias (1996). *Zwischen Kartellen und Konkurrenz. Der Schuman-Plan und die Ursprünge der europäischen Einigung 1944–1952*, Berlin: Duncker & Humblot.

Kirschbaum, Stanislav J. (ed.) (2007). *Central European History and the European Union. The Meaning of Europe*, Palgrave: Basingstoke.

Kitzinger, Uwe (1961). *The Challenge of the Common Market*, Oxford: Blackwell.

Kitzinger, Uwe (1969). *The Second Try. Labour and the EEC*, Oxford: Pergamon Press.

Kitzinger, Uwe (1973). *Diplomacy and Persuasion. How Britain Joined the Common Market*, London: Thames & Hudson.

Klinkhammer, Lutz (2004). Novecento statt Storia contemporana? Überlegungen zur italienischen Zeitgeschichte, in Alexander Nützenadel and Wolfgang Schieder (eds), *Zeitgeschichte als Problem. Nationale Traditionen und Perspektiven der Forschung in Europa*, Göttingen: Vandenhoeck & Ruprecht, 107–27.

Klotzbach, Kurt (1988). Die deutsche Sozialdemokratie und der Schuman-Plan, in Klaus Schwabe (ed.), *The Beginnings of the Schuman-Plan 1950/51*, Baden-Baden: Nomos, 333–44.

Knudsen, Ann-Christina L. (2001) Creating the Common Agricultural Policy. Story of Cereal Prices, in Wilfried Loth (ed.), *Crises and Compromises. The European Project 1963–1969*, Baden-Baden: Nomos, 131–56.

Knudsen, Ann-Christina L. (2001). Defining the Policies of the Common Agricultural Policy. A Historical Study, PhD, Florence: European University Institute.

Knudsen, Ann-Christina L. (2009). *Farmers on Welfare. The Making of Europe's Common Agricultural Policy*, Ithaca, NY: Cornell UP.

Knudsen, Ann-Christina L. and Morten Rasmussen (2008). A European Political System in the Making. The Relevance of Emerging Committee Structures, *Journal of European Integration History*, vol. 14, no. 1, 51–67.

Kohli, Martin (2000). The Battlegrounds of European Identity, *European Societies*, vol. 2, no. 2, 113–37.

Krüger, Dieter (2003). *Sicherheit durch Integration? Die wirtschaftliche und politische Zusammenarbeit Westeuropas 1947 bis 1957/58*, Munich: Oldenbourg.

Kunz, Diana B. (1997). *Butter and Guns. America's Cold War Economic Diplomacy*, New York: The Free Press.

Küsters, Hanns Jürgen (1982a), *Die Gründung der Europäischen Wirtschaftsgemeinschaft*, Baden-Baden: Nomos.

Küsters, Hanns Jürgen (1982b). The Federal Republic of Germany and the EEC-Treaty, in Enrico Serra (ed.), *The Relaunching of Europe and the Treaties of Rome*, Brussels: Bruylant, 495–506.

Küsters, Hanns Jürgen (1993). Zwischen Vormarsch und Schlaganfall. Das Projekt der Europäischen Politischen Gemeinschaft und die Haltung der Bundesrepublik Deutschland (1951–1954), in Gilbert Trausch (ed.), *The European Integration from the Schuman-Plan to the Treaties of Rome*, Baden-Baden: Nomos, 259–93.

Küsters, Hanns Jürgen (2000). *Der Integrationsfriede. Viermächte-Verhandlungen über die Friedensregelung mit Deutschland 1945–1990*, Munich: Oldenbourg.

Lacroix-Riz, Annie (1988). Paris et Washington au début du Plan Schuman (1950–1951), in Klaus Schwabe (ed.), *The Beginnings of the Schuman-Plan 1950/51*, Baden-Baden: Nomos, 241–68.

Lafféach, François-Xavier (2009). An Avant-Garde for Europe. The Young European Federalists and the Emergence of a European Consciousness, 1948–72, in Ann-Christina L. Knudsen and Morten Rasmussen (eds), *The Road to a United Europe. Interpretations of the Process of European Integration*, Berne: Peter Lang, 38–50.

Lager, Carole (1995). *L'Europe en quête de ses symboles*, Berne: Peter Lang.

Lamb, Richard (1995). *The Macmillan Years 1957–1963. The Emerging Truth*, London: Murray.

Lamberts, Emiel (ed.) (1997). *Christian Democracy in the European Union 1945–1995*, Leuven: Leuven UP.

Landuyt, Ariane and Daniela Preda (eds) (2000). *I movimenti per l'unità europea 1970–1986*, Bologna: Il Mulino.

Lappenküper, Ulrich (2001). *Die deutsch-französischen Beziehungen 1949–1963. Von der 'Erbfeindschaft' zur 'Entente élémentaire'*, 2 vols, Munich: Oldenbourg.

Laschi, Guiliana (1999). *L'agricoltura italiana e l'integrazione europea*, Brussels: Peter Lang.

Laski, Harold (1917). *Studies in the Problem in Sovereignty*, Yale: Yale UP.

Laursen, Johnny (1996). The Great Challenge. The Social and Political Foundations of Denmark's Application for EEC Membership, 1961–63, in Stuart Ward and Richard T. Griffiths (eds), *Courting the Common Market. The first Attempt to Enlarge the European Community, 1961–63*, London: Lothian Foundation Press, 211–27.

Laursen, Johnny (2000). Det danske tilfælde: en Studie i dansk Europapolitiks begrebsdannelse, 1956–57, in Johnny Laursen (ed.), *I tradition og kaos. Festskrift til Henning Poulsen*, Aarhus: Universitetsforlag, 238–77.

Laursen, Johnny (2001). Denmark, Scandinavia and the Second Attempt to Enlarge the EEC, 1966–67, in Wilfried Loth (ed.), *Crises and Compromises. The European Project 1963–1969*, Baden-Baden: Nomos, 407–36.

Laursen, Johnny (2004). A Kingdom Divided: Denmark, in Wolfram Kaiser and Jürgen Elvert (eds), *European Union Enlargement. A Comparative History*, London: Routledge, 31–52.

Laursen, Johnny (2009a). The Enlargment of the European Community, 1950–95, in Wilfried Loth (ed.), *Experiencing Europe. 50 Years of European Construction 1957–2007*, Baden Baden: Nomos, 269–304.

Laursen, Johnny (2009b). The Supranational Seven? Denmark, Scandinavia and the Schuman Plan, 1950–53, in Michael Gehler (ed.), *Vom gemeinsamen Markt zur europäischen Unionsbildung. 50 Jahre Römische Verträge 1957–2007*, Vienna, Cologne and Weimar: Böhlau, 197–223.

Lee, Sabine (1999). Germany and the First Enlargement Negotiations 1961–1963, in Anne Deighton and Alan S. Milward (eds), *Widening, Deepening and Acceleration. The European Economic Community 1957–1963*, Baden-Baden: Nomos, 167–83.

Leonard, Mark (2005). *Why Europe Will Run the 21st Century*, New York: Public Affairs.

Leonardi, Laura and Antonio Varsori (eds) (2005). *Lo spazio sociale europeo*, Florence: Florence UP.

Leucht, Brigitte (2008). Transatlantic Policy Networks and the Formation of Core Europe, PhD, Portsmouth: University of Portsmouth.

Leucht, Brigitte (2009a). Transatlantic Policy Networks in the Creation of the First European Anti-trust Law, in Wolfram Kaiser, Brigitte Leucht and Morten Rasmussen (eds), *The History of the European Union. Origins of a Trans- and Supranational Polity, 1950–1972*, London: Routledge, 56–73.

Leucht, Brigitte (2009b). Transatlantische Politiknetzwerke und europäische Integration, 1950–57, in Michael Gehler (ed.), *Vom gemeinsamen Markt zur Europäischen Unionsbildung. 50 Jahre Römische Verträge 1957–2007*, Vienna, Cologne and Weimar: Böhlau, 63–84.

Leucht, Brigitte and Katja Seidel (2008). Du Traité de Paris au règlement 17/1962: ruptures et continuités dans la politique européenne de concurrence, 1950–1962, *Histoire, Economie et Société*, vol. 27, no. 1, 35–46.

Levi, Lucio (1992), *Altiero Spinelli, Mario Albertini and the Italian Federalist School*, in Andrea Bosco (ed.), *The Federal Idea*, vol. 2, London: Lothian Foundation Press, 217–34.

Levi, Lucio (2002). *Il pensiero federalista*, Rome: Laterza.

Levi, Lucio (ed.) (1990). *Altiero Spinelli and Federalism in Europe and in the World*, Franco Angeli: Milan.

Levi, Lucio and Umberto Morelli (eds) (1994). *L'unificazione europea. Cinquant'anni di storia*, Turin: Celid.

Lidegaard, Bo (2001–02). *Jens Otto Krag 1914–1978*, 2 vols, Copenhagen: Gyldendal Publisher.

Lieber, Robert J. (1970). *British Politics and European Unity. Parties, Elites, and Pressure Groups*, Berkeley, CA: University of California Press.

Lieshout, R. H., M. L. R. Segers and A. M. van der Vleuten (2004). De Gaulle, Moravcsik and The Choice for Europe. Soft Sources, Weak Evidence, *Journal of Cold War Studies*, vol. 6, no. 4, 89–139.

Lightfoot, Simon (2005). *Europeanizing Social Democracy. The Rise of the Party of European Socialists*, London: Routledge.

Lindberg, Leon (1963). *The Political Dynamics of European Economic Integration*, Stanford, CA: Stanford UP.

Lipgens, Walter (ed.) (1980). *Sources for the History of European Integration (1945–1955)*, Brussels: Bruylant.

Lipgens, Walter (ed.) (1982). *A History of European Integration*, vol. 1, *The Formation of the European Unity Movement*, Oxford: Clarendon Press [German 1977].

Lipgens, Walter (ed.) (1985). *Documents on the History of European Integration*, vol. 1, *Continental Plans for European Union 1939–1945*, Berlin and New York: de Gruyter.

Lipgens, Walter (ed.) (1986). *Documents on the History of European Integration*, vol. 2, *Plans for European Union in Great Britain and in Exile 1939–1945*, Berlin and New York: de Gruyter.

Lipgens, Walter and Wilfried Loth (eds) (1988). *Documents on the History of European Integration*, vol. 3, *The Struggle for European Union by Political Parties and Pressure Groups in Western European Countries 1945–1950*, Berlin and New York: de Gruyter.

Lipgens, Walter and Wilfried Loth (eds) (1991). *Documents on the History of European integration*, vol. 4, *Transnational Organizations of Political Parties and Pressure Groups in the Struggle for European Union, 1945–1950*, Berlin and New York: de Gruyter.

Loth, Wilfried (1989). Deutsche Europa-Konzeptionen in der Gründungsphase der EWG, in Enrico Serra (ed.), *The Relaunching of Europe and the Treaties of Rome*, Brussels: Bruylant, 585–602.

Loth, Wilfried (2001). Beiträge der Geschichtswissenschaft zur Deutung der europäischen Integration, in idem and Wolfgang Wessels (eds), *Theorien europäischer Integration*, Opladen: Leske & Buderich, 87–106.

Loth, Wilfried (2006). *Walter Lipgens (1925–1984)*, in Heinz Duchardt et al. (eds), *Europa-Historiker. Ein biographisches Handbuch*, vol. 1, Göttingen: Vandenhoeck & Ruprecht, 317–36.

Loth, Wilfried (2007). European Political Co-operation and European Security in the Policies of Willy Brandt and Georges Pompidou, in Jan van der Harst (ed.), *Beyond the Customs Union. The European Community's Quest for Deepening, Widening and Completion, 1969–1975*, Brussels: Nomos, 21–34.

Loth, Wilfried (2008). Explaining European Integration. The Contribution from Historians, *Journal of European Integration History*, vol. 14, no. 1, 8–26.

Loth, Wilfried (ed.) (2001). *Crises and Compromises. The European Project, 1963–1969*, Baden-Baden: Nomos.

Loth, Wilfried (ed.) (2005a), *La gouvernance supranationale dans la construction européenne*, Brussels: Bruylant.

Loth, Wilfried (ed.) (2005b). *Europäische Gesellschaft. Grundlagen und Perspektiven*, Wiesbaden: VS Verlag für Sozialwissenschaften.

Loth, Wilfried (ed.) (2009). *Experiencing Europe. 50 Years of European Construction 1957–2007*, Baden-Baden: Nomos.

Loth, Wilfried and Jürgen Osterhammel (eds) (2000). *Internationale Geschichte: Themen – Ergebnisse – Aussichten*, Munich: Oldenbourg.

Loth, Wilfried, William Wallace and Wolfgang Wessels (eds) (1995). *Walter Hallstein. Der vergessene Europäer*, Bonn: Europa Union Verlag.

Loth, Wilfried, William Wallace and Wolfgang Wessels (eds) (1998). *Walter Hallstein. The Forgotten European?* London: Macmillan.

Lothian, Philip Henry Kerr (1935). *Pacifism is not Enough, nor Patriotism Either*, London: Burge Memorial Lecture.

Lucarelli, Sonia (2007). The EU in the Eyes of the Others. Towards Filling a Gap in the Literature, *European Foreign Affairs Review*, vol. 12, no. 3, 249–70.

Ludlow, N. Piers (1997). *Dealing with Britain. The Six and the First UK Application to the EEC*, Cambridge: CUP.

Ludlow, N. Piers (2005a). Mieux que six ambassadeurs. L'émergence du COREPER durant les premières années de la CEE, in Laurence Badel, Stanislas Jeannesson and N. Piers Ludlow (eds), *Les administrations nationales et la construction européenne. Une approche historique (1919–1975)*, Brussels: Peter Lang, 337–55.

Ludlow, N. Piers (2005b). The Making of the CAP: Towards a Historical Analysis of the First EU's Major Policy, *Contemporary European History*, vol. 14, no. 3, 347–71.

Ludlow, N. Piers (2006). *The European Community and the Crises of the 1960s. Negotiating the Gaullist Challenge*, London: Routledge.

Ludlow, N. Piers (2007). The Emergence of a Commercial Heavy-weight: The Kennedy Round Negotiations and the European Community of the 1960s, *Diplomacy & Statecraft*, vol. 18, no. 2, 351–68.

Ludlow, N. Piers (2009). Widening, Deepening and Opening out: Towards a Fourth Decade of European Integration History, in Wilfried Loth (ed.), *Experiencing Europe. 50 Years of European Construction 1957–2007*, Baden-Baden: Nomos, 33–44.

Ludlow, Peter (1982). *The Making of the European Monetary System. A Case Study of the Politics of the European Community*, London: Butterworth.

Ludlow, Peter (2004). *The Making of the New Europe*, Brussels: EuroComment.

Lundestad, Geir (1986). Empire by Invitation? The United States and Western Europe, 1945–1952, *Journal of Peace Research*, vol. 23, no. 3, 263–77.

Lundestad, Geir (1998). *'Empire' by Integration. The United States and European Integration 1945–1997*, Oxford: OUP.

Lundestad, Geir (2003). *The United States and Western Europe since 1945. From 'Empire' by Invitation to Transatlantic Drift*, Oxford: OUP.

Lynch, Frances (1997). *A History of the French Economy. From Vichy to Rome, 1944–58*, London: Routledge.

Maas, Willem (2007). *Creating European Citizens*. Landham, MD: Rowan & Littlefield Publishers.

MacKay, R.W.G. (1961). *Towards a United States of Europe. An Analysis of Britain's Role in European Union*, London: Hutchinson.

Maes, Ivo (2004). Macroeconomic and Monetary Policy-Making at the European Commission – From the Rome Treaties to the Hague Summit, *National Bank of Belgium Working Papers*, no. 58.

Magagnoli, Ralf (1998). Anregungen zu einer Neubewertung der Europapolitik Alcide De Gasperis, *Journal of European Integration History*, vol. 4, no. 1, 27–53.

Maier, Charles (2000). Consigning the 20th Century to History. Alternative Narratives for the Modern Era, *American Historical Review*, vol. 165, no. 3, 807–31.

Majocchi, Luigi Vittorio and Francesco Rossolillo (1979). *Il Parlamento europeo. Significato storico di un'elezione*, Naples: Guida.

Malmborg, Mikael af (1994). *Den ståndaktiga nationalstaten. Sverige og den västeuropeiska integrationen 1945–1959*, Lund: Lund UP.

Malmborg, Mikael af and Bo Stråth (eds) (2002). *The Meaning of Europe. Variety and Contention within and among Nations*, Oxford: Berg.

Marcussen, Martin (2000). *Ideas and Elites. The Social Construction of Economic and Monetary Union*, Aalborg: Aalborg UP.

Marten, Hans (1979). *Danmarks ja, Nordes nej. EF folkeafstemningerne i 1972*, Copenhagen: Munksgaard.

Masala, Carlo (1997). *Italia und Germania. Die deutsch-italienischen Beziehungen 1963–1969*, Cologne: SH-Verlag.

Mau, Stefan (2007). *Transnationale Vergesellschaftung. Die Entgrenzung sozialer Lebenswelten*, Frankfurt am Main: Campus.

Mayne, Richard (1962). *The Community of Europe,* London: Gollancz.

Mayne, Richard and John Pinder (1990). *Federal Union. The Pioneers. A History of Federal Union*, London: Macmillan.

Mazower, Mark (1998). *Dark Continent. Europe's Twentieth Century*, London: Allen Lane.

Mazower, Mark (2008). Whatever Happened to Old Europe? The Struggle to Understand How Even a United Continent is Far from a Place at the Centre of the World, *The Times*, April 30.

Mechi, Lorenzo (2003). *L'Europa di Ugo La Malfa. La via italiana alla modernizazione, 1942–1979*, Milan: Angeli.

Mechi, Lorenzo (2004). Le politiche sociali della CECA, in Ruggero Ranieri and Luciano Tosi (eds), *La Comunità Europea del Carbone e dell'Acciaio (1952–2002). Gli esiti del trattato in Europa e in Italia*, Padua: CEDAM, 105–26.

Mechi, Lorenzo (2006). Les États membres, les institutions et les débuts du Fonds Social Européen, in Antonio Varsori (ed.), *Inside the European Community.*

Actors and Policies in the European Integration, 1957–1972, Baden-Baden: Nomos, 95–116.

Mechi, Lorenzo (2008). Dai fondi Ceca al Fondo Sociale Europeo: l'Italia e la nascita di un principio comunitario di redistribuzione, in Luciano Tosi (ed.), *L'Italia e la dimensione sociale nell'integrazione europea*, Padua: CEDAM, 233–49.

Mechi, Lorenzo (2009). Abilità diplomatica, insuccessi economici, progressi amministrativi. Appunti per una storia dell'Italia e i fondi strutturali, in Piero Craveri and Antonio Varsori (eds), *L'Italia nella costruzione europea. Un bilancio storico (1957–2007)*, Milan: Franco Angeli, 187–210.

Mélandri, Pierre (1975). *Les Etats-Unis et le 'défi' européen, 1955–1958*, Paris: Presses Universitaires de France.

Mélandri, Pierre (1980). *Les Etats-Unis face à l'unification de l'Europe, 1945–1954*, Paris: A. Pedone.

Melchionni, Maria Grazia (2000). *Fonti e luoghi della documentazione europea. Istruzioni per l'uso*, Rome: Università La Sapienza.

Meyer, Jan-Henrik (2010). *The European Public Sphere. Media and Transnational Communication in European Integration, 1969–1991*, Stuttgart: Franz Steiner.

Middlemas, Keith (1995). *Orchestrating Europe. The Informal Politics of the European Union, 1973–95*, London: Fontana.

Migani, Guia (2008a). *La France et l'Afrique sub-saharienne, 1957–1963*, Brussels: Peter Lang.

Migani, Guia (2008b). Un nuovo modello di cooperazione Nord-Sud? Lomé, la CEE ed i paesi ACP, in Giuliana Laschi, Gabriele D'Ottavio and Alessandra Bitumi (eds), *La Comunità europea e le relazioni esterne, 1957–1992*, Bologna: CLUEB, 173–93.

Miljan, Toivo (1977). *The Reluctant Europeans. The Attitudes of the Nordic Countries towards European Integration*, London: Hurst.

Milward, Alan S. (1984). *The Reconstruction of Western Europe, 1945–51*, London: Routledge.

Milward, Alan S. (1992). *The European Rescue of the Nation-State*, London: Routledge.

Milward, Alan S. (1993). Conclusions: the Value of History, in Alan S. Milward et al. (eds), *The Frontier of National Sovereignty. History and Theory 1945–1992*. London: Routledge, 182–201.

Milward, Alan S. (1995). Allegiance – The Past and the Future, *Journal of European Integration History*, vol. 1, no. 1, 7–19.

Milward, Alan S. (2002a). Historical Teleologies, in Mary Farrell, Stefano Fella and Michael Newman (eds), *European Integration in the 21st Century. Unity in Diversity*, London: Sage, 15–28.

Milward, Alan S. (2002b). *The United Kingdom and the European Community*, vol. 1, *The Rise and Fall of a National Strategy, 1945–1963*, London: Frank Cass.

Milward, Alan S. (2005). *Politics and Economics in the History of the European Union*, London: Routledge.

Milward, Alan S. (2007). History, Political Science and European Integration, in *Handbook of European Union Politics*, London: Sage, 99–103.

Milward, Alan S. and George Brennan (1996). *Britain's Place in the World. A Historical Enquiry into Import Controls 1945–1960*, London: Routledge.

Milward, Alan S. and Vibeke Sørensen (1993), Interdependence or Integration? A National Choice, in Alan S. Milward et al. (eds), *The Frontier of National Sovereignty. History and Theory 1945–1992*, London: Routledge, 1–32.

Milward, Alan S. et al. (1993). *The Frontier of National Sovereignty. History and Theory 1945–1992*, London: Routledge.

Misa, Thomas J. and Johan Schot (2005). Inventing Europe. Technology and the Hidden Integration of Europe, *History and Technology*, vol. 21, no. 1, 1–21.

Mittag, Jürgen (ed.) (2006). *Politische Parteien und europäische Integration. Entwicklung und Perspektiven transnationaler Parteienkooperation in Europa*, Essen: Klartext.

Möckli, Daniel (2007). Speaking with one Voice? The Evolution of a European Foreign Policy, in Gérard Bossuat and Anne Deighton (eds), *The EC/EU. A World Security Actor*, Paris: Soleb, 132–51.

Möckli, Daniel (2008). *European Foreign Policy During the Cold War. Heath, Brandt, Pompidou and the Dream of Political Unity*, London: I.B. Tauris.

Moguen-Toursel, Marine (ed.) (2007). *Stratégies d'entreprise et action publique dans l'Europe integrée (1950–1980). Affrontement et apprentisssage des acteurs*, Brussels: Peter Lang.

Moon, Jeremy (1985). *European Integration in British Politics 1950–1963. A Study of Issue Change*, Aldershot: Gower.

Moravcsik, Andrew (1998). *The Choice for Europe. Social Purpose and State Power from Messina to Maastricht*, Ithaca, NY: Cornell UP.

Moravcsik, Andrew (2000). De Gaulle between Grain and *Grandeur*. The Political Economy of French EC Policy, 1958–1970, *Journal of Cold War Studies*, vol. 2, no. 2, 3–43; vol. 2, no. 3, 4–68.

Morlino, Leonardo (1998). *Democracy between Consolidation and Crisis. Parties, Groups, and Citizens in Southern Europe*, Oxford: OUP.

Müller-Härlin, Maximilian (2008). *Nation und Europa in Parlamentsdebatten zur Europäischen Integration. Identifikationsmuster in Deutschland, Frankreich und Großbritannien nach 1950*, Baden-Baden: Nomos.

Muñoz-Sánchez, Antonio (2009). A European Answer to the Spanish Question. The SPD and the End of the Franco Dictatorship, in *Journal of European Integration History*, vol. 15, no. 1, 77–93.

Nehring, Holger (2004). Westernization. A New Paradigm for Interpreting West European History in a Cold War Context, *Cold War History*, vol. 4, no. 2, 175–90.

Nehring, Holger and Helge Pharo (2008) Introduction: A Peaceful Europe? Negotiating Peace in the Twentieth Century, *Contemporary European History*, vol. 17, no. 3, 277–99.

Nielson, Gunnar P. (1966). Denmark and European Integration: A Small Country at the Crossroads, PhD, Berkeley, CA: University of California at Berkeley.

Noël, Gilbert (1988). *Du pool vert à la politique agricole commune. Les tentatives de Communauté agricole européenne entre 1945 et 1955*, Paris: Economica.

Noël, Gilbert (1995). French Agricultural Pressure Groups and the Project for a European Agricultural Organisation, in Richard T. Griffiths and Brian Girvin (eds), *The Green Pool and the Origins of the Common Agricultural Policy*, Bloomsbury: Lothian Press, 51–77.

Noël, Gilbert (2006). Les finalités de la politique agricole commune (1958–1972). Marché et cohésion économique et sociale, in Antonio Varsori (ed.), *Inside the*

European Community. Actors and Policies in the European Integration, 1957–1972, Baden-Baden: Nomos, 283–300.

North, Douglas (1990). *Institutions, Institutional Change and Economic Performance*, Cambrigde: CUP.

Nuti, Leopoldo (1999). *Gli Stati Uniti e l'apertura a sinistra. Importanza e limiti della presenza americana in Italia*, Rome: Laterza.

Nuttal, Simon (2000). *European Poreign Policy*, Oxford: OUP.

Olesen, Thorsten and Poul Villaume (eds) (2005). *Under the Bloc Division. Danish Foreign Policy History 1945–1972*, vol. 5, Copenhagen: Gyldendal.

Olivi, Bino and Roberto Santaniello (2005). *Storia dell'integrazione europea: dalla guerra fredda alla costituzione europea*, Bologna: Il Mulino.

Ortuño Anaya, Pilar (2001). *European Socialists and Spain. The Transition to Democracy, 1959–77*, Basingstoke: Palgrave.

Outhwaite, William (2008). *European Society*, Cambridge: Polity.

Paavonen, Tapani (2001). From Isolation to the core. Finland's Position towards European Integration, 1960–95, *Journal of European Integration History*, vol. 7, no. 1, 53–76.

Padoa Schioppa, Antonio (2007). *Ricordo di Mario Albertini*, in Fabio Zucca (ed.), *Europeismo e federalismo in Lombardia dal Risorgimento all'Unione Europea*, Bologna: Il Mulino, 443–8.

Padoa Schioppa, Tommaso (2007). *L'Europa forza gentile*, Bologna: Il Mulino.

Palayret, Jean-Marie (1996). *Un'università per l'Europa. Le origini dell'Istituto Universitario Europeo di Firenze (1948–1976)*, Rome: Presidenza del Consiglio dei Ministri.

Palayret, Jean-Marie (2006). Mondialisme contre régionalisme. CEE et ACP dans les négociations de la convention de Lomé, 1970–75, in Antonio Varsori (ed.), *Inside the European Community. Actors and Policies in the European Integration, 1957–1973*, Brussels: Bruylant, 369–98.

Palayret, Jean-Marie, Helen Wallace and Pascaline Winand (eds) (2006). *Visions, Votes, and Vetoes. The Empty Chair Crisis and the Luxembourg Compromise Forty Years on*, Brussels: Peter Lang.

Paoli, Simone (2006). La forza di due debolezze. Il ruolo del Parlamento Europeo nella nascita di una politica comunitaria dell'istruzione (1957–1972), in Antonio Varsori (ed.), *Sfide del mercato e identità europea. Le politiche di educazione e formazione professionale nell'Europa comunitaria*, Milan: Franco Angeli, 11–52.

Paoli, Simone (2007). La nascita di una dimensone educativa comunitaria tra interessi nazionali e istanze di movimento (1969–1976), in Antonio Varsori (ed.), *Alle origini del presente. L'Europa occidentale nella crisi degli anni Settanta*, Milan: Franco Angeli, 221–50.

Paolini, Edmondo (1988). *Altiero Spinelli. Appunti per una biografia*, Bologna: Il Mulino.

Paolini, Edmondo (1996). *Altiero Spinelli. Dalla lotta antifascista alla battaglia per la Federazione europea, 1920–1948: documenti e testimonianze*, Bologna: Il Mulino.

Pasquinucci, Daniele (2000). *Europeismo e democrazia. Altiero Spinelli e la sinistra europea 1950–1986*, Bologna: Il Mulino.

Pasquinucci, Daniele (2006). A passage to the West. The Italian Socialists and European Integration in the Sixties, in Antonio Varsori (ed.), *Inside the European Community. Actors and Policies in the European Integration 1957–1972*, Baden-Baden: Nomos, 161–76.

Pasquinucci, Daniele and Luca Verzichelli (2004). *Elezioni europee e classe politica sovranazionale 1979–2004*, Bologna: Il Mulino.

Passerini, Luisa (ed.) (1998). *Identità culturale europea. Idee, sentimenti, relazioni*, Florence: La Nuova Italia.

Passerini, Luisa (ed.) (2003). *Figures d'Europe. Images and Myths of Europe*, Brussels: Peter Lang.

Pastorelli, Pietro (1987). *La politica estera italiana del dopoguerra*, Milan: Franco Angeli.

Pastorelli, Pietro (1998). *Dalle prima alla seconda guerra mondiale. Momenti e problemi della politica estera italiana (1914–1943)*, Milan: LED edizioni Universitaria.

Pastorelli, Pietro (2009). *Il ritorno dell'Italia nell'Occidente. Raccanto della politica estera italiana dal 15 settembre 1947 al 21 novembre 1949*, Milan: LED edizioni Universitaria.

Pasture, Patrick (1995). À la recherche du temps perdu? La CISC face à l'intégration européenne, in Andrea Ciampani (ed.), *L'altra via per l'Europa: forze sociali e organizzazione degli interessi nell'integrazione europea (1947–1957)*, Milan: Franco Angeli, 171–99.

Patel, Kiran Klaus (2008). Überlegungen zu einer transnationalen Geschichte, in Jürgen Osterhammel (ed.), *Weltgeschichte*, Stuttgart: Franz Steiner, 67–89.

Patel, Kiran Klaus (2009a). *Europäisierung wider Willen. Die Bundesrepublik in der Agrarintegration der EWG 1955–1975*, Munich: Oldenbourg.

Patel, Kiran Klaus (2009b). Veto Player No. 1? Germany and the Creation of the EEC's Common Agricultural Policy 1957–1964, in Michael Gehler (ed.), *Vom gemeinsamen Markt zur europäischen Unionsbildung. 50 Jahre Römische Verträge 1957–2007*, Vienna, Cologne and Weimar: Böhlau, 349–70.

Patel, Kiran Klaus (ed.) (2009c). *Fertile Ground for Europe? The History of European Integration and the Common Agricultural Policy since 1945*, Baden-Baden: Nomos.

Pentland, Charles (1973). *International Theory and European Integration*, London: Faber & Faber.

Perron, Régine (ed.) (2004). *The Stability of Europe. The Common Market. Towards European Integration of Industrial and Financial Markets? (1958–1968)*, Paris: Presses l'Université de Paris-Sorbonne.

Peterson, John (2008). José Manuel Barroso. Political Scientist and ECPR Member, *European Political Science*, vol. 7, no. 1, 64–75.

Petrini, Francesco (2005). *Il liberismo a una dimensione. La confindustria e l'integrazione europea (1947–1957)*, Milan: Franco Angeli.

Pinder, John (1961). *Britain and the Common Market*, London: The Cresset Press.

Pinder, John (1985). Unione europea. Gradualismo e costituzione, *Il Federalista*, vol. 27, no. 3, 160–72.

Pinder, John (1989). Federalism in Britain and Italy. Radicals and the English Liberal Tradition, in Peter M.R. Stirk (ed.), *European Unity in Context. The Interwar Period*, London: Pinter, 201–23.

Pinder, John (1991). *European Community. The Building of a Union*, Oxford: OUP.

Pinder, John (1996). I federalisti e la loro rete conducono gli inglesi verso la Comunità, in Sergio Pistone (ed.), *I movimenti per l'unità europea 1954–1969*, Pavia: Jaca Book, 81–112.

Pinder, John (1998). *Altiero Spinelli and the British Federalists. Writings by Beveridge, Robbins and Spinelli 1937–1943*, London: Federal Trust.

Pinder, John (2005). Tre fasi nella storia del federalismo britannico, in Daniela Preda and Cinzia Rognoni Vercelli (eds), *Storia e percorsi del federalismo. L'eredità di Carlo Cattaneo*, Bologna: Il Mulino, 367–402.

Pinder, John and Roy Pryce (1969). *Europe After de Gaulle. Towards a United States of Europe*, Harmondsworth: Penguin.

Pine, Melissa (2007). Britain, Europe and the 'Special Relationship'. Finding a Role 1967–1972, in Jan van der Harst (ed.), *Beyond the Customs Union. The European Community's Quest for Deepening, Widening and Completion, 1969–1975*, Brussels: Bruylant, 107–33.

Pisani, Edgar (2004). *Un vieil homme et la terre*, Paris: Seuil.

Pistone, Sergio (1977). L'importanza dell'opera storiografica di Lipgens sugli inizi del processo di unificazione europea, *Il Federalista*, vol. 19, no. 3, 155–70.

Pistone, Sergio (1985). *L'Italia e l'Unità Europea dalle origini alla elezione del Parlamento Europeo*, Turin: Loescher.

Pistone, Sergio (1993). Il ruolo di Altiero Spinelli nella genesi dell'art. 38 della Communità Europea di Difesa e del progetto di Communità Politica Europea, in Gilbert Trausch (ed.), *The European Integration from the Schuman-Plan to the Treaties of Rome*, Baden-Baden: Nomos, 393–413.

Pistone, Sergio (1996). I movimento per l'unità europea in Italia, in idem (ed.), *I movimenti per l'unità europea 1954–1969*, Pavia: PIME, 17–53.

Pistone, Sergio (1999). *L'integrazione europea. Uno schizzo storico*, Torino: UTET.

Pistone, Sergio (2000). I movimenti per l'unità europea in Italia, in Ariane Landuyt and Daniela Preda (eds), *I movimenti per l'unità europea 1970–1986*, Bologna: Il Mulino, 39–119.

Pistone, Sergio (ed.) (1992). *I movimenti per l'unità europea 1945–1954*, Milan: Jaca Book.

Pistone, Sergio (ed.) (1996). *I movimenti per l'unità europea 1954–1969*, Pavia: Pime.

Poggiolini, Ilaria (2004). *Alle origini dell'Europa allargata. La Gran Bretagna e l'adesione alla CEE (1972–1973)*, Milan: Edizioni Unicopli.

Poidevin, Raymond (1986). *Robert Schuman. Homme d'Etat*, Paris: Imprimerie nationale.

Poidevin, Raymond (1988). *Robert Schuman*, Paris: Beauchesne.

Poidevin, Raymond (1990). Die europäischen Initiativen Frankreichs des Jahres 1950. Aus einer Zwangslage geboren?, in Ludolf Herbst, Werner Bührer and Hanno Sowade (eds), *Vom Marshallplan zur EWG. Die Eingliederung der Bundesrepublik Deutschland in die westliche Welt*, Munich: Oldenbourg, 247–62.

Poidevin, Raymond (ed.) (1986). *Origins of the European Integration, March 1948–May 1950*, Brussels: Bruylant.

Poidevin, Raymond and Jacques Bariéty (eds) (1977). *Les relations franco-allemandes 1815–1975*, Paris: Colin.

Pons, Vittorio (2006). The Italian Communist Party between Brussels and Moscow, in Antonio Varsori (ed.), *Inside the European Community. Actors and Policies in the European Integration 1957–1972*, Baden-Baden: Nomos, 151–60.

Preda, Daniela (1990). *Storia di una speranza. La battaglia per la CED e la Federazione europea,* Milan: Jaca Book.

Preda, Daniela (1994). *Sulla soglia dell'unione. La vicenda della Comunità politica europea (1952–1954)*, Milan: Jaca Book.

Preda, Daniela (2004). *Alcide De Gasperi federalista europeo*, Bologna: Il Mulino.
Preda, Daniela and Vercelli Cinzia Rognoni (eds) (2005). *Storia e percorsi del feder-alismo. L'eredità di Carlo Cattaneo*, 2 vols, Bologna: Il Mulino.
Pryce, Roy (1962). *The Political Future of the European Community*, London: Marshbank for the Federal Trust.
Pryce, Roy (1987). *The Dynamics of European Union*, London: Croom Helm.
Pryce, Roy (1994). The Maastricht Treaty and the New Europe, in Andrew Duff, John Pinder and Roy Pryce (eds), *Maastricht and Beyond. Building the European Union*, London: Routledge, 36–52.
Putnam, Robert W. (1988). Diplomacy and Domestic Politics. The Logic of Two-Level Games, *International Organization*, vol. 42, no. 3, 427–60.
Ramirez Pérez, Sigfrido (2009). The French Automobile Industry and the Treaty of Rome. Between Welfare State and Multinational Corporations 1955–1958, in Michael Gehler (ed.), *Vom gemeinsamen Markt zur europäischen Unionsbildung. 50 Jahre Römische Verträge 1957–2007*, Vienna, Cologne and Weimar: Böhlau, 169–94.
Ramírez Pérez, Sigfrido (2010). *Multinational Corporations and the State in the History of European Integration. The Automobile Industry from Fascism to the Treaty of Rome (1939–1958)*, Brussels: Peter Lang.
Ranieri, Ruggero (1988). The Italian Steel Industry and the Schuman Plan Negotiations, in Klaus Schwabe (ed.), *The Beginnings of the Schuman-Plan 1950/51*, Baden-Baden: Nomos, 345–56.
Ranieri, Ruggero (1999). Italian Industry and the EEC, in Anne Deighton and Alan S. Milward (eds), *Widening, Deepening and Acceleration. The European Economic Community 1957–1963*, Baden-Baden: Nomos, 185–98.
Ranieri, Ruggero and Luciano Tosi (eds) (2004). *La Comunità europea de carbone e dell'acciaio, 1952–2002. Gli esiste del trattato in Europa e in Italia*, Padova: CEDAM.
Ranieri, Ruggero, et al. (eds) (2005). *L'Europa e l'industria. L'amministrazione pub-blica italiana di fronte ai problemi di politica industriale posti dall'integrazione europea: l'esperienza della CECA*, Rome: Scuola Superiore della Pubblica Amministrazione.
Rappaport, Armin (1981). The United States and European Integration: the first Phase, *Diplomatic History*, vol. 5, no. 2, 121–50.
Rapport d'activité 2006 du Ministère d'Etat (March 2007). http://www.gouvernement.lu/publications/informations_gouvernementales/rapports_activite/rapport_activite2006/01me/me.pdf (accessed 6 April 2009).
Rasmussen, Morten (2003). How Denmark Made Britain Pay the Bills, in Jørgen Sevaldsen, Claus Bjørn and Bo Bjørke (eds), *Britain and Denmark. Political, Economic and Cultural Relations in the 19th and 20th Centuries*, Copenhagen: Museum Tusculanum Press, 617–37.
Rasmussen, Morten (2005). The Hesitant European. History of Denmark's Accession to the European Communities 1970–1973, *Journal of European Integration History*, vol. 11, no. 2, 47–74.
Rasmussen, Morten (2008). The Origins of a Legal Revolution. The Early History of the European Court of Justice, *Journal of European Integration History*, vol. 14, no. 2, 77–98.
Rasmussen, Søren H. (1997). *Sære Alliancer. Politiske bevægelser i efterkrigstidens Danmark*, Aarhus: Aarhus Universitetsforlag.

Rey, Marie-Pierre (2005). Le retour à l'Europe? Les décideurs soviètiques face à l'intégration ouest-européenne, 1957–1991, *Revue de l'intégration européenne*, vol. 11, no. 1, 7–28.

Rhenisch, Thomas (1999). *Europäische Integration und industrielles Interesse.* Stuttgart: Franz Steiner.

Rifkin, Jeremy (2004). *The European Dream. How Europe's Vision of the Future is Quietly Eclipsing the American Dream*, New York: Tarcher and Penguin.

Risse, Thomas (2010). *We the European Peoples? The Europeanization of Identities and Public Spheres*, Ithaca, NY: Cornell UP.

Rittberger, Berthold (2005). *Building Europe's Parliament. Democratic Representation Beyond the Nation-State*, Oxford: OUP.

Robertson, Paul L. and John Singleton (1999). Britain, the Dominions and the EEC, 1961–1963, in Anne Deighton and Alan S. Milward (eds), *Widening, Deepening and Acceleration. The European Economic Community 1957–1963*, Baden-Baden: Nomos, 107–22.

Rochard, Bertrand (2003). *L'Europe des Commissaires. Réflexions sur l'identité européenne des traités de Rome au traité d'Amsterdam*, Brussels: Bruylant.

Rognoni Vercelli, Cinzia (2008). *Luciano Bolis dall'Italia all'Europa*, Bologna: Il Mulino.

Rollings, Neil (2008). *British Business in the Formative Years of European Integration, 1945–1973*, Cambridge: CUP.

Rollings, Neil and Matthias Kipping (2004). Networks of Peak Industrial Federations. The Council of Directors of European Industrial Federations and the Council of European Industrial Federations, in Michel Dumoulin (ed.), *Réseaux économiques et construction européenne*, Brussels: Peter Lang, 277–300.

Rollings, Neil and Matthias Kipping (2008). Private Transnational Governance in the Heyday of the Nation-State. The Council of European Industrial Federations (CEIF), *Economic History Review*, vol. 61, no. 2, 409–31.

Romano, Angela (2009). *From Détente in Europe to European Détente. How the West Shaped the Helsinki Final Act*, Brussels: Peter Lang.

Romero, Federico (1991). *Emigrazione e integrazione europea 1945–1973*, Rome: Edizione Lavori.

Romero, Federico (1993). Interdependence and Integration in American Eyes From the Marshall Plan to Currency Convertibility, in Alan S. Milward et al. (eds), *The Frontier of National Sovereignty*, London: Routledge, 155–81.

Romero, Federico (2007). The Twilight of American Cultural Hegemony. A Historical Perspective on Western Europe's Distancing from America, in David Farber (ed.), *What They Think of Us. International Perceptions of the United States since 9/11*, Princeton, NJ: Princeton UP, 153–76.

Romero, Federico and Antonio Varsori (eds) (2005–2006). *Nazione, interdipendenza, integrazione. Le relazioni internazionali dell'Italia (1917–1989)*, 2 vols, Rome: Carocci.

Rosamond, Ben (2007). European Integration and the Social Science of EU Studies: the Disciplinary Politics of a Subfield, *International Affairs*, vol. 83, no. 2, 231–52.

Rostow, Walt W. (1960). *The Stages of Economic Growth. A Non-Communist Manifesto*, Cambridge: CUP.

Roussel, Eric (1996). *Jean Monnet 1888–1979*, Paris: Fayard.

Rücker, Katrin and Laurent Warlouzet (eds) (2006), *Quelle(s) Europe(s). Nouvelles approches en histoire de l'intégration européenne*, Brussels and Berne: PIE-Peter Lang.

Rumford, Chris (2002). *The European Union. A Political Sociology*, Malden, MA: Blackwell.

Rye, Lise (2009). The Origins of Community Information Policy. Educating Europeans, in Wolfram Kaiser, Brigitte Leucht and Morten Rasmussen (eds), *The History of the European Union. Origins of a Trans- and Supranational Polity 1950–72*, London: Routledge, 148–66.

Sandkühler, Thomas (ed.), *Europäische Integration. Deutsche Hegemonialpolitik gegenüber Westeuropa 1920–1960*, Göttingen: Wallstein.

Sassoon, Donald (1997). *One Hundred Years of Socialism. The West European Left in the Twentieth Century*, New York: New Press.

Saunier, Georges (2003). François Mitterrand, un projet socialiste pour l'Europe? L'équipe européenne de François Mitterrand, 1981–1984, in Gérard Bossuat and Georges Saunier (eds), *Inventer l'Europe: histoire nouvelle des groupes d'influence et des acteurs de l'unité européenne*, Brussels: Peter Lang, 431–48.

Scarano, Frederico (2009). Italien, die italienische Linke und die Römischen Verträge im historischen Rückblick, in Michael Gehler (ed.), *Vom gemeinsamen Markt zur europäischen Unionsbildung. 50 Jahre Römische Verträge 1957–2007*, Vienna, Cologne and Weimar: Böhlau, 557–72.

Schaad, Martin (2000). *Bullying Bonn. Anglo-German Diplomacy on European Integration, 1955–1961*, London: Macmillan.

Schabert, Tilo (2002). *Wie die Weltgeschichte gemacht wird. Frankeich und die deutsche Einheit*, Stuttgart: Klett-Cotta.

Schmidt, Heide-Irene and Helge Pharo (2003). Introduction, *Contemporary European History*, vol. 12, no. 4, 395–412.

Schönwald, Matthias (2001). Walter Hallstein and the 'Empty Chair' Crisis 1965/66, in Wilfried Loth (ed.), *Crises and Compromises. The European Project, 1963–1969*, Baden-Baden: Nomos, 157–71.

Schulte, Markus (1999). Challenging the Common Market Project. German Industry, Britain and Europe 1957–1963, in Anne Deighton and Alan S. Milward (eds), *Widening, Deepening and Acceleration. The European Economic Community 1957–1963*, Baden-Baden: Nomos, 167–83.

Schulz-Forberg, Hagen (2007). The EU and the European Public Sphere. A Historical Reflection on a Current Issue, in Hans-Ake Persson and Bo Stråth (eds), *Reflections on Europe. Defining a Political Order in Time and Space*, Brussels: PIE-Peter Lang, 183–200.

Schulzinger, Robert D. (2002). *U.S. Diplomacy since 1900*, New York: OUP.

Schwabe, Klaus (1995). The United States and European Integration, 1947–1957, in Clemens Wurm (ed.), *Western Europe and Germany. The Beginnings of European Integration, 1945–1960*, Oxford: Berg, 115–36.

Schwabe, Klaus (1998). Atlantic Partnership and European Integration. American-European Policies and the German Problem, 1947–1966, in Geir Lundestad (ed.), *No End to Alliance. The United States and Western Europe. Past, Present and Future*, Basingstoke: Macmillan, 38–80.

Schwabe, Klaus (2001). The Cold War and European Integration, 1947–1963, *Diplomacy & Statecraft*, vol. 12, no. 4, 18–34.

Schwabe, Klaus (ed.) (1988). *The Beginnings of the Schuman-Plan 1950/51*, Baden-Baden: Nomos.

Schwartz, Thomas A. (2003) *Lyndon Johnson and Europe. In the Shadow of Vietnam*, Cambridge, MA: Harvard UP.

Schwarz, Hans-Peter (1979). Adenauer und Europa, *Vierteljahrshefte für Zeitgeschichte*, vol. 27, 471–523.

Schwarz, Hans-Peter (1981). *Die Ära Adenauer. Gründerjahre der Republik 1949–1957*, Stuttgart: Brockhaus.

Schwarz, Hans-Peter (1983). Die Europäische Integration als Aufgabe der Zeitgeschichtsforschung, *Vierteljahrshefte für Zeitgeschichte*, vol. 31, 555–72.

Schwarz, Hans-Peter (1986–91). *Adenauer*, 2 vols, Stuttgart: DVA.

Scichilone, Laura (2008). *L'Europa e la sfida ecologica. Storia della politica ambientale europea (1969–1998)*, Bologna: Il Mulino.

Seidel, Katja (2010). *The Process of Politics in Europe. The Rise of European Elites and Supranational Institutions*, London: I.B. Tauris.

Serra, Enrico (ed.) (1989). *The Relaunching of Europe and the Treaties of Rome*, Brussels: Bruylant.

Shanks, Michael and John Lambert (1962). *Britain and the New Europe. The Future of the Common Market*, London: Chatto & Windus.

Shipway, Martin (2008). *Decolonization and Its Impact. A Comparative Approach to the End of the Colonial Empires*, Oxford: Blackwell.

Shore, Cris (2000). *Building Europe. The Cultural Politics of European Integration*, London: Routledge.

Singh M. (1962). India and the European Common Market, *Journal of Common Market Studies*, vol. 1, no. 3, 62–72.

Sørensen, Anders Thornvig (1998). *Denmark and the Green Pool. Et spørgsmæl om suverænitet: Danmark, landbruget og Europa, 1950–53*, Aarhus: Aarhus Universitetsforlag.

Sørensen, Vibeke (2001). *Denmark's Social Democratic Government and the Marshall Plan. 1947–50*, Copenhagen: Tusculanum's Press.

Soutou, Georges-Henri (1996). *L'alliance incertaine. Les rapports politico-stratégiques franco-allemands, 1954–1996*, Paris: Fayard.

Soutou, Georges-Henri (1999). Le général de Gaulle et le plan Fouchet d'union politique européenne. Un projet stratégique, in Anne Deighton and Alan S. Milward (eds), *Widening, Deepening and Acceleration. The European Economic Community 1951–1963*, Baden-Baden: Nomos, 55–71.

Soutou, Georges-Henri (2001). La France et la défense européenne du traité de l'Elysée au retrait de l'OTAN (1963–1966), in Wilfried Loth (ed.), *Crises and Compromises. The European Project 1963–1969*, Baden-Baden: Nomos, 21–46.

Spierenburg, Dirk and Raymond Poidevin (1993). *Histoire de la Haute Autorité de la Communauté Européenne du Charbon et de l'Acier. Une expérience supranationale*, Brussels: Bruylant.

Spinelli, Altiero (1987). *Come ho tentato di diventare saggio. La goccia e la roccia*, ed. Edmondo Paolini, Bologna: Il Mulino.

Stein, Eric (1981). Lawyers, Judges and the Making of a Transnational Constitution, *American Journal of International Law*, vol. 75, no. 1, 1–27.

Steininger, Rolf (1985). *Eine Chance zur Wiedervereinigung? Die Stalin-Note vom 10. März 1952. Darstellung und Dokumentation auf der Grundlage unveröffentlichter britischer und amerikanischer Akten*, Bonn: Verlag Neue Gesellschaft.

Stirk, Peter M.R. (1996). *A History of European Integration since 1914*, London: Pinter.

Stråth, Bo (ed.) (2000). *After Full Employment. European Discourses on Work and Flexibility*, Brussels: Peter Lang.

Stråth, Bo and Thomas Sandkühler (2002). Europäische Integration. Grundlinien und Interpretationen, in Thomas Sandkühler (ed.), *Europäische Integration. Deutsche Hegemonialpolitik gegenüber Westeuropa 1920–1960*, Göttingen: Wallstein, 19–39.

Telò, Mario (2006). *Europe, a Civilian Power? European Union, Global Governance, World Order*, New York: Palgrave.

Theiler, Tobias (2005). *Political Symbolism and European Integration*, Manchester: MUP.

Thiemeyer, Guido (1999). *Vom 'Pool Vert' zur Europäischen Wirtschaftsgemeinschaft. Europäische Integration, Kalter Krieg und die Anfänge der Gemeinsamen Europäischen Agrarpolitik 1950–1957*, Munich: Oldenbourg.

Thiemeyer, Guido (2005). West German Perceptions of Africa and the Association of the Overseas Territories with the Common Market 1956/57, in Marie-Thérèse Bitsch and Gérard Bossuat (eds), *L'Europe unie et l'Afrique. De l'idée d'Eurafrique à la convention de Lome I*, Brussels: Bruylant, 269–85.

Thiemeyer, Guido (2007) The Mansholt Plan, the Definite Financing of the Common Agricultural Policy and the Enlargement of the Community, 1969–1973, in Jan van der Harst (ed.), *Beyond the Customs Union. The European Community's Quest for Deepening, Widening and Completion, 1969–1975*, Baden-Baden: Nomos, 197–224.

Thiemeyer, Guido (2009). *Internationalismus und Diplomatie. Währungspolitische Kooperation im europäischen Staatensystem 1865–1900*, Munich: Oldenbourg.

Thoß, Bruno (1995). *Vom Kalten Krieg zur deutschen Einheit. Analysen und Zeitzeugenberichte zur deutschen Militärgeschichte 1945 bis 1995*, Munich: Oldenbourg.

Thoß, Bruno and Hans-Erich Volkmann (eds) (1988). *Zwischen Kaltem Krieg und Entspannung. Sicherheits- und Deutschlandpolitik der Bundesrepublik im Mächtesystem der Jahre 1953–1956*, Boppard am Rhein: Boldt.

Torquati, Emanuele (2006). L'azione Jean Monnet, unicum nelle iniziative della Commissione Europea per l'università, in Antonio Varsori (ed.), *Sfide del mercato e identità europea. Le politiche di educazione e formazione professionale nell'Europa comunitaria*, Milan: Franco Angeli, 111–44.

Trachtenberg, Marc (1999). *A Constructed Peace. The Making of the European Settlement, 1945–1963*, Princeton, NJ: Princeton UP.

Tranholm-Mikkelsen, Jeppe (1991). Neo-functionalism: Obstinate or Obsolete?, *Millenium. Journal of International Studies*, vol. 20, no. 1, 1–22.

Tratt, Jacqueline (1996). *The Macmillan Government and Europe. A Study in the Process of Policy Development*, Basingstoke: Macmillan.

Trausch, Gilbert (ed.) (1993). *The European Integration from the Schuman-Plan to the Treaties of Rome*, Brussels: Bruylant.

Trausch, Gilbert (ed.) (2005). *Small Countries in Europe. Their Role and Place in the XXth Century*, Baden-Baden: Nomos.

Trenz, Hans-Jörg (2002). *Zur Konstitution politischer Öffentlichkeit in der Europäischen Union. Zivilgesellschaftliche Subpolitik oder schaupolitische Inszenierung?*, Baden-Baden: Nomos.

Trenz, Hans-Jörg (2005). *Europa in den Medien. Die europäische Integration im Spiegel nationaler Öffentlichkeit*, Frankfurt: Campus.

Trouvé, Matthieu (2008). *L'Espagne et l'Europe. De la dictature de Franco à l'Union européenne*, Brussels: Peter Lang.

Trunk, Achim (2007). *Europa, ein Ausweg. Politische Eliten und europäische Integration in den 1950er Jahren*, Munich: Oldenbourg.

Tsoukalis, Loukas (1981). *The European Community and Its Mediterranean Enlargement*, London: Allen & Unwin.

Turpin, Frédéric (2007). Alle origini della politica europea di cooperazione allo sviluppo: la Francia e la politica di associazione Europa-Africa (1957–1975), *Ventunesimo Secolo*, vol. 6, no. 14, 47–65.

Uri, Pierre (ed.) (1971). *Un avenir pour l'Europe agricole*, Paris: L'Institut Atlantique.

Vaicbourdt, Nicolas (2002). Les ambitions américaines pour l'Europe, 1945–1960, in Gérard Bossuat and Nicolas Vaicbourdt (eds), *Etats-Unis, Europe et Union européenne: Histoire et avenir d'un partenariat difficile (1945–1999)*, Brussels: PIE-Peter Lang, 17–49.

Vaïsse, Maurice (1998). *La grandeur. Politique étrangère du général de Gaulle (1958–1969)*, Paris: Fayard.

Van Laer, Arthe (2006). Liberalization or Europeanization? The EEC Commission's Policy on Public Procurement in Information Technology and Telecommunications (1957–1984)', *Journal of European Integration History*, vol. 12, no. 2, 107–30.

Vanke, Jeffrey W. (2001). An Impossible Union. Dutch Objections to the Fouchet Plan, 1959–62, *Cold War History*, vol. 2, no. 1, 95–112.

Varsori, Antonio (1988). *Il Patto di Bruxelles 1948. Fra integrazione europea e alleanza atlantica*, Rome: Bonacci.

Varsori, Antonio (1997). *L'Italia nelle relazioni internazionali dal 1947 al 1992*, Rome and Bari: Laterza.

Varsori, Antonio (2001a). La questione europea nella politica italiana (1969–1979), *Studi storici*, vol. 42, no. 4, 953–71.

Varsori, Antonio (2001b). La storiografia sull'integrazione europea, *Europa Europe*, vol. 10, no. 1, 69–93.

Varsori, Antonio (2006). Alle origini di un modello sociale europeo. La Comunità europea e la nascita di una politica sociale (1969–1974), *Ventunesimo secolo*, vol. 5, no. 9, 17–47.

Varsori, Antonio (2007a). The EC/EU and the United States 1947–2006, in Anne Deighton and Gérard Bossuat (eds), *The EC/EU. A World Security Actor?*, Paris: Soleb, 24–51.

Varsori, Antonio (2007b). European Regional Policy. The Foundations of Solidarity, in Michel Dumoulin (ed.), *The European Commission 1958–72. History and Memories*, Luxembourg: OPOCE, 411–25.

Varsori, Antonio (2007c). Per una storia della politica sociale europea, in Giorgio Petracchi (ed.), *Vaghe stelle d'Europa. Quali confini, quale identità, quale economia?*, Gorizia: LEG, 209–30.

Varsori, Antonio (2008). Cold War History in Italy, *Cold War History*, vol. 8, no. 2, 157–88.

Varsori, Antonio (2009). Development of European Social Policy, in Wilfried Loth (ed.), *Experiencing Europe. 50 Years of European Construction, 1957–2007*, Baden-Baden: Nomos, 169–92.

Varsori, Antonio (ed.) (2000). *Il Comitato Economico e Sociale nella costruzione europea*, Venice: Marsilio.

Varsori, Antonio (ed.) (2004). *Towards a History of Vocational Education and Training in Europe in a Comparative Perspective*, vol. 2, Luxembourg: OPOCE.

Varsori, Antonio (ed.) (2006a). *Sfide del mercato e identità europea. Le politiche di educazione e formazione professionale nell'Europa comunitaria*, Milan: Franco Angeli.

Varsori, Antonio (ed.) (2006b). *Inside the European Community. Actors and Policies in the European Integration from the Rome Treaties to the Creation of the 'Snake' 1958–1972*, Baden-Baden, Nomos.

Varsori, Antonio (ed.) (2007). *Alle origini del presente. L'Europa occidentale nella crisi degli anni Settanta*, Milan: Franco Angeli.

Varsori, Antonio and Lorenzo Mechi (eds) (2008). *Lionello Levi Sandri e la politica sociale europea*, Milan: FrancoAngeli.

Verdun, Amy (2002). *The Euro. European Integration Theory and Economic and Monetary Union*, London: Rowman & Littlefield.

Vigezzi, Brunello (ed.) (1985). *Opinion publique et politique extérieure*, vol. 3, *1945–1981*, Milan and Rome: Università di Milano and École Française de Rome.

Volkmann, Hans-Erich (1999). Adenauer, Frankreich und die Europäische Verteidigungsgemeinschaft, in Andreas Wilkens (ed.), *Interessen verbinden. Jean Monnet und die europäische Integration der Bundesrepublik Deutschland*, Bonn: Bouvier, 161–86.

Warleigh-Lack, Alex (2009). Interdisciplinarity in EU Studies. Politics, History and Prospects for Collaboration, in Wolfram Kaiser, Brigitte Leucht and Morten Rasmussen (eds), *The History of the European Union. Origins of a Trans- and Supranational Polity 1950–72*, London: Routledge, 206–20.

Warlouzet, Laurent (2008). Relancer la CEE avant la chaise vide. Néo-fonctionnalistes vs. fédéralistes au sein de la Commission européenne (1964–1965), *Journal of European Integration History*, vol. 14, no. 1, 69–86.

Warlouzet, Laurent (2009). France and the Treaty of Rome: Negotiation and Implementation 1956–74, in Michael Gehler (ed.), *Vom gemeinsamen Markt zur europäischen Unionsbildung. 50 Jahre Römische Verträge 1957–2007*, Vienna, Cologne and Weimar: Böhlau, 541–56.

Warlouzet, Laurent (2010). *Le choix de la CEE par la France. Les débats économiques, 1955–1969*, Paris: Comité pour l'histoire économique et financière de la France.

Warner, Geoffrey (1993). Eisenhower, Dulles and the Unity of Western Europe, 1955–1957, *International Affairs*, vol. 69, no. 2, 319–29.

Wasserstein, Bernard (2007). *Barbarism and Civilization. A History of Europe in Our Time*, Oxford: OUP.

Weber, Max (2001), L''oggettività' conoscitiva della scienza sociale e della politica sociale, in idem., *Saggi sul metodo delle scienze storico-sociali*, ed. Pietro Rossi, Turin: Edizioni di Comunità, 157–208 [German 1904].

Wehler, Hans-Ulrich (1987). *Vom Feudalismus des Alten Reiches bis zur defensiven Modernisierung der Reformära 1700–1815*, Munich: Beck.

Weilemann, Peter (1983). *Die Anfänge der Europäischen Atomgemeinschaft: Zur Gründungsgeschichte von Euratom 1955–1957*, Baden-Baden: Nomos.

Weilemann, Peter (1989). Die Deutsche Haltung während der Euratom-Verhandlungen, in Enrico Serra (ed.), *The Relaunching of Europe and the Treaties of Rome*, Brussels: Bruylant, 531–45.

Weiler, Joseph H.H. (1991). The Transformation of Europe, *The Yale Law Journal*, vol. 100, no. 8, 2405–83.

Weinachter, Michèle (2007). Valéry Giscard d'Estaing, la construction européenne et l'opinion publique: de l'Europe 'd'en haut' à l'Europe des citoyens? (1974–2004), in Marie-Thérèse Bitsch, Wilfried Loth and Charles Barthel (eds), *Cultures politiques, opinions publiques et intégration européenne*, Brussels: Bruylant, 247–61.

Werner, Michael and Bénédicte Zimmermann (2006). Beyond Comparison. Histoire croisée and the Challenge of Reflexivity, *History and Theory*, vol. 45, no. 1, 51–71.

Wesseling, Henk L. (1985). Les Pays-Bas après la décolonisation: politique extérieure et forces profondes, in Brunello Vigezzi (ed.), *Opinion publique et politique extériure*, vol. 3, *1945–1981*, Milan – Rome: Università di Milano and École Française de Rome, 219–39.

Wessels, Wolfgang (ed.) (1977). *Europa und der Nord-Süd-Dialog*, Bonn: Europa Union Verlag.

Westad, Arne (ed.) (2000). *Reviewing the Cold War. Approaches, Interpretations and Theories*, London: Frank Cass.

Wheare, Kenneth C. (1946). *Federal Government*, Oxford: OUP.

White, Jonathan P.J. (2003). Theory Guiding Practice. The Neofunctionalists and the Hallstein EEC Commission, *Journal of European Integration History*, vol. 9, no. 1, 111–31.

Wiggershaus, Norbert (1986). Zur Frage der militärischen Integration Westdeutschlands (vor Mai 1950), in Raymond Poidevin (ed.), *Origins of the European Integration, March 1948-May 1950*, Brussels: Bruylant, 343–66.

Wilkens, Andreas (1999). Westpolitik, Ostpolitik and the Project of the Economic and Monetary Union. Germany's European Policy in the Brandt Era (1969–1974), *Journal of European Integration History*, vol. 5, no. 1, 73–102.

Wilkens, Andreas (ed.) (1997). *Die deutsch-französischen Wirtschaftsbeziehungen 1945–1960*, Sigmaringen: Thorbecke.

Wilkens, Andreas (ed.) (2004). *Le plan Schuman dans l'histoire. Intérêts nationaux et projet européen*, Brussels: Bruylant.

Wilson, Jérôme (2004). Le groupe de Bellagio. Origines et premiers pas (1960–1964), in Michel Dumoulin (ed.), *Réseaux économiques et construction européenne*, Brussels: PIE-Peter Lang, 391–410.

Winand, Pascaline (1993). *Eisenhower, Kennedy and the United States of Europe*, New York: St. Martin's Press.

Winand, Pascaline (1997). American 'Europeanists', Monnet's Action Committee and British Membership, in George Wilkes (ed.), *Britain's Failure to Enter the European Community 1961–1963*, London: Frank Cass, 164–90.

Winand, Pascaline (2006). Kennedy's Atlantic Partnership, the EEC Empty Chair Crisis and the French/NATO Problem, in Jean-Marie Palayret, Helen Wallace and Pascaline Winand (eds), *Visions, Votes and Vetoes. The Empty Chair Crisis and the Luxembourg Compromise Forty Years On*, Brussels: Peter Lang, 183–218.

Winkler, Heinrich-August (2000). *Der lange Weg nach Westen. Deutsche Geschichte vom Ende des Alten Reiches bis zum Untergang der Weimarer Republik 1806–1933*, Munich: Beck.

Wistrich, Ernest (1994). *The United States of Europe*, London: Routledge.

Witschke, Tobias (2009). *Gefahr für den Wettbewerb? Die Fusionskontrolle der Europäischen Gemeinschaft für Kohle und Stahl und die 'Rekonzentration' der Ruhrstahlindustrie 1950–1963*, Berlin: Akademie Verlag.

Wurm, Clemens (1995). Two Paths to Europe. Great Britain and France from a Comparative Perspective, in idem. (ed.), *Western Europe and Germany. The Beginnings of European Integration 1945–1960*, Oxford: Berg, 175–200.

Yakemtchouk, Romain (2005). *La politique étrangère de l'Union européenne*, Paris: L'Harmattan.

Yamamoto, Takeshi (2007). Détente or Integration? EC Response to Soviet Policy Change towards the Common Market, 1970–75, *Cold War History*, vol. 7, no. 1, 75–94.

Young, John W. (2000). *Britain and European Unity 1945–1999*, Basingstoke: Palgrave.

Zampoli, Davide (2007). I primi passi della Cooperazione politica europea: problematiche ed evoluzione istituzionale, in Antonio Varsori (ed.), *Alle origini del presente. L'Europa occidentale nella crisi degli anni Settanta*, Milan: Franco Angeli, 169–93.

Zeller, Adrien (1970). *L'imbroglio agricolo del Mercato comune*, Milan: Arnoldo Mondadori.

Zimmermann, Hubert (2002), *Money and Security. Troops, Monetary Policy, and West Germany's Relations with the United States and Britain, 1950–1971*, Cambridge: CUP.

Zimmermann, Hubert (2003). Western Europe and the American Challenge. Conflict and Cooperation in Technology and Monetary Policy, 1965–1973, in Marc Trachtenberg (ed.), *Between Empire and Alliance. America and Europe in the Cold War*, Lanham, MD: Rowman & Littlefield, 127–55.

Zucca, Fabio (2001). *Autonomie locali e federazione sovranazionale. La battaglia del Conseil des Communes et Regions d'Europe per la federazione europea*, Bologna: Il Mulino.

Zysman, John (1977). *Political Strategies for Industrial Order. State, Market and Industry in France*, Berkeley, CA: University of California Press.

Index

254   *Index*

France – *continued*
 dollar hoards 181
 and EDC treaty 74, 88, 175,
   179, 192
 EEC and industry and economy 92,
   93, 104
 and Empty Chair crisis 144
 European policy 90–3, 115, 136
 Fifth Republic 93
 foreign policy 197
 historical research in 90–3
 integration and post-war
   recovery 10
 and LDCs 195
 as leader of European
   integration 173, 178
 nationalism in 180
 and NATO 92
 opposition to
   supranationalism 105
 post-war nationalism 71
 and rehabilitation of Germany
   172, 179
 relations with US 91, 92
Frank, Robert 9, 16, 17, 22, 154–5
Franz Steiner Verlag 19, 41
Free Democrats (Germany) 69
Free French 55
free movement of people 60, 96, 153,
   154, 166, 167
free trade 88, 104, 146, 176, 179, 195
French language, in
   publications 30–1, 40
Friedrich, Carl J. 80–1
Friedrich Ebert Foundation 205
frontiers *see* border controls
Fulbright, William J. 172
functionalism 53

G7 summits 202, 205
Garavini, Giuliano 5, 91, 108, 181,
   186, 190–208
GATT *see* General Agreement on
   Tariffs and Trade
Gaullism 90, 93, 117, 198
Gavin, Francis 184
Gehler, Michael 4, 85–108, 109
General Agreement on Tariffs and
   Trade (GATT) 146, 191, 197

 and ECSC 192
 and EEC 194
 Kennedy Round 115, 124, 194, 195
 Malfatti Round 205
 Uruguay Round 196
general elections, determining
   factors 132–3
George, Stephen 99
Gerbet, Pierre 12, 50
German language, in publications
   30, 40
Germany
 19th-century unification of 69, 86
 bilateral relations with France 88,
   90, 91, 99, 115, 119, 140,
   143, 144
 and CAP 89–90
 Christian Democrats 69
 constitution and federal
   structure 88–9
 control of military potential 88
 economic reconstruction 87–8
 and ECSC 173
 European policy 86–90, 103
 European Studies in 50–1
 Federal Republic 86–7, 172, 173, 174
 federalist movement 87
 foreign policy 199
 historical research in 86–90
 influence of industry on policy-
   making 87–8
 JEIH in 29
 joins EEC 87
 membership of NATO 87, 88
 national socialism 78
 plans for 'Fourth Reich' 50
 relations with Britain 119
 relations with Italy 119
 reunification of 16, 89, 90, 103
 support for EEC enlargement 88
 US and post-war rehabilitation
   of 172, 173, 174
 world wars 104
Geyer, Martin 86
Giauque, Jeffrey 183
Gilbert, Mark 4–5, 169–89, 190, 194
Gillingham, John 48, 87, 173, 190
Girault, René 8–10, 13, 14, 16–17, 18,
   20, 21, 22, 23, 30, 62, 130, 138, 147

peace
European capabilities for peace-
making 190, 199, 200, 203
ideal of 75, 79
Pentagon 181
Pentland, Charles 53
Per un'Europa libera e unita see
Manifesto di Ventotene
Peter Lang 41
Pharo, Helge 190
philosophy, and European
identity 155
Pinder, John 67, 81
Pine, Melissa 99
Pisani, Edgar 196
Pistone, Sergio 12, 67, 78
Pleven Plan 91
pluralism 155
Poidevin, Raymond 12, 13, 14, 30, 37,
50, 111, 112, 118, 192, 193
Poland 35
policy-making
bilateral aspects of 119
conservative character of 57
cross-policy linkage 124
cultural and identity aspects of 99
evolution of common 39
focus on individual policy
areas 124
influence of economic and political
science theory on 52
informal network-type character
of 54, 58
and past decision-making 56–7
in pluralist democracies 43
remoteness of supranational 1
social developments and 60
social impact of common 4, 46,
151, 161–6, 168
societal constraints on 130
socio-economic aspects of 130
and transnational networks 158–9
political actors 56, 115, 131–2, 204
political change 96
political crises 85
political economy, of
integration 128–9
political entrepreneurship 58
political militancy 66

political parties
cooperation of 43
European leverage for domestic
ends 127
and foreign affairs 204–5
and integration 97, 99, 106, 150,
151, 158
transnational networks 58, 158–9,
204–5
political science
cross-disciplinarity with 152
and European integration 54, 57,
114, 116, 204
gap between contemporary history
and 50, 51–2
sociological turn in 58
study of 51
theoretical approach 55
and working of EU 121
political sociology, national paradigm
in 59
political symbols 61
political system
European 4, 121–7
interface between European and
national 127
polity, EU as 46, 49, 54, 143, 148
Pompidou, Georges 88, 186, 198
Portugal
democratization 203, 205
and EFTA 197
joins EU 42, 103, 135, 136, 191, 202
post-war period, interest in 36, 40
poverty 161
power politics, research into 9–10
pre-federal institutions 79
pre-war years, interest in 36–7,
39–40
Preda, Daniela 75
predictions 51, 63
press
British 97
coverage of European issues
167, 168
coverage of summits 157
pressure groups 166
price subsidies 56
Prodi, Romano 73, 94
Programme of Social Action 163

United States (US) – *continued*
  as European partner or rival 181–6
  European view of 188
  Europhilia 174
  federal model 78, 169, 179
  foreign policy 169, 170, 177, 186, 188, 194, 197, 199, 200
  and GATT 194, 195
  as great power 9, 171
  imports from EEC 176, 185
  influence on networks 160
  internal market 171
  investment in Europe 176
  isolationist alternative 178–80
  Italian Left and 96–7
  multinationals 146
  post-war policy towards Germany 91
  and post-war recovery 140, 177
  response to EU 86
  role in European integration 4–5, 71, 83, 105, 169–89, 190
  and shape of post-war Europe 8
  social model 165
  souring of transatlantic relationship 170, 188–9, 199
  'special relationship' with UK 97, 104–5
  studies comparing Europe with 165
  and world financial crisis 48
  in World Wars 171, 177
unity in diversity 61
universities
  academic mobility 31
  access to *JEIH* in 29
  chairs funded by EU 6, 15, 17, 47, 61
  provision of study at 153
Uri, Pierre 13, 196
US *see* United States

Van Laer, Arthe 118–19
Varsori, Antonio 3–4, 6–25, 26, 30, 31, 38, 41, 47, 53, 55, 60, 61, 62, 86, 95, 96, 97, 112, 115, 133, 138, 161, 164, 166, 177, 187, 198
Vichy government 90

Vietnam War 183, 184, 185, 188, 195
Vigezzi, Brunello 9, 206
vocational training 10, 164, 166, 168

Warlouzet, Laurent 52, 93, 115, 125
Warner, Geoffrey 9, 12
Watt, Donald 9, 12, 14
Weber, Max 83
websites
  CERE 29
  on European integration 17, 22
Weilemann, Peter R. 50, 87
Weiler, Joseph 122–3
welfare benefits 133
welfare states
  Danish 101
  decline of 106
  different types of 133, 142
  emergence of 130, 160
  financing of 137
  impact on allegiance 133
  integration and provisions 153
  Lisbon Strategy 165–6
  provision at EU level 62
  transformation of 2
Wells, H.G. 78
Wesseling, Henk 206
Wessels, Wolfgang 87
western defence system 8
Western European Union (WEU) 88
WEU *see* Western European Union
Wheare, Kenneth C. 73, 79
White, Jonathan P.J. 52
Wilson, Harold 99
Wilson, Jerome 160
Winand, Pascaline 174, 175, 182–3
Woolf, Leonard 78
Wootton, Barbara 79
World Bank 191, 192, 201, 208
World War II
  archival sources 8
  articles in *JEIH* 36
  connections across 50, 70, 138
  German invasion of Benelux countries 104
  plans for post-war Europe 39, 50, 70